COLONIALISM/POSTCOLONIALISM

This accessible volume provides a vital introduction to the historical dimensions and theoretical concepts associated with colonial and postcolonial discourses.

Ania Loomba examines the key features of the ideologies and history of colonialism, and the relationship of colonial discourse to literature. She goes on to consider the challenges to colonialism, surveying anti-colonial discourses, and recent developments in postcolonial theories and histories. Looking at how sexuality is figured in the texts of colonialism, *Colonialism/Postcolonialism* shows how contemporary feminist ideas and concepts intersect with those of postcolonialist thought.

This clear and concise volume is a must for any student needing to get to grips with this crucial and complex area.

Ania Loomba is Catherine Bryson Professor of English, University of Pennsylvania, USA.

THE NEW CRITICAL IDIOM

SERIES EDITOR: JOHN DRAKAKIS, UNIVERSITY OF STIRLING

The New Critical Idiom is an invaluable series of introductory guides to today's critical terminology. Each book:

- provides a handy, explanatory guide to the use (and abuse) of the term
- offers an original and distinctive overview by a leading literary and cultural critic
- relates the term to the larger field of cultural representation

With a strong emphasis on clarity, lively debate and the widest possible breadth of examples, *The New Critical Idiom* is an indispensable approach to key topics in literary studies.

- Also available in this series:

COLONIALISM/ POSTCOLONIALISM

Ania Loomba

Routledge
Taylor & Francis Group

LONDON AND NEW YORK

First published 1998
by Routledge
11 New Fetter Lane, London EC4P 4EE

Simultaneously published in the USA and Canada
by Routledge
29 West 35th Street, New York, NY 10001

Reprinted 1998, 2000, 2001, 2002, 2004

Routledge is an imprint of the Taylor & Francis Group

Typeset in Garamond by Routledge
Printed and bound in Great Britain by TJ International Ltd, Padstow, Cornwall

British Library Cataloguing in Publication Data
A catalogue record for this book is available from the British Library

Library of Congress Cataloguing in Publication Data
A catalogue record has been requested for this title

ISBN 0–415–12808–0 (hbk)
ISBN 0–415–12809–9 (pbk)

For Suvir and for Tariq

Contents

SERIES EDITOR'S PREFACE

The New Critical Idiom is a series of introductory books which seeks to extend the lexicon of literary terms, in order to address the radical changes which have taken place in the study of literature during the last decades of the twentieth century. The aim is to provide clear, well-illustrated accounts of the full range of terminology currently in use, and to evolve histories of its changing usage.

The current state of the discipline of literary studies is one in which there is considerable debate concerning basic questions of terminology. This involves, among other things, the boundaries which distinguish the literary from the non-literary; the position of literature within the larger sphere of culture; the relationship between literatures of different cultures; and questions concerning the relation of literary to other cultural forms within the context of inter-disciplinary studies.

It is clear that the field of literary criticism and theory is a dynamic and heterogeneous one. The present need is for individual volumes on terms which combine clarity of exposition with an adventurousness of perspective and a breadth of application. Each volume will contain as part of its apparatus some indication of the direction in which the definition of particular terms is likely to move, as well as expanding the disciplinary boundaries within which some of these terms have been traditionally contained. This will involve some resituation of terms within the larger field of cultural presentation, and will introduce examples from the area of film and the modern media in addition to examples from a variety of literary texts.

ACKNOWLEDGEMENTS

It is a pleasure to thank the various people whose intellectual and emotional support made it possible for this book to survive, and even benefit from, inter-continental oscillations: John Drakakis for his encouragement and comments; Suvir Kaul, Neeladri Bhattacharya and Priyamvada Gopal for their engaged readings of drafts; Ranita Lochan for always being there to help, and Vilashini Cooppan and Isabel Hofmeyr for sharing their work with me. I have learnt a lot from conversations with Shalini Advani, Nivedita Menon, Martin Orkin and Tanika Sarkar. Bindia Thapar has always provided me with a home away from home, and so, now, have Kaushalya and Bhavanesh Kaul. In the early days of this project Primla Loomba asked me what this 'post-colonialism question was all about': her own commitment and work have continually reminded me what is at stake in discussing such issues. Tariq Thachil's scepticism about 'post-colonialism' has been as important as his amiability and companionship. Suvir Kaul I thank for thinking through so many ideas with me, and for attempting to re-shape both my prose and the globe so that we can share our lives.

INTRODUCTION

A great deal of excitement as well as confusion and scepticism surrounds the relatively new field of postcolonial studies. Many people are not clear what is new about these studies – after all, writing about colonialism is almost as old as colonialism itself. Others are able to identify what is new and do not like what they read – including the fact that these new ways of studying colonialism and its aftermath have become fashionable within universities the world over. A recent essay by Russell Jacoby complains that the term 'postcolonial' has become 'the latest catchall term to dazzle the academic mind' (1995: 30). 'Oh, its something postcolonial' is what Jacoby's friend was told when she inquired about a piece of pottery. Squabbles over the definitions of 'colonialism', and even over the meaning of 'post' extend to a confusion over 'postcolonial studies' so that 'its enthusiasts themselves don't know what it is'. He adds that lots of the theory is written in a confusing manner, it is marked by infighting among the critics who all accuse each other of complicity with colonial structures of thought, and although its declared intentions are to allow the voices of once colonised peoples and their descendants to be heard, it in fact closes off both their voices and any legitimate place from which critics can speak.

Now, despite the fact that this attack only barely disguises the author's disciplinary and political conservatism, many of these criticisms are shared by those who are sympathetic to postcolonial studies, including many students new to the field or those who are outside the academy, particularly those outside the Western academy. I am routinely irritated when objects, food or clothes (and perhaps ideas) from my part of the world become 'ethnic' in Europe or North America; within India, 'ethnic' applies to the cultures and objects of tribal, or rural folk, especially when they are displayed in trendy markets. In other words, is it the case that terms like 'ethnic' and 'postcolonial' have become shorthand for something (fashionably) marginal? Academic discussions of post-coloniality have had an impact on, and been shaped by, a wide range of social and cultural practices outside the universities although some of the most important or landmark essays in 'post-colonial studies' are notoriously difficult to read, especially in the classroom. Those not directly concerned with English studies tend to be especially critical of this difficulty, particularly because this 'field' intersects with that of critical or literary theory in general, which is also regarded as full of jargon, confusing, and removed from daily reality. It may be true that 'Western theory' has been transformed as a result of its encounter with 'non-Western cultures' (Lloyd: 1994). But many 'Third World' academics continue to be wary of even this transformed theory, including post-colonial theory, because of its perceived distance from situations in their part of the world, and because of its supposed overlaps with 'post-modernism'. Post-modernism in this view is a specifically Western malaise which breeds angst and despair instead of aiding political action and resistance. There have been sharp critiques of postcolonial theory along similar lines from academics within the Western academy. The 'field' therefore is as beleaguered as it is fashionable. The concept, Stuart Hall says, 'has become the bearer of such powerful unconscious investments – a sign of desire for some, and equally for others, a signifier of danger' (1996a: 242).

It is true that the term 'postcolonialism' has become so heterogeneous and diffuse that it is impossible to satisfactorily describe what its study might entail. This difficulty is partly due to the inter-disciplinary nature of postcolonial studies which may range from literary analysis to research in the archives of colonial government, from the critique of medical texts to economic theory, and usually combine these and other areas. But it is also true that the newer critical languages are not merely 'jargon', even though it may sometimes appear that communication is not a priority for many of those who speak them. The continuing suspicion of academic discussions can often be traced to a reluctance to expand or change one's political and conceptual vocabulary. These languages have emerged from recent developments both in the social sciences and literary and linguistic studies, and therefore cannot simply be replaced by an everyday terminology. Nevertheless, it is important to continuously try and discuss the issues at stake in a language that is more 'user-friendly'. As the editors of a recent reader of postcolonial studies put it, postcolonial theory does not have to be 'depressingly difficult' (Williams and Chrisman 1994: ix). This book is written in that belief, and in the hope that it will help readers to think about the intellectual and political possibilities of these recent developments.

Modern European colonialism was distinctive and by far the most extensive of the different kinds of colonial contact that have been a recurrent feature of human history. By the 1930s, colonies and ex-colonies covered 84.6 per cent of the land surface of the globe. Only parts of Arabia, Persia, Afghanistan, Mongolia, Tibet, China, Siam and Japan had never been under formal European government (Fieldhouse 1989: 373). Such a geographical and historical sweep makes summaries impossible. It also makes it very difficult to 'theorise' colonialism – some particular instance is bound to negate any generalisation we may make about the nature of colonialism or of resistances to it. There is always a certain amount of reduction in any attempt to simplify, schematise or summarise complex debates and histories, and the study of colonialism is especially vulnerable to such problems on account of colonialism's heterogeneous practices and impact over the last four centuries. Each scholar of colonialism, depending on her disciplinary affiliation, geographic and institutional location and identity, is likely to come up with a different set of examples, emphasis and perspective on the question. In this book, I have not attempted to provide watertight definitions or

to offer comprehensive accounts of colonial histories and ideologies. Instead, I present important terms, events and issues by
focusing on some key debates and scholarship which will help
readers to get a sense of the complexity of each of them as well as
the connections between them.

Just because colonial studies encompass such a vast area, it
does not mean that we should only confine ourselves to study of
particular cases, without any attempt to think about the larger
structures of colonial rule and thought. How do we weave together the general and the particular? It is sometimes assumed
that older accounts of colonialism are untheoretical because they
are based on empirical study of specific events while recent studies are theoretical because they do not confine themselves to actual events. This is a misunderstanding – conventional studies of
colonialism are also theoretical in the sense that they too rest on
larger assumptions about the nature of colonial contact or quarrel
about certain issues such as whether or not colonial rule was economically profitable for the 'mother' country. What then is the
difference between them? Sometimes critics of postcolonial studies claim that these studies are doing nothing new, at other times
they suggest that the innovations are not always helpful in understanding this large and complex area of human history. Of course,
admirers see the new initiatives as not only offering fresh perspectives on the past, but as enabling us to understand the continuing
changes around the world.

There are certain dangers attendant upon these perspectives
becoming institutionalised, especially within English depart-
ments. Ella Shohat points out one negative implication of the
very acceptability of the term 'postcolonial' in the Western
academy: it serves to keep at bay more sharply political terms
such as 'imperialism', or 'geopolitics' (Shohat 1993: 99). Terry
Eagleton (1994) makes a related accusation that within 'postcolonial
thought' one is 'allowed to talk about cultural differences, but not –
or not much – about economic exploitation'. Has 'postcolonialism'

then begun to function within academia as a term of compromise that allows us to take the easy way out? Eagleton's own use of the term 'postcolonial thought' to designate an academic trend is unsatisfactory: many postcolonial writers and academics do write extensively about economic exploitation, although their work is often not included within what is becoming institutionalised as 'postcolonial studies'.

A second, related, problem is that (despite the sophisticated work done in this area), in the classroom the 'postcolonial' functions in increasingly formulaic or reductive terms that are abstracted from concrete situations. It is often seen as something that has to be appended to existing syllabi. This means enormous condensation – one week to do the 'race' thing in a Shakespeare or a literary theory course, or even the one token course to go through the whole theoretical field, or one faculty member to represent the entire spectrum of literary and intellectual production outside of Anglo-America. It seems far too inconvenient, in such a scenario, to attend to differences within the 'rest of the world' or to details of specific situations. Metropolitan postcolonial theory obliges by locating itself in some general 'colonial' or 'postcolonial' location rather than asking for extensive work on the details and specificities of far-away locales. Peter Hulme suggests that this is because non-European texts are generally taught only in juxtaposition to, or as offering a critique of, European literatures (1994: 72). Specific local details, ironically, would be well within the compass of conventional 'area studies' specialists, who, however, rarely work with colonialism as a theoretical parameter.

A third result of the boom in postcolonial studies has been that essays by a handful of name-brand critics have become more important than the field itself – students feel the pressure to 'do' Edward Said, Gayatri Spivak or Homi Bhabha or to read only the very latest article. What Barbara Christian (1990) has called 'the race for theory' is detrimental to thinking about the area itself. It is the star system of the Western and particularly the United States academy that is partly responsible for this, and partly the nature of theoretical work itself, which can be intimidating and often self-referential. Thus although most students feel obliged to take some note of postcolonial theory, not all of them are inspired to be creative with it perhaps because they often lack expertise in colonial and postcolonial histories and cultures.

This book aims to work through some of these problems. I have tried to place the genesis and parameters of contemporary theories of postcoloniality and the problems which confront them within other intellectual debates such as those about ideology or representation, gender or agency, rather than attempt to summarise the sprawling history of colonialism or resistance. The work of individual critics is located within specific debates, and will crop up in different sections. Thus, for instance, the writings of Frantz Fanon are discussed in the multiple contexts of gender and sexuality, nationalism and hybridity. The section divisions also do not indicate watertight compartments, so the intersection of gender and colonialism for example, or the issue of alterity, is dealt with throughout. I have tried to emphasise the need to incorporate an awareness of historical and geographic difference into our attempts to 'theorise'. Of course, one's own disciplinary training or identity is bound to shape one's knowledge of the field – I felt myself turning to early modern Europe or to modern India for my examples. The point, however, is not that we need to know the entire historical and geographic diversity of colonialism in order to theorise, but rather, that we must build our theories with an awareness that such diversity exists, and not expand the local to the status of the universal. But of course, we must not romanticise the category of the local. As Bruce Robbins warns us 'thinking small is not enough' and while we must stay clear of the 'easy generalization' we should 'retain the right to *difficult* generalization' (1992: 174–176).[1]

This book is divided into three main chapters, each of which is further subdivided into smaller sections. The first chapter discusses the different meanings of terms such as colonialism, imperialism and postcolonialism, and the controversies surrounding them. It connects colonial discourse studies to key debates on ideology, subjectivity and language, showing why both a new terminology and a new reaching across disciplinary boundaries became necessary in relation to the study of colonialism. The relationship between colonialism and literary studies is discussed in some detail. The literary inception as well as inflection of colonial discourse studies have resulted in exciting innovations in thinking about colonial representations and subjectivity, but they have also generated certain problems, which are taken up by the last section of this chapter. This chapter will introduce readers to aspects of post-structuralist, Marxist, feminist and post-modern thought which have become important or controversial in relation to post-colonial studies.

The second chapter considers the complexities of colonial and postcolonial subjects and identities. How does the colonial encounter restructure ideologies of racial, cultural, class and sexual difference? In what ways are patriarchal oppression and colonial domination conceptually and historically connected to one another? What is the relationship between capitalism and colonialism? Is racial difference produced by colonialist domination, or did colonialism generate racism? What frameworks can we adopt for locating the complex restructuring of individual subjects during colonialism? Is psychoanalysis useful for understanding colonial subjectivities? How can we understand the now fashionable concept of hybridity in the light of these issues? These are some of the questions this chapter will address, with a view to opening up the larger debate on the relationship between material and economic processes and human subjectivities.

In the third chapter, processes of decolonisation and the problems of recovering the viewpoint of colonised subjects from a 'postcolonial' perspective are examined. Various theories of resistance are approached here, not in a descriptive manner but by considering the crucial debates they engender about authenticity and hybridity, the nation, ethnicity and colonial identities. Theories of nationalism and pan-nationalism are then considered, as are the complexities within colonised countries, and how nationalism is fractured by gender, class and ideological divides. This chapter will look at some recent writings that discuss the relationship between literary production and nationalist thought. One of the most vexed questions in postcolonial studies is the agency of the colonised subject, or 'subaltern', and whether it can be recovered and represented by postcolonial intellectuals. Another is the relationship between post-modernism and postcolonial studies, and the last two sections will consider these questions and connect them to previous discussions of agency and representation.

Although this volume does not even attempt the impossible task of 'covering' every major thinker, event or controversy, I hope its selection of the major debates and issues will stimulate and enable its readers to explore, and to critique, further afield.

1

SITUATING COLONIAL AND POSTCOLONIAL STUDIES

DEFINING THE TERMS: COLONIALISM, IMPERIALISM, NEO-COLONIALISM, POSTCOLONIALISM

Colonialism and imperialism are often used interchangeably. The word colonialism, according to the *Oxford English Dictionary* (*OED*), comes from the Roman 'colonia' which meant 'farm' or 'settlement', and referred to Romans who settled in other lands but still retained their citizenship. Accordingly, the *OED* describes it as,

> a settlement in a new country ... a body of people who settle in a new locality, forming a community subject to or connected with their parent state; the community so formed, consisting of the original settlers and their descendants and successors, as long as the connection with the parent state is kept up.

This definition, quite remarkably, avoids any reference to people other than the colonisers, people who might already have been living in those places where colonies were established. Hence it evacuates the word 'colonialism' of any implication of an encounter between peoples, or of conquest and domination. There is no hint that the 'new locality' may not be so 'new' and that the process of 'forming a community' might be somewhat unfair. Colonialism was not an identical process in different parts of the world but everywhere it locked the original inhabitants and the newcomers into the most complex and traumatic relationships in human history. In *The Tempest*, for example, Shakespeare's single major addition to the story he found in certain pamphlets about a shipwreck in the Bermudas was to make the island inhabited before Prospero's arrival (Hulme 1986b: 69). That single addition turned the adventure story into an allegory of the colonial encounter. The process of 'forming a community' in the new land necessarily meant *unforming* or re-forming the communities that existed there already, and involved a wide range of practices including trade, plunder, negotiation, warfare, genocide, enslavement and rebellions. Such practices produced and were produced through a variety of writings – public and private records, letters, trade documents, government papers, fiction and scientific literature. These practices and writings are an important part of all that contemporary studies of colonialism and postcolonialism try to make sense of.

So colonialism can be defined as the conquest and control of other people's land and goods. But colonialism in this sense is not merely the expansion of various European powers into Asia, Africa or the Americas from the sixteenth century onwards; it has been a recurrent and widespread feature of human history. At its height in the second century AD, the Roman Empire stretched from Armenia to the Atlantic. Under Genghis Khan in the thirteenth century, the Mongols conquered the Middle East as well as China. The Aztec Empire was established when, from the fourteenth to the sixteenth centuries, one of the various ethnic groups who settled in the valley of Mexico subjugated the others. Aztecs extracted tributes in services and goods from conquered regions, as did the Inca Empire which was the largest pre-industrial state in the Americas. In the fifteenth century too, various kingdoms in southern India came under the control of the Vijaynagara Empire, and the Ottoman Empire, which began as a minor Islamic principality in what is now western Turkey, extended itself over most of Asia Minor and the Balkans. At the beginning of the eighteenth century, it still extended from the Mediterranean to the Indian ocean, and the Chinese Empire was larger than anything Europe had seen. Modern European colonialism cannot be sealed off from these earlier histories of contact – the Crusades, or the Moorish invasion of Spain, the legendary exploits of Mongol rulers or the fabled wealth of the Incas or the Mughals were real or imagined fuel for the European journeys to different parts of the world. And yet, these newer European travels ushered in new and different kinds of colonial practices which altered the whole globe in a way that these other colonialisms did not.

How do we think about these differences? Was it that Europeans established empires far away from their own shores? Were they more violent or more ruthless? Were they better organised? Or a superior race? All of these explanations have in fact been offered to account for the global power and drastic effects of European colonialisms. Marxist thinking on the subject locates a crucial distinction between the two: whereas earlier colonialisms were pre-capitalist, modern colonialism was established alongside capitalism in Western Europe (see Bottomore 1983: 81–85). Modern colonialism did more than extract tribute, goods and wealth from the countries that it conquered – it restructured the economies of the latter, drawing them into a complex relationship with their own, so that there was a flow of human and natural resources between colonised and colonial countries. This flow worked in both directions – slaves and indentured labour as well as raw materials were transported to manufacture goods in the metropolis, or in other locations for metropolitan consumption, but the colonies also provided captive markets for European goods. Thus slaves were moved from Africa to the Americas, and in the West Indian plantations they produced sugar for consumption in Europe, and raw cotton was moved from India to be manufactured into cloth in England and then sold back to India whose own cloth production suffered as a result. In whichever direction human beings and materials travelled, the profits always flowed back into the so-called 'mother country'.

These flows of profits and people involved settlement and plantations as in the Americas, 'trade' as in India, and enormous global shifts of populations. Both the colonised and the colonisers moved: the former not only as slaves but also as indentured labourers, domestic servants, travellers and traders, and the colonial masters as administrators, soldiers, merchants, settlers, travellers, writers, domestic staff, missionaries, teachers and scientists. The essential point is that although European colonialisms involved a variety of techniques and patterns of domination, penetrating deep into some societies and involving a comparatively superficial contact with others, all of them produced the economic imbalance that was necessary for the growth of European capitalism and industry. Thus we could say that colonialism was the midwife that assisted at the birth of European capitalism, or that without colonial expansion the transition to capitalism could not have taken place in Europe.

The distinction between pre-capitalist and capitalist colonialisms is often made by referring to the latter as imperialism. This is somewhat misleading, because imperialism, like colonialism, stretches back to a pre-capitalist past. Imperial Russia, for example, was pre-capitalist, as was Imperial Spain. Some commentators place imperialism as *prior* to colonialism (Boehmer 1995: 3). Like 'colonialism', this concept too is best understood not by trying to pin it down to a single semantic meaning but by relating its shifting meanings to historical processes. Early in its usage in the English language it simply means 'command or superior power' (Williams 1976: 131). The *OED* defines 'imperial' as simply 'pertaining to empire', and 'imperialism' as the 'rule of an emperor, especially when despotic or arbitrary; the principal or spirit of empire; advocacy of what are held to be imperial interests'. As a matter of fact, the connection of *imperial* with *royal* authority is highly variable. While royalty were both financially and symbolically invested in early European colonisations, these ventures were in every case also the result of wider class and social interests. Thus although Ralegh named Virginia after his Queen, and trading privileges to the English in India or Turkey were sought and granted not simply in the name of the East India Company but to Englishmen as representatives of Elizabeth I or James I, it was a wider base of English merchants, traders, financiers as well as feudal lords that made English trade and colonialism possible. The same is true even of the Portuguese empire, where royal involvement was more spectacular.

In the early twentieth century, Lenin and Kautsky (among other writers) gave a new meaning to the word 'imperialism' by linking it to a particular stage of the development of capitalism. In *Imperialism, the Highest Stage of Capitalism* (1947), Lenin argued that the growth of 'finance-capitalism' and industry in the Western countries had created 'an enormous superabundance of capital'. This money could not be profitably invested at home where labour was limited. The colonies lacked capital but were abundant in labour and human resources. Therefore it needed to move out and subordinate non-industrialised countries to sustain its own growth. Lenin thus predicted that in due course the rest of the world would be absorbed by European finance capitalists. This global system was called 'imperialism' and constituted a particular stage of capitalist development – the 'highest' in Lenin's understanding because rivalry between the various imperial wars would catalyse their destruction and the demise of capitalism. It is this Leninist definition that allows some people to argue that capitalism is the distinguishing feature between colonialism and imperialism.

Direct colonial rule is not necessary for imperialism in this sense, because the economic (and social) relations of dependency and control ensure both captive labour as well as markets for European industry as well as goods. Sometimes the words 'neo-imperialism' or 'neo-colonialism' are used to describe these situations. In as much as the growth of European industry and finance-capital was achieved through colonial domination in the first place, we can also see that imperialism (in this sense) is the highest stage of colonialism. In the modern world then, we can distinguish between colonisation as the take over of territory, appropriation of material resources, exploitation of labour and interference with political and cultural structures of another territory or nation, and imperialism as a global system. However, there remains enormous ambiguity between the economic and political connotations of the word. If imperialism is defined as a political system in which an imperial centre governs colonised countries, then the granting of political independence signals the end of empire, the collapse of imperialism. However, if imperialism is primarily an economic system of penetration and control of markets, then political changes do not basically affect it, and may even redefine the term as in the case of 'American imperialism' which wields enormous military and economic power across the globe but without direct political control. The political sense was predominant however in the description of the relations between the former USSR and other Eastern European countries as 'Soviet imperialism'. As we will discuss in later sections, the tensions between economic and political connotations of imperialism also spill over into the understanding of racial oppression, and its relationship with class or other structures of oppression.

Thus, imperialism, colonialism and the differences between them are defined differently depending on their historical mutations. One useful way of distinguishing between them might be to not separate them in temporal but in spatial terms and to think of imperialism or neo-imperialism as the phenomenon that originates in the metropolis, the process which leads to domination and

control. Its result, or what happens in the colonies as a conse-
quence of imperial domination is colonialism or neo-colonialism.
Thus the imperial country is the 'metropole' from which power
flows, and the colony or neo-colony is the place which it penetrates and controls. Imperialism can function without formal
colonies (as in United States imperialism today) but colonialism
cannot.

These fluctuations also complicate the meanings of the term
'postcolonial', a term that is the subject of an ongoing debate,
which we shall unravel slowly. It might seem that because the age
of colonialism is over, and because the descendants of once-
colonised peoples live everywhere, the whole world is postcolonial. And yet the term has been fiercely contested on many
counts. To begin with, the prefix 'post' complicates matters because it implies an 'aftermath' in two senses – temporal, as in
coming after, and ideological, as in supplanting. It is the second
implication which critics of the term have found contestable: if
the inequities of colonial rule have not been erased, it is perhaps
premature to proclaim the demise of colonialism. A country may
be both postcolonial (in the sense of being formally independent)
and neo-colonial (in the sense of remaining economically and/or
culturally dependent) at the same time. We cannot dismiss the
importance of either formal decolonisation, or the fact that unequal relations of colonial rule are reinscribed in the contemporary imbalances between 'first' and 'third' world nations. The new
global order does not depend upon direct rule. However, it does
allow the economic, cultural and (to varying degrees) political
penetration of some countries by others. This makes it debatable
whether once-colonised countries can be seen as properly 'postcolonial' (see McClintock 1992).

Even in the temporal sense, the word postcolonial cannot be
used in any single sense. Formal decolonisation has spanned three
centuries, ranging from the eighteenth and nineteenth centuries
in the Americas, Australia, New Zealand and South Africa, to the

1970s in the case of Angola and Mozambique. Pointing to this fact, Ella Shohat trenchantly asks, 'When exactly, then, does the "postcolonial" begin?' (1993: 103). This is not just a rhetorical question; Shohat's point is that these diverse beginnings indicate that colonialism was challenged from a variety of perspectives by people who were not all oppressed in the same way or to the same extent. Thus the politics of decolonisation in parts of Latin America or Australia or South Africa where white settlers formed their own independent nations is different from the dynamics of those societies where indigenous populations overthrew their European masters. The term is not only inadequate to the task of defining contemporary realities in the once-colonised countries, and vague in terms of indicating a specific period of history, but may also cloud the internal social and racial differences of many societies. Spanish colonies in Latin America, for example, became 'mixed' societies, in which local born whites (or 'creoles') and mestizos, or 'hybrids', dominated the native working population. Hybridity or mestizaje here included a complex internal hierarchy within various mixed peoples. As J. Jorge Klor de Alva explains, one's experience of colonial exploitation depended on one's position within this hierarchy:

> In most places, the original inhabitants, who logically grouped themselves into separate cultural units (i.e. ethnicities), all but disappeared after contact, wiped out physically by disease and abuse, and later, genetically and socially by miscegenation, and lastly, culturally, by the religious and political practices of the Europeans and their mixed progeny. Even in the regions where native peoples survived as corporate groups in their own greatly transformed communities, especially in the 'core' areas of Mesoamerica and the Andes, within two or three generations they were greatly reduced in number and politically and socially marginalized from the new centers of power. Thus, those who escaped the orbit of native communities but

were still the most socially and economically proximate to these dispossessed peoples could be expected to distance themselves from them wherever possible.

(1995: 243)

The term 'postcolonial' does not apply to those at the bottom end of this hierarchy, who are still 'at the far economic margins of the nation-state' so that nothing is 'post' about their colonisation. On the other hand, those elites who won the wars of independence from Spain, Alva argues, 'were never colonial subjects' and they 'established their own nation-states in the image of the mother-land, tinged by the local color of some precontact practices and symbols, framed by many imperial period adaptations and suffused with European ideals, practices and material objects' (1995: 270). The elite creoles, writes another critic, Mary Louise Pratt, 'sought esthetic and ideological grounding as white Americans' and attempted to create 'an independent, decolonised American society and culture, while retaining European values and white supremacy' (1992: 175). The quarrels of these Americans with colonial powers were radically different from anti-colonial struggles in parts of Africa or Asia and so, Alva concludes, they cannot be considered 'postcolonial' in the same sense.

In Australia, New Zealand or Canada, 'hybridity' is less evident between descendants of white settlers and those of the original inhabitants. But because the former also feel estranged from Britain (or France) they want to be considered postcolonial subjects. However, we cannot explore in what ways they are postcolonial without also highlighting internal differences within these countries (Mishra and Hodge 1991: 413). White settlers were historically the agents of colonial rule, and their own subsequent development – cultural as well as economic – does not simply align them with other colonised peoples. No matter what their differences with the mother country, white populations here were not subject to the genocide, economic exploitation, cultural decimation and political exclusion felt by indigenous peoples or by other colonies. Although we cannot equate its history with those of these other settler-countries, the most bizarre instance of this may be South Africa, where nationalist Afrikaners 'continued to see themselves as victims of English colonisation and . . . the imagined continuation of this victimization was used to justify the maintenance of apartheid' (Jolly 1995: 22).[1]

These internal fractures and divisions are important if 'post-colonialism' is to be anything more than a term signifying a technical transfer of governance. But at the same time, we cannot simply construct a global 'white' culture either. There are important differences of power and history between New Zealand or Canada and the European (or later United States) metropolis. Internal fractures also exist in countries whose postcolonial status is not usually contested, such as India. Here the ruptures have to do with class and ethnicity in a different sense. In a moving story, 'Shishu' (Children) the Bengali writer Mahasweta Devi describes how tribal peoples have been literally and figuratively crippled in post-independence India. National 'development' has no space for tribal cultures or beliefs, and the attitude of even the well-meaning government officer, Mr Singh, towards the tribals replicates colonialist views of non-Western peoples – to him, they are mysterious, superstitious, uncivilised, backward. In other words, they are like children who need to be brought in line with the rest of the country. The rebellious among them have literally been pushed into the forests and have been starving there for years. At the chilling climax of the tale, we are brought face to face with these 'children' who thrust their starved bodies towards Mr Singh, forcing the officer to recognise that they are not children at all but adult citizens of free India, and stunted by free India:

> Fear – stark, unreasoning, naked fear – gripped him. Why this silent creeping forward? Why didn't they utter one word? . . . Why were they naked? And why such long hair? Children, he

had always heard of children, but how come that one had white hair? Why did the women – no, no, girls – have dangling, withered breasts? . . . 'We are not children. We are Agarias of the Village of Kuva. . . . There are only fourteen of us left. Our bodies have shrunk without food. Our men are impotent, our women barren. That's why we steal the relief [the food Singh brings from the Government to distribute to the more docile among the tribals]. Don't you see we need food to grow to a human size again?' . . . .

They cackled with savage and revengeful glee. Cackling, they ran around him. They rubbed their organs against him and told him they were adult citizens of India . . . .

Singh's shadow covered their bodies. And the shadow brought the realization home to him.

They hated his height of five feet and nine inches.

They hated the normal growth of his body.

His normalcy was a crime they could not forgive.

Singh's cerebral cells tried to register the logical explanation but he failed to utter a single word. Why, why this revenge? He was just an ordinary Indian. He didn't have the stature of a healthy Russian, Canadian or American. He did not eat food that supplied enough calories for a human body. The World Health Organization said that it was a crime to deny the human body of the right number of calories . . . .

(Mahasweta Devi 1993: 248–250)

Even as it is careful to demarcate between what is available to citizens of different nations, the story reminds us that anti-colonial movements have rarely represented the interests of all the peoples of a colonised country. After independence, these fissures can no longer be glossed over, which is why, like some of their Indian counterparts, African novelists since the 1960s can also be regarded as 'no longer committed to the nation' (Appiah 1996: 66). The newly independent nation-state makes available the fruits of

liberation only selectively and unevenly: the dismantling of colonial rule did not automatically bring about changes for the better
in the status of women, the working class or the peasantry in
most colonised countries. 'Colonialism' is not just something that
happens from outside a country or a people, not just something
that operates with the collusion of forces inside, but a version of
it can be duplicated from within. So that 'postcolonialism', far
from being a term that can be indiscriminately applied, appears
to be riddled with contradictions and qualifications.

It has been suggested that it is more helpful to think of postcolonialism not just as coming literally after colonialism and signifying its demise, but more flexibly as the contestation of
colonial domination and the legacies of colonialism. Such a position would allow us to include people geographically displaced
by colonialism such as African-Americans or people of Asian or
Caribbean origin in Britain as 'postcolonial' subjects although
they live within metropolitan cultures. It also allows us to incorporate the history of anti-colonial resistance with contemporary
resistances to imperialism and to dominant Western culture.
Jorge de Alva suggests that postcoloniality should 'signify not so
much subjectivity "after" the colonial experience as a subjectivity
of oppositionality to imperializing/colonizing (read: subordinat-
ing/subjectivizing) discourses and practices'. He justifies this by
arguing that new approaches to history have discredited the idea
of a single linear progression, focusing instead on 'a multiplicity
of often conflicting and frequently parallel narratives'. Therefore,
he suggests that we should 'remove postcoloniality from a dependence on an antecedent colonial condition' and 'tether the term to
a post-structuralist stake that marks its appearance. That, I believe, is the way postcoloniality must be understood when applied to United States Latinos or Latin American hybrids' (Alva
1995: 245).

This statement is worth unpacking for it leads us into the
heart of the controversy surrounding postcolonial studies today.

Although we shall only discuss this controversy later in the book, we can take a quick look at the direction in which some current debates are moving. Alva wants to de-link the term postcoloniality from formal decolonisation because he thinks many people living in both once-colonised and once colonising countries are still subject to the oppressions put into place by colonialism. And he justifies this expansion of the term by referring to post-structuralist approaches to history which have suggested that the lives of various oppressed peoples can only be uncovered by insisting that there is no single history but a 'multiplicity of histories'. It was not only post-structuralists who discredited master narratives, feminists also insisted that such narratives had hidden women from history. Anti-colonial intellectuals also espoused a similar view. However, the idea has received its most sustained articulation within post-structuralist writing. Thus Alva suggests that postcoloniality is, and must be more firmly connected to, post-structuralist theories of history.

Recently, many critics of postcolonial theory have in fact blamed it for too much dependence upon post-structuralist or post-modern perspectives (which are often read as identical). They claim that the insistence on multiple histories and fragmentation within these perspectives has been detrimental to thinking about the global operation of capitalism today. The increasing fragmentation and mobility of communities and peoples needs to be contextualised in terms of the new ways in which global capitalism works. According to this argument, an accent on a multiplicity of histories serves to obfuscate the ways in which these histories are being connected anew by the international workings of multinational capital. Without this focus, the global imbalances of power are glossed over, and the world rendered 'seemingly shapeless' (Dirlik 1994: 355). A too-quick enlargement of the term postcolonial can indeed paradoxically flatten both past and contemporary situations. All 'subordinating' discourses and practices are not the same either over time or across the globe.

Erstwhile colonial powers may be restructured by contemporary imperialism but they are not the same phenomena. Opposition to colonial rule was spearheaded by forms of nationalist struggle which cannot offer a blueprint for dealing with inequities of the contemporary world order. In fact, as the Mahasweta Devi story quoted above exemplifies, many struggles in the postcolonial world are sceptical about precisely those forces and discourses that were responsible for formal decolonisation.

And so, we might ask not only when does the postcolonial begin, but where is postcoloniality to be found? Although 'minority' peoples living in the West (and they may not in every place be literally a minority at all) and the peoples living in 'third world' countries share a history of colonial exploitation, may share cultural roots, and may also share an opposition to the legacy of colonial domination, their histories and present concerns cannot simply be merged. African-Americans and South African blacks, for example, may both be engaged in the reconstruction of their cultures, yet how can we forget that blacks in South Africa are the marginalised majority of the population or that African-Americans are citizens of the world's mightiest state although their own position within it might be marginal? These differences are highlighted by a production of Shakespeare's *Othello* by the South African actress Janet Suzman. Suzman had been living in Britain for many years when she returned home to mount the play for the Market Theatre in Johannesburg, in which she cast a black actor in the central role. In the context of a long history of *Othello* productions where the hero is played by a white man, or which simply gloss over the racial politics of the play in favour of the 'universal' themes of male jealousy, doomed love, and devoted female victims, and especially in the context of South Africa's laws against mixed marriages, this production was radical. And to place Othello in one of the cultures of 'his' origin is to allow us to rethink the entire history of the play. But at the same time, Shakespeare's drama is about a black man trying to live in a white society, assimilating yet maintaining his identity. His loneliness is an integral feature of the play – he is isolated from other black people, from his history and culture. To place Shakespeare's *Othello* in South Africa is to open up a powerful new reading of the play, but also to elide two different kinds of marginality: the one which arises out of displacement and another in which black people and cultures were victimised but not literally isolated from each other.

Othello's situation of course does not translate exactly into today's European context because so-called metropolitan societies are now literally changing their colours. Othello's successors are not so alone. And yet, British Asians face a different sort of pressure on their self-definition than people within India or Pakistan or Bangladesh. Further, by now there are as many differences between each of these groups as there are similarities. Similarly anti-colonial positions are embedded in specific histories, and cannot be collapsed into some pure oppositional essence. They also depended on the nature of colonial rule so that nationalist struggles in Algeria against the French were different from Indian resistance to the British, and neither can be equated to Vietnamese opposition to French and United States imperialism. As we will see, many writings on postcolonialism emphasise concepts like 'hybridity' and fragmentation and diversity, and yet they routinely claim to be describing 'the postcolonial condition', or 'the postcolonial subject' or 'the postcolonial woman'. At best, such terms are no more than a helpful shorthand, because they do not allow for differences between distinct kinds of colonial situations, or the workings of class, gender, location, race, caste or ideology among people whose lives have been restructured by colonial rule.

As mentioned earlier, by the 1930s colonialism had exercised its sway over 84.6 per cent of the land surface of the globe. This fact alone reminds us that it is impossible for European colonialism to have been a monolithic operation. Right from its earliest years it deployed diverse strategies and methods of control and of representation. European discourses about 'the other' are accordingly variable. But because they produced comparable (and sometimes uncannily similar) relations of inequity and domination the world over, it is sometimes overlooked that colonial methods and images varied hugely over time and place. Most contemporary commentators continue to generalise about colonialism from their specific knowledge of it in a particular place or time. Thus, for some critics such as Gayatri Spivak, nineteenth-century India, and particularly nineteenth-century Bengal, has become a privileged model for the colonised world. Laura Chrisman finds that 'an Oriental/Occidental binarism, in which continents and colonies which do not belong to this West/East axis are nonetheless absorbed into it' is detrimental to recovering the specificity of certain situations in Africa. Although such homogenising might partially have arisen from the desire to emphasise how colonial discourses themselves blur difference, its effect, as Chrisman points out, is to overlook how these discourses also deploy strategies of exaggerating and playing off differences among diverse others:

> It is just as important to observe differences between imperial practices – whether it be geographical/national (for example, the differences between the French imperialism of Baudelaire and the English imperialism of Kipling) or historical (say the differences between the early-nineteenth-century imperialism, prior to its formal codification, and late-nineteenth-century imperialism) – as it is to emphasize what all these formations have in common.
>
> (Chrisman 1994: 500)

The legacies of colonialism are thus varied and multiple even as they obviously share some important features.

If the term postcolonial is taken to signify an oppositional position or even desire, as Alva suggests, then it has the effect of collapsing various locations so that the specificities of all of them are blurred. Moreover, thought of as an oppositional stance, 'postcolonial' refers to specific groups of (oppressed or dissenting) people (or individuals within them) rather than to a location or a social order, which may include such people but is not limited to them. Postcolonial theory has been accused of precisely this: it shifts the focus from locations and institutions to individuals and their subjectivities. Postcoloniality becomes a vague condition of people anywhere and everywhere, and the specificities of locale do not matter. In part the dependence of postcolonial theory upon literary and cultural criticism, and upon post-structuralism is responsible for this shift. So we are back to the critique articulated earlier – that post-structuralism is responsible for current inadequacies in theorising postcoloniality. We will return to this issue when some of the terms in the debate have been further clarified. For now, we can see some of the problems with expanding the term postcolonial to signify a political position.

There is yet another issue at stake in the term, and this time the problem is not with 'post' but with 'colonial'. Analyses of 'postcolonial' societies too often work with the sense that colonialism is the only history of these societies. What came before colonial rule? What indigenous ideologies, practices and hierarchies existed alongside colonialism and interacted with it? Colonialism did not inscribe itself on a clean slate, and it cannot therefore account for everything that exists in 'postcolonial' societies. The food, or music, or languages, or arts of any culture that we think of as postcolonial evoke earlier histories or shades of culture that elude the term 'colonial'. Critics such as Gayatri Spivak have repeatedly cautioned against the idea that pre-colonial cultures are something that we can easily recover, warning that 'a nostalgia for lost origins can be detrimental to the exploration of social realities within the critique of imperialism' (1988: 211–313). Spivak is suggesting here that the pre-colonial is always reworked by the history of colonialism, and is not available to us in any pristine form that can be neatly separated from the history of colonialism. She is interested in emphasising the worlding (i.e. both the violation and the creation) of the 'third world' by colonial powers and therefore resists the romanticising of once-colonised societies 'as distant cultures, exploited but with rich intact heritages waiting to be recovered . . . '. Other critics such as Kwame Anthony Appiah (1991) have also criticised the tendency to eulogise the pre-colonial past or romanticise native culture. Such 'nativism', they suggest is espoused by both certain intellectuals within postcolonial societies and some First World academics. But while such caution is necessary, it can also lead to a reverse simplification, whereby the 'Third World' is seen as a world defined entirely by its relation to colonialism. Its histories are then flattened, and colonialism becomes their defining feature, whereas in several parts of the once-colonised world, historians are inclined to regard colonialism 'as a minor interruption' in a long, complex history (Vaughan 1993: 47).

Postcolonialism, then, is a word that is useful only if we use it with caution and qualifications. In this it can be compared to the concept of 'patriarchy' in feminist thought, which is applicable to the extent that it indicates male domination over women. But the ideology and practices of male domination are historically, geographically and culturally variable. English patriarchal structures were different in the sixteenth century from what they are today, and they varied also between classes, then and now. All of these are further distinct from patriarchy in China, which is also variable over time and social groupings. But of course all of these also have something in common, so feminist theory has had to weave between analysing the universals and the particulars in the oppression of women. Patriarchy then becomes a useful shorthand for conveying a structure of inequity, which is, in practice, highly variable because it always works alongside other social structures. Similarly, the word 'postcolonial' is useful as a generalisation to the extent that 'it refers to a *process* of disengagement from the whole colonial syndrome, which takes many forms and is probably inescapable for all those whose worlds have been marked by that set of phenomena: "postcolonial" is (or should be) a descriptive not an evaluative term' (Hulme 1995: 120).

Postcolonial studies have shown that both the 'metropolis' and the 'colony' were deeply altered by the colonial process. *Both* of them are, accordingly, also restructured by decolonisation. This of course does not mean that both are postcolonial *in the same way*. Postcoloniality, like patriarchy, is articulated alongside other economic, social, cultural and historical factors, and therefore, in practice, it works quite differently in various parts of the world. Frankenburg and Mani (1993) and Hulme (1995) make this point by tracing some of the ways in which the meaning of the term shifts across different locations. Hulme argues that, contrary to Alva's suggestion, the American continent is postcolonial, even though its anti-colonial wars were not fought by the indigenous peoples. American postcoloniality, in Hulme's argument, is simply *different* from the one that operates in India, and it also includes enormous variety within itself (the USA is the world's leading imperialist power but it once was anti-colonial in a limited sense; the Caribbean and Latin America still struggle with the effects of colonial domination and neo-colonialism). To impose a single understanding of decolonisation would in fact erase the differences within that term. In this view, there is a productive tension between the temporal and the critical dimensions of the word postcolonial, but postcoloniality is not, Hulme points out, simply a 'merit badge' that can be worn at will. We can conclude, then, that the word 'postcolonial' is useful in indicating a general process with some shared features across the globe. But if it is uprooted from specific locations, 'postcoloniality' cannot be meaningfully investigated, and instead, the term begins to obscure the very relations of domination that it seeks to uncover.

FROM COLONIALISM TO COLONIAL DISCOURSE

What is new about the current ways of discussing colonialism and its aftermath? Is there anything new at all? In order to answer such questions it is necessary to place postcolonial studies within two broad (and overlapping) contexts. The first is the history of decolonisation itself. Intellectuals and activists who fought against colonial rule, and their successors who now engage with its continuing legacy, challenged and revised dominant definitions of race, culture, language and class in the process of making their voices heard. The second context is the revolution, within 'Western' intellectual traditions, in thinking about some of the same issues – language and how it articulates experience, how ideologies work, how human subjectivities are formed, and what we might mean by culture. These two revolutions are sometimes counterpoised to one another, but it is impossible to understand the current debates in postcolonial studies (whether or not we approve of them) without making the connections between them. It is obviously difficult to summarise these developments for they entail not only the history of the social sciences in the West over the last hundred years, but also political movements that cover most of the globe. However, this section will outline some of the key areas of debate and conceptual innovation around issues of ideology, language and culture, which have had an impact upon the analysis of colonialism. The intersections of such intellectual developments with anti-colonial articulation will become evident both here and in later sections.

So far, we have defined colonialism as the forcible takeover of land and economy, and, in the case of European colonialism, a restructuring of non-capitalist economies in order to fuel European capitalism. This allows us to understand modern European colonialism not as some transhistorical impulse to conquer but as an integral part of capitalist development. But such a definition leaves many questions unanswered. In placing colonialism within

the trajectory of capitalism, most Marxist thinkers tended to regard colonialism, as indeed they did capitalism, as an exploitative yet necessary phase of human social development. History,
in their view, was a teleological movement that would culminate in communism. This would not happen automatically, but
as a result of a fierce struggle between opposing classes. In certain respects, 'progress' was understood in similar ways by capitalists as well as socialists — for both, it included a high level of
industrialisation, the mastery of 'man' over 'nature', the modern
European view of science and technology. Colonialism, in as
much as it was the vehicle for the export of Western technologies, also spelt the export of these ideas. Hence Marx himself regarded colonialism as a brutal precondition for the liberation of
these societies: 'England, it is true, in causing a social revolution
in Hindustan was actuated only by the vilest interests, and was
stupid in her manner of enforcing them. But that is not the
question. The question is, can mankind fulfil its destiny without
a fundamental revolution in the social state of Asia? If not,
whatever may have been the crimes of England she was the unconscious tool of history in bringing about that revolution'
(1973: 306).

Many nineteenth- and twentieth-century writers equated the
advance of European colonisation with the triumph of science and
reason over the forces of superstition, and indeed many colonised
peoples took the same view. An Education Despatch of 1854 explicitly connected 'the advance of European knowledge' in India
to the economic development of the subcontinent. English education would 'teach the natives of India the marvellous results of
the employment of labour and capital', and 'rouse them to emu-
late us in the development of the vast resources of the country'
(quoted Adas 1989: 284). The Indian reformer Raja Rammohan
Roy had already written to the Governor-General Lord Amherst
some thirty years earlier that the government policy of support to
Sanskrit and Arabic-Persian education would serve only to 'keep

[India] in darkness'. Thus, across the colonial spectrum, European technology and learning was regarded as progressive.

However, Marxism's penetrating critique of colonialism as capitalism was inspirational for many anti-colonial struggles. Aimé Césaire's moving and powerful *Discourse on Colonialism* (first published in 1950) indicts colonial brutality in terms that are clearly inflected by Marxist analysis of capitalism. Marx emphasised that under capitalism money and commodities begin to stand in for human relations and for human beings, objectifying them and robbing them of their human essence. Similarly, Césaire claims that colonialism not only exploits but dehumanises and objectifies the colonised subject, as it degrades the coloniser himself. He explains this by a stark 'equation: colonisation = "thingification" ' (1972: 21). But at the same time, for anti-colonial intellectuals, the Marxist understanding of class struggle as the motor of history had to be revised because in the colonial context the division between the haves and the have-nots was inflected by race. Thus, in *The Wretched of the Earth*, Fanon writes:

> this world cut in two is inhabited by two different species. The originality of the colonial context is that economic reality, inequality and the immense difference of ways of life never come to mask the human realities. When you examine at close quarters the colonial context, it is evident that what parcels out the world is to begin with the fact of belonging to or not belonging to a given race, a given species. In the colonies the economic substructure is also a superstructure. The cause is the consequence; you are rich because you are white, you are white because you are rich. This is why Marxist analysis should always be slightly stretched every time we have to do with the colonial problem.
>
> (1963: 32)

Here Fanon maps race and class divisions on to one another. But such mapping is extremely difficult to grasp in all its complexity without a specific understanding of race, which did not find much space in classical Marxism. If in the colonies, whiteness and wealth dovetailed, it clearly did not do so within European countries. And yet, white working classes could display as much racism as their masters. In the colonies, as the Prime Minister of Cape colony remarked in 1908, white workers were 'delighted on arrival . . . to find themselves in a position of an aristocracy of colour' (Ranger 1983: 213). Was such racial consciousness created by colonial hierarchies, or was it integral to the whiteness of the European working classes?

These questions obviously demanded more than a 'slight stretching' of Marxist analysis. But such 'stretching' did not come easily: while some analysts emphasised class as primary, others insisted that the world was basically split along racial lines. For example, although he was a staunch member of the Martiniquan Communist Party, Césaire places 'Africa' as the binary opposite of 'Europe', a Europe that is 'decadent', 'stricken' and 'morally, spiritually indefensible' (1972: 9). For Césaire was also one of the founders of the Negritude movement, which emphasised the cultural antagonism between Europe and its 'others'. If, in Kipling's words, 'East is East, and West is West and ne'er the twain shall meet', then Negritude angrily endorsed this conceptual distance. Césaire issues a sweeping indictment of Europe on the one hand, and a 'systematic defense of the non-European civilizations' on the other, claiming that they were 'communal', 'anti-capitalist', 'democratic', 'co-operative' and 'federal' before they were invaded by European colonialism, capitalism and imperialism. Thus, it is suggested, the difference between Europe and its others can be understood as a difference between capitalist and non-capitalist societies. Césaire shares something here with his fellow Martiniquan Frantz Fanon, who also emphasised the dehumanising aspect of colonialism, thus pushing its analysis into the realm of the psyche and the subjectivity of colonised people, as well as of their masters. *Black Skin, White Masks* thus defines colonised people as not simply those whose labour has been appropriated but those 'in whose soul an inferiority complex has been created by the death and burial of its local cultural originality' (Fanon 1967: 18).

Analogous debates have marked the relationship of class and gender. Although Marxist thought had paid a great deal of attention to the oppression of women, it failed to theorise the *specificity* of gender oppression. For feminists, the question of culture and ideologies was vital for a variety of reasons: women's oppression had hitherto been seen as simply a matter of culture and as taking place within the family – the exploitation of their labour power was obscured by a gender-blind economic analysis which could not integrate class with other forms of social division. But, on the other hand, there was no serious analysis of the family or culture or sexuality, and of how precisely women were marginalised. Women's oppression was, consequently, seriously undertheorised within Marxism, but also of course in the wider intellectual sphere. The crucial question – how does the oppression of women connect with the operations of capitalism (or other economic systems) – remained unanswered till feminists began to interrelate the economic and the ideological aspects of women's oppression. The question of race and colonialism also demanded rethinking for similar reasons. The impact of colonialism on culture is intimately tied up with its economic processes but the relationship between them cannot be understood unless cultural processes are theorised as fully and deeply as the economic ones. In recent years, some of the fiercest disagreements among scholars are about this interrelation. Colonised intellectuals consistently raised the question of their cultures, both as the sites of colonial oppression, and as vital tools for their own resistance. Thus the analysis of colonialism demanded that the categories developed for understanding capitalism (such as class) be revised, but also that the relation between the realm of 'culture' or 'ideology' and the sphere of 'economics' or 'material reality' be re-examined.

Ideology does not, as is often assumed, refer to political ideas alone. It includes all our 'mental frameworks', our beliefs, concepts, and ways of expressing our relationship to the world. It is one of the most complex and elusive terms in social thought, and the object of continuing debates. Yet the central question at the heart of these debates is fairly straightforward: how can we give an account of how our social ideas arise? Here we shall discuss in an extremely condensed fashion only those strands that are especially important for understanding developments in discussions of colonialism and race.[2]

In *The German Ideology* (written in 1846), Marx and Engels had suggested that ideology is basically a distorted or a false consciousness of the world which disguises people's real relationship to their world. This is so because the ideologies that most circulate or gain currency in any society reflect and reproduce the interests of the dominant social classes. Hence, for example a factory worker, the fruits of whose hard labour are appropriated daily by his or her master still believes in the virtue of hard work or of being rewarded in heaven. These beliefs both persuade workers to continue to work and blind them to the truth about their own exploitation; hence they reflect the interests of their master, or of the capitalist system. Similarly, a battered wife (although Marx and Engels do not consider such an example) may believe that single women are more vulnerable to danger and violence, and more lonely and unhappy than married women, and this belief impels her not to rebel against her situation, and even allows her to expound on the necessity for women to be married. Or a white worker might mistakenly think that his joblessness is the fault of black immigrants. Thus ideology has the function of obscuring from the working (and other oppressed) classes the 'real' state of their own lives and exploitation.

Marx and Engels used the metaphor of the *camera obscura* to explain the processes of such obfuscation or misrepresentation: 'If in ideology men and their realizations appear upside down as in a *camera obscura*, this phenomenon arises just as much from their historical life-process as the inversion of objects on their retina does from the physical life-process' (Marx and Engels 1976, vol. 5: 37). Such a comparison implies that the human mind spontaneously and necessarily inverts reality. Marx and Engels emphasised strongly that our ideas come from the world around us, that 'It is not consciousness that determines life, but life that determines consciousness' (1976, vol. 5: 36). All our ideas, including our self-conceptions, spring from the world in which we live. And this world, under capitalism, itself gives rise to a series of illusions. Money has the power to distort, even invert reality. Marx illustrated this with a speech from Shakespeare's play *Timon of Athens* in which Timon, outcast and abandoned by his friends after he has lost his wealth speculates that 'yellow glittering gold' is a 'visible god' which has the power to make

> Black white, foul fair, wrong right,
> Base noble, old young, coward valiant . . . .
> . . . . This yellow slave
> Will knit and break religions, bless th'accurs'd,
> Make the hoar leprosy ador'd, place thieves
> And give them title, knee and approbation
> With senators on the bench . . . .
>
> (IV, iii, 26–38)[3]

As capitalism advances, money and commodities increasingly displace, stand in for, and are mistaken for human values. Thus they become fetishised (fetishes being objects which we invest with human qualities). In this view, ideology is not a failure to perceive reality, for reality (capitalism) itself is ideological, disguising its essential features in a realm of false appearances.

If reality itself leads us to a distorted perception of it, is it at all possible to hold subversive ideas, or to see things as they are? If our material being holds the key to our ideas, then the latter cannot change unless the former does. Marx does not regard all ideas as ideological or false. He contrasts ideology to science, which has the capacity to cut through illusions. The Hungarian theoretician Georg Lukács offered an alternative view of ideology in which it is not always understood as false consciousness. Rather, the validity or falsity of an ideology depends upon the 'class situation' of the collective subject whose view it represents. Thus, if bourgeois ideology expressed the distorted nature of capitalism, the proletariat was capable of a more scientific view which would express the true nature of reality. Ideologies are not therefore always false consciousness, but in every case, they are still the product of economic and social life. The problem with such reasoning was of course that it simply asserted, rather than demonstrated, the cognitive superiority of the proletarian view. It also posited a very formulaic correspondence between particular classes and ideologies.

In fact, no correspondence between ideologies and classes can be taken for granted. Classes are heterogeneous groups, fissured by gender, race and other divides. Different people within the same class do not hold the same relationship to the production process, or to other aspects of reality. Their ideologies cannot, accordingly, be the same. There could be no uniform ideology of the working class, for example, since this class was split along racial lines. Moreover, as the Russian critic Volosinov wrote, 'different classes will use one and the same language. As a result, differently oriented accents intersect in every ideological sign. Sign becomes the arena of class struggle' (1973: 23). This insight has obvious implications for the question of racial and colonial difference, where 'differently oriented accents' have laid claim to and appropriated not only different languages such as English or French, but also other 'signs' such as art, music, food and politics. Similarly, ideologies are also fields of 'intersecting accents' coming from several different directions. For example, men on both sides of the colonial divide could share certain patriarchal assumptions about women and their sexuality. Thus languages and ideologies are 'multi-accentual'.

In many ways, it was the work of the Italian communist Antonio Gramsci that made it possible to think about how ideologies can cut across different classes and how, also, the same class can hold many, even contradictory, ideologies. Gramsci's views do not form part of a finished philosophy and are scattered in his various prison diaries or *Prison Notebooks*, written between 1929 and 1935 (1971). Gramsci questioned the primacy of the economic (conceptualised as 'base' in classical Marxist thought) over the ideological (conceived of as 'superstructure') because he was trying to understand the failure of the revolution in Western Europe, despite the economic conditions being ripe for the same. This does not mean that Gramsci ignored the role of economic changes. Rather, he did not believe that they alone create historic events, rather, they can only create conditions which are favourable for certain kinds of ideologies to flourish.

Gramsci drew a distinction between various kinds of ideologies, suggesting that while ideology in general works to maintain social cohesion and expresses dominant interests, there are also particular ideologies that express the protest of those who are exploited. The proletariat or oppressed subject possesses a dual consciousness – that which is beholden to the rulers, and complicit with their will, and that which is capable of developing into resistance. If social realities, including social conflicts, are grasped by human beings via their ideologies, then ideologies are also the site of social struggle. (Later, Raymond Williams discussed how these ideological contradictions could fuel resistance on the part of individual and collective subjects.)

In trying to probe these nuances within the 'class subject' (which had previously been seen in rather unitary terms) Gramsci makes a crucial distinction between 'philosophy' and 'common sense' – two floors or levels on which ideology operates. The former is a specialised elaboration of a specific position. 'Common sense', on the other hand, is the practical, everyday, popular consciousness of human beings. Most of us think about 'common sense' as that which is obviously true, common to everybody, or normative. Gramsci analyses how such 'common sense' is formed. It is actually a highly contradictory body of beliefs that combines 'elements from the Stone Age and principles of a more advanced science, prejudices from all past phases of history at the local level and intuitions of a future philosophy which will be that of the human race united the world over'. Common sense is thus an amalgam of ideas 'on which the practical consciousness of the masses of the people is actually formed' (Hall 1996b: 431).

But if ideologies and classes do not neatly overlap, why is it that, as Marx and Engels put it, 'the ideas of the ruling class are in every epoch the ruling ideas' (1976: 59)? How is it that ordinary people come to be persuaded of a specific view of things? In other words, the crucial question about ideology is not whether it is 'real' or 'false' but how it comes to be believed in, to be lived out? It was in trying to understand these questions that Gramsci formulated his concept of 'hegemony'. Hegemony is power achieved through a combination of coercion and consent. Playing upon Machiavelli's suggestion that power can be achieved through both force and fraud, Gramsci argued that the ruling classes achieve domination not by force or coercion alone, but also by creating subjects who 'willingly' submit to being ruled. Ideology is crucial in creating consent, it is the medium through which certain ideas are transmitted and more important, held to be true. Hegemony is achieved not only by direct manipulation or indoctrination, but by playing upon the common sense of people, upon what Raymond Williams calls their 'lived system of meanings and values' (1977: 110). Gramsci thus views ideologies as more than just reflections of material reality. Rather, ideologies are conceptions of life that are manifest in all aspects of individual and collective existence. By suggesting this, Gramsci is not simply interested in *expanding* the meaning of ideology, but in understanding also how ideologies animate social relations 'organize human masses, and create the terrain on which men move, acquire consciousness of their position, struggle, etc.' (Gramsci 1971: 324, 377).

Stuart Hall perceptively draws out the importance of these ideas for thinking about the relationship between race, ethnicity and colonialism on the one hand, and capital and class on the other (see Hall 1996b). In trying to formulate reasons for the failure of the Italian revolution, Gramsci needed to differentiate between Italy and the rest of Europe as well as different regions in Italy, laying the ground for thinking about national and regional issues as an important part of capitalist development. Thus he did not treat 'labour' as a homogeneous category (Hall 1996b: 436). Capitalism works *through* and because of 'the culturally specific character of labour power' or, to put it more simply, class and race are mutually constitutive and shaping forces. Gramsci's attempt to think about the so-called backwardness of his own birthplace, Sardinia (and of southern Italy in general) in relation to a more affluent north, is useful for us in considering how racial and cultural differences operate within the same class, or mode of production. How did colonial regimes differentiate between races and groups but also simultaneously incorporate them all within a general system? For example, how did Bantustans function to spur the development of advanced capitalism in South Africa? In the next chapter, we will examine in greater detail how race and class function together. Here I only want to point out that Gramsci's notion that ideologies 'create the terrain on which men move' helps us to locate racism not just as an effect of capitalism but as more complexly intertwined with it.

Gramsci's ideas have been employed by a wide range of writers to analyse race and colonialism. Errol Lawrence (1982) for example, has used them to discuss the 'common-sense' ideas about black people in postwar Britain, which he shows to be a combination of older prejudices and newer responses formulated within contemporary economic and cultural crisis. Scholars at the Centre for Contemporary Cultural Studies have used Gramsci to analyse contemporary political formations in Europe, as has the Subaltern Studies group of Indian historians to revise existing theories of nationalism and postcolonial social formations (Hall *et al*. 1978; Guha 1982). Similarly Latin American and South African historians find Gramsci useful in thinking about the nature of the colonial and postcolonial state (Mallon 1994; Cooper 1994). Today, historians are increasingly interested in probing how colonial regimes achieved domination through creating partial consent, or involving the colonised peoples in creating the states and regimes which oppressed them. Gramsci's notion of hegemony is of obvious interest to these scholars, even though they often invoke it in order to emphasise how *dissimilar* colonial situations were from the European ones analysed by Gramsci (see Engels and Marks 1994). Colonial domination involved much repression and coercion, and thus is sometimes analysed as a process which did not involve the consent of the colonised. However, recent scholarship has suggested that in colonial societies, harsh coercion worked 'in tandem with a "consent" that was part voluntary, part contrived' (Arnold 1994: 133). Colonial regimes tried to gain the consent of certain groups, while excluding others from civil society. But even the most repressive rule involved some give-and-take. Gramscian notions of hegemony stress the incorporation and transformation of ideas and practices belonging to those who are dominated, rather than simple imposition from above. Such transformations are being increasingly seen as central to colonial rule. The dimension of Gramsci's work that has most inspired revisionary analyses of colonial societies is his understanding that subjectivity and ideology are absolutely central to the processes of domination. We will return later to some of this material. At this point, though, we need to stay with the question of ideology for a while and trace how some subsequent debates about it shaped key 'post-structuralist' notions of power, whose place within postcolonial studies is so contentious today.

The work of the French communist theorist Louis Althusser on ideology has been both influential as well as controversial. Althusser explored further the dialectic between ideas and material existence. In doing so he opened up certain important and new areas of inquiry such as *how* ideologies are internalised, how human beings make dominant ideas 'their own', how they express socially determined views 'spontaneously'. Althusser was interested in how subjects and their deepest selves are 'interpellated' (the term is borrowed from Freud), positioned (the term is Lacan's), and shaped by what lies outside them. Ideologies may express the interests of social groups, but they work through and upon individual people or 'subjects'. In fact subjectivity, or personhood, Althusser suggested, is itself formed in and through ideology. For him, psychoanalysis was most valuable in suggesting that the human being has no essential 'centre', 'except in the imaginary misrecognition of the "ego", i.e. in the ideological formations in which it "recognizes" itself'. This 'structure of misrecognition' was, for Althusser, most important in understanding ideology (1971: 218–219). He explicitly borrowed from Lacanian psychoanalysis and its account of subject-formation through language (and its slippages) in probing how ideology might work.

It still remains extremely difficult to bring together questions of human subjectivity with those of human collectivity. There is still a split between psychoanalytically inflected critiques of the 'insides' of people, and the Marxist discourses of their 'outsides'. Stuart Hall astutely suggests that Althusser's influential essay 'Ideological State Apparatuses' may in fact have contributed to such a bifurcation by adopting a two-part structure, the first addressing ideology and the reproduction of the social relations of production, and the second how ideology creates us as subjects (1985: 91–114). But we can also argue that it was Althusser's very juxtaposition of these disparate vocabularies which put their interrelation on the agenda. However, Althusser's work was also deeply problematic and contradictory in its effects. He tried to explore further Gramsci's suggestion that ideas are transmitted via certain social institutions. Gramsci had suggested, you will recall, that hegemony is achieved via a combination of 'force' and 'consent'. Althusser argued that in modern capitalist societies, the former is achieved by 'Repressive State Apparatuses' such as the army and the police, but the latter is enforced via 'Ideological State Apparatuses' such as schools, the Church, the family, media and political systems. These ideological apparatuses assist in the reproduction of the dominant system by creating subjects who are ideologically conditioned to accept the values of the system. Such an idea is immensely useful in demystifying certain apparently innocent and apolitical institutions and has subsequently influenced analyses of schools, universities, family structures, and (via the work of Althusser's friend Pierre Macherey) literary texts. But it also effects a closure by failing to account for ideological struggle and oppositional ideas. If subjects are entirely the creation of dominant ideologies then there is no scope for any ideas outside of these ideologies, and thus no scope for social change. Thus we can say that Althusser's ideas about ideological apparatuses are too functionalist: they stress the function but not the complexity of either institutions or human subjects.

In pursuing Gramsci's suggestion that ideas can mould material reality Althusser argued that ideology has a 'relative autonomy' from the material base. He then expanded this idea and suggested that ideology 'has a material existence' in the sense that 'an ideology always exists in an apparatus, and its practice, or practices' (1971: 166). Some of Althusser's admirers began to employ the notion of the material effect of ideology in a way that suggested that ideology and material practices were practically identical. This blurring stems from some of Athusser's own formulations.[4] In many post-Althusserian formulations, however, 'material in its effect' begins to be read as 'material in itself'. This shift in meaning is problematic; after all, it makes no sense to say that ideology is material in its effect if the two terms are the same thing to begin with. The problem is an important one for post-colonial theory, which, as we shall see, has been accused of being unable to maintain any distinction between ideas (culture, representation and language) and material realities (economic systems). This is obviously a difficult and tricky issue because on the one hand there is the need to interrelate the two so that issues of culture and economics are seen as mutually constitutive, and on the other hand there is also the need to maintain some distinction so that the specificity of each is not eroded.

Althusser's work and the renewed interest it sparked in issues of ideologies, language and subjectivity have had a somewhat contradictory effect. It certainly opened up innovative ways of analysing institutions as well as ideas. At the same time, following upon Althusser's interest in language and psyche, subject-formation is often taken to be an effect of language and ideas, and a matter of individual psychic development alone. These innovative as well as reductive effects are both visible in postcolonial studies, often refracted through the writings of Althusser's student Michel Foucault. Foucault's work stands at the intersection of innovations in theories of ideology, subjectivity and language, and has exerted an important (some would say even definitive) influence on the shaping of post-modernist and post-structuralist ideas and, via Edward Said's *Orientalism* (1978), on postcolonial studies.

Foucault pushed to an extreme the idea of human beings being determined by the conditions of their existence. Like Marx and Engels, and Althusser after them, he tried to understand how the human subject is not an autonomous, free entity. However, his search led him to reject the distinction between ideas and material existence altogether and to abandon entirely the category of 'ideology'. All human ideas, and all fields of knowledge, are structured and determined by 'the laws of a certain code of knowledge' (Foucault 1970: ix). Thus no subject is 'free' and no utterance undetermined by a predetermined order or code. It is in this sense that Foucault pronounces the death of the author, for no single individual is the sole source of any utterance. This view intersects with certain important innovations in linguistics which also challenged conventional ways of thinking about human utterance. According to one critic, it is 'the triple alliance' between Althusserian Marxism, Lacanian psychoanalysis and Saussurean linguistics which spawns discourse analysis (Elliot 1996: 255).

The Swiss linguist Ferdinand de Saussure had argued that the relation between the 'signifier' (which is a sound image) and the 'signified' (which is the concept to which it refers) is arbitrary, which it is to say that words achieve their meaning from an association in the mind, not from any natural or necessary reference to entities in the real world. These associations work through the principle of exclusion, which is to say that any sign achieves meaning diacritically, or through a system of differentiation from other signs. Thus, language is not a nomenclature, or a way of naming things which already exist, but a system of signs, whose meaning is relational. Only a social group can produce signs, because only a specific social usage gives a sign any meaning. So, if 'in Welsh the colour glas (blue), like the Latin glaucus, includes elements which the English would identify as green or gray', the different meanings are put into place by the different communities using these words (Belsey 1980: 39). The sign, or words, need a community with shared assumptions to confer them with meaning; conversely, a social group needs signs in order to know itself as a community. On this basis, we can think of language as ideological rather than as objective.

Several influential thinkers such as Lévi-Strauss attempted to systematise Saussure's ideas and suggest that there were general laws that governed how any and all signs worked, so that with the same general understanding, any cultural or signifying practice – from hair styles to myths – could be studied. This assumption, that there are general and 'scientific' laws underlying all cultural production (known as structuralism) was criticised from several different directions. The French Marxist Pierre Macherey objected to it on the grounds that no single system of meaning can work in every place and at every time. To find such a system would be to imply that texts acquire meaning even before they are written. Instead, Macheray suggested that texts can only be understood in the context of their utterance. The literary text 'is not created by an intention (objective or subjective); it is produced under determinate conditions' (1978: 78). When and where a text is written, the language in which it is inscribed, the traditions and debates within which it intervenes all come together to create a textual fabric. What a text can say is as determined by these factors as what it cannot say. Jacques Derrida also criticised Lévi-Strauss for implying that there was a secure outside ground from which different representations could be studied, but the grounds of his criticism are different. He said that Lévi-Strauss had not gone far enough in confronting the implications of the instability of the sign. Instead, Derrida read Saussure more radically to suggest that no sign is identical with what it signifies, and there is always a gap between the two. The slippage between words or signs and their meaning is evident in every representation, every utterance. Accordingly, no utterance or text is capable of perfectly conveying its own meaning. But all texts, if analysed closely enough, or deconstructed, reveal their own instability, and their contradictions (Derrida 1994: 347–358). Meaning, in other words, is not self-present in the sign, or in text, but is the result of this gap, slippage or what Derrida calls 'différance'.

These are complex questions, which provoked sprawling and nuanced responses. For our purposes, the important point is that although these thinkers differ from each other on questions of politics as well as method, they share some important features. All of them question the humanist assumption that individuals are the sole source of meaning or action.[5] Language emerges not as the creation of the speaking subject; rather the subject becomes so only by schooling his speech to a socially determined system of linguistic prescriptions. The primacy of language over subjectivity was also confirmed by Lacanian psychoanalysis according to which the child learns to see itself as distinct from the rest of the world by regarding its own mirror image, but becomes a full subject only when it enters the world of language. Thus from a variety of different intersecting perspectives, language is seen to *construct* the subject. Perhaps the most radical result of these interconnecting but diverse ways of thinking about language was that no human utterance could be seen as innocent. Any set of words could be analysed to reveal not just an individual but a historical consciousness at work. Words and images thus become fundamental for an analysis of historical processes such as colonialism.

We can see the ways in which these intellectual developments dovetail with the ideology debates. Together, they suggested that ideological and social practices are interconnected, indeed that they constitute each other. The place of language, culture and the individual in political and economic processes could no longer be seen as simply derivative or secondary, even though the exact ways in which they come together are still a matter of sharp controversy and debate. I want to keep this element of heterogeneity and debate constantly in view, and emphasise that the intellectual positions I have summarised do not always share a political agenda or methodology. They do intensify and sharpen debates about the social fabric, and make it imperative for us to weave the economic realities of colonialism with all that was hitherto excluded from 'hard' social analysis – sexuality, subjectivity, psychology and language. They remind us that the 'real' relations of society do not exist in isolation from its cultural or ideological categories. And these various radical ways of thinking about language and ideology do share this much: they challenge any rigid demarcation of event and representation, or history and text.

This brings us back to Foucault, for whom such a demarcation is impossible. We have already discussed how Foucault collapses the notion of ideology. All ideas are ordered through 'some material medium' (1970: 100). This ordering imposes a pattern on them: a pattern which Foucault calls 'discourse'. The *OED* tells us that 'discourse', after the Latin cursus or 'running to and fro', carries several meanings – onward course, process or succession of time, events, actions; the faculty of reasoning or rationality; communication of thought by speech or conversation; a narrative, tale or account; familiarity, and a spoken or written treatment of a subject in which it is treated or handled at length. This last meaning, the dictionary tells us, is the prevailing sense of the word today. In the work of Michel Foucault, some of the earlier meanings are restored and others added to the word. It is in this expanded sense that 'discourse' has currently become central to critical theory and postcolonial criticism, especially after Said's use of it in *Orientalism*.

Foucault's notion of discourse was born from his work on madness, and from his desire to recover an inner perspective on the subject, or the voice of insane people, rather than what others had said about them. This was a difficult task – how might one recover voices that have been deemed not worthy of social circulation? Foucault found that literary texts were one of the rare places where they might be heard. He started to think about how madness as a category of human identity is produced and reproduced by various rules, systems and procedures which create and separate it from 'normalcy'. Such systems form what he called 'the order of discourse', or the entire conceptual territory on which knowledge is formed and produced. This includes not just what is thought or said but the rules which govern what can be said and what not, what is included as rational and what left out, what is thought of as madness or insubordination and what is seen as sane or socially acceptable.

Discourse in this sense is a whole field or domain within which language is used in particular ways. This domain is rooted (as is Gramsci's or Althusser's notion of ideology) in human practices, institutions and actions. Thus, the discourse on madness in modern society is anchored in institutions such as madhouses, and in practices such as psychiatry. Discursive practices make it difficult for individuals to think outside them – hence they are also exercises in power and control. This element of control should not be taken to mean that a discourse as a domain of utterance is either static or cannot admit of contradictions. Consider as an example the discourse on the burning of widows on their husbands' pyres in India. This would include the entire spectrum of writing or utterance upon this subject: those in favour of widow immolation and those against it, Hindu reformers and nationalists, the Hindu orthodoxy and British administrators. All of these groups engaged in contentious debates with one another, but at the same time they all worked within a shared conceptual order in which women's burning was seen as part of the Hindu tradition, and women were regarded as creatures whose interests needed to be represented by men. As a result, women's own voices could find no representation during the colonial debates on this subject. Today, the discourse on widow burning in India reveals both a continuity from the colonial times and some radical changes. A whole spectrum of women are very much part of contemporary discussions. To analyse the changes between nineteenth-century and recent debates is to map the historical, cultural and political shifts between then and now as well as between India and the West (Mani 1989; Loomba 1993). As Hayden White puts it in a different context, discourse constitutes 'the ground whereon to decide what shall count as a fact in the matters under consideration and to determine what mode of comprehension is best suited to the understanding of the facts thus constituted' (1987: 3). The historian and the critic, then, are also part of a discursive order rather than outsiders – what they say, indeed what they *can* say is also determined and shaped by their circumstances. Thus the concept of discourse extends the notion of a historically and ideologically inflected linguistic field – no utterance is innocent and every utterance tells us something about the world we live in. But equally, the world we live in is only comprehensible to us via its discursive representations.

In various permutations and combinations, the intellectual developments outlined in this section (and various crucial strands have been excluded) had a revolutionary impact on different disciplines – for literary criticism, it meant that history does not just provide a background to the study of texts, but forms an essential part of textual meaning; conversely, texts or representations have to be seen as fundamental to the creation of history and culture. For historical study it meant that claims to objectivity and truth would have to be tempered as historical writing could now be seen as subject to the same rules, slippages and strategies as other narratives. The lines between 'fact' and 'fiction' were becoming blurred, or at least were subject to intense scrutiny. Such a move was perhaps especially liberating for Anglo-American literary studies, which had been dominated by different versions of idealist criticism according to which literary texts were stable carriers of culture and meaning.

Finally, the point from which we began: these developments cannot be seen in isolation from the growth of certain political movements such as feminism or anti-colonial struggles. Both women and colonised peoples functioned in economies which rested on their labour, and both were subject to ideologies which justified this exploitation. So both feminist and anti-colonial movements needed to challenge dominant ideas of history, culture and representation. They too questioned objectivity in dominant historiography, they too showed how canonical literary texts disguised their political affiliations, and they too broke with dominant Western, patriarchal, philosophies. Post-structuralists' suspicion of established truths was shared by various new social movements which also challenged the 'meta-narratives' that excluded them. Anti-colonial or feminist struggles emphasised culture as a site of conflict between the oppressors and the oppressed. The decentring of the human subject was important to them because such a subject had been dominantly theorised by European imperialist discourses as male and white. They also paid attention to language as a tool of domination and as a means of constructing identity.

But, on the other hand, anti-colonial and feminist activists and intellectuals were invested not only in questioning totalising frameworks but also in the possibility of social change. Foucault's notion of discourse, and his ideas about social power were highly problematic in this regard. Foucault argued that after the beginning of the nineteenth century (which he characterises as inaugurating the 'modern' epoch), the dominant structures of Western societies reproduce themselves by working insidiously rather than spectacularly upon the human subject and especially the human body. Human beings internalise the systems of repression and reproduce them by conforming to certain ideas of what is normal and what is deviant. Thus our ideas about madness, criminality or sexuality are regulated through institutions such as the madhouse or the prison, and also by certain ideological 'regimes'. Power does not emanate from some central or hierarchical structure but flows through society in a sort of capillary action: 'Power is everywhere; not because it embraces everything, but because it comes from everywhere' (Foucault 1990: 93).

Such a conception of power was useful for feminists and others who were interested in focusing upon the repressive aspects of everyday life and of institutions such as the family. But it did not help explain how various institutions and discursive formations, different 'regimes of truth' come together to create a social fabric. While Foucault breaks away from a reductive conception of social unity, he does not present an alternative, more complex, consideration of a social *formation*. As soon as we think about society not as a unitary whole but as a complex amalgam, or a formation, we are obliged to think about the relations of power *between* different social structures as well as within each social structure:

> The question of the relative power and distribution of different regimes of truth in the social formation at any one time – which have certain effects for the maintenance of power in the social order – that's what I call 'the ideological effect'. So I go on using the term 'ideology' because it forces me to continue thinking about that problem. By abandoning the term, I think that Foucault has let himself off the hook of having to retheorize it in a more radical way: i.e. he saves for himself 'the political' with his insistence on power, but he denies himself *a politics* because he has no idea of the 'relations of force'.
>
> (Hall 1996d: 136)

This is an important point, because without thinking about such relations, it is hard to think about resistance in any systematic way. Thus Hall calls Foucault's position 'proto-anarchist' because it makes resistance an arbitrary affair. Accordingly, in various Foucaultian analyses, emancipation is conceptualised as a personal affair, understandable only to those who resist, something that cannot be analysed or represented by anyone else. At other times the idea of power is rendered so diffuse that it cannot be either understood or challenged: one feminist argues that in Foucault, 'Power is everywhere, and so ultimately nowhere' (Hartsock 1990: 170).

In certain post-modern writings, these tendencies are taken even further. The human being is decentred, society is conceptualised as totally fragmented and utterance as unstable. When plurality, slippage and deferral of meaning become enshrined as philosophical beliefs they can deny the very possibility of human understanding. Decentring the subject allows for a social reading of language and representations, but it can also make it impossible to think about a subject capable of acting and challenging the *status quo*. These issues are again open to multiple interpretations, and we will return to them later. The important point is that these tensions about power and subjectivity have become central to the study of colonialism. More recently, Edward Said alleges that 'all the energies poured into critical theory, into novel and demystifying theoretical praxes like the new historicism and deconstruction and Marxism have avoided the major, I would say determining, political horizon of modern Western culture, namely imperialism' (1995: 37). This critique is somewhat ironic, given that it was Said's earlier book, *Orientalism* (1978) which used some of these new perspectives (including Foucault's insights) to offer a new critique of colonialist thought, and to become a foundational text for a new area of inquiry – that of 'colonial discourse'.

COLONIAL DISCOURSE

Knowledge is not innocent but profoundly connected with the operations of power. This Foucaultian insight informs Edward Said's foundational work *Orientalism*, which points out the extent to which 'knowledge' about 'the Orient' as it was produced and circulated in Europe was an ideological accompaniment of colonial 'power'. This is a book not about non-Western cultures, but about the Western representation of these cultures, particularly in the scholarly discipline called Orientalism. Said shows how this discipline was created alongside the European penetration into the 'Near East' and how it was nurtured and supported by various other disciplines such as philology, history, anthropology, philosophy, archeology and literature.

Orientalism uses the concept of discourse to re-order the study of colonialism. It examines how the formal study of the 'Orient' (what is today referred to as the Middle East), along with key literary and cultural texts, consolidated certain ways of seeing and thinking which in turn contributed to the functioning of colonial power. These are not materials that traditional analysts of colonialism have considered, but which can now, thanks both to *Orientalism* and to the changing perspectives on ideology and culture outlined above, be seen as central to the making and functioning of colonial societies. Said explains that certain texts are accorded

> the authority of academics, institutions, and governments . . . . Most important, such texts can create not only knowledge but also the very reality they appear to describe. In time such knowledge and reality produce a tradition, or what Michel Foucault calls a discourse, whose material presence or weight, not the originality of a given author, is really responsible for the texts produced out of it.
>
> (1978: 94)

Said accords a greater importance to individual authors than does Foucault, but, like Foucault, he also wishes to connect them to structures of thought and to the workings of power. Accordingly, he brings together a range of creative writers, statesmen, political thinkers, philologists and philosophers who contributed to Orientalism as an institution which then provided the lens through which the 'Orient' would be viewed, and controlled; but equally this control itself spawned these ways of knowing, studying, believing and writing. Thus knowledge about and power over colonised lands are related enterprises.

Orientalism can be said to inaugurate a new kind of study of colonialism. Said argues that representations of the 'Orient' in European literary texts, travelogues and other writings contributed to the creation of a dichotomy between Europe and its 'others', a dichotomy that was central to the creation of European culture as well as to the maintenance and extension of European hegemony over other lands. Said's project is to show how 'knowledge' about non-Europeans was part of the process of maintaining power over them; thus the status of 'knowledge' is demystified, and the lines between the ideological and the objective blurred. It was not, Said suggests, that Europeans were 'telling lies', or that they individually disliked non-Western peoples or cultures. In the case of Richard Burton (the translator into English of books like *The Arabian Nights*, *The Rubaiyat of Omar Khayyam* and *The Kama Sutra*) for example, Said points out that

> no man who did not know Arabic and Islam as well as Burton could have gone as far as he did in actually becoming a pilgrim to Mecca and Medina. So what we read in Burton's prose is the history of a consciousness negotiating its way through an alien culture by virtue of having successfully absorbed its systems of information and behaviour . . . . [Yet] every one of Burton's footnotes, whether in the *Pilgrimage* or in his translation of *The Arabian Nights* . . . was meant to be testimony to his victory over the same scandalous system of Oriental knowledge, a system he had mastered by himself.
>
> (1978: 195–196)

So the impressive knowledge of Orientalists was filtered through their cultural bias, for the 'study' of the Orient was not objective but

> a political vision of reality whose structure promoted the difference between the familiar (Europe, the West, 'us') and the strange (the Orient, the East, 'them') . . . . When one uses categories like Oriental and Western as both the starting and the end points of analysis, research, public policy . . . the result is usually to polarize the distinction – the Oriental becomes more Oriental, the Westerner more Western – and limit the human encounter between different cultures, traditions, and societies.
>
> (1978: 45–46)

Said argued that knowledge of the East could never be innocent or 'objective' because it was produced by human beings who
were necessarily embedded in colonial history and relationships.
Some such point had also been made, albeit less 'theoretically', by
the Indian nationalist Bipin Chandra Pal earlier in this century
when he pointed out that

> When . . . the European scientist studies the physical features
> of our land, when he mensurates our fields, trignometrates
> our altitudes and undulations, investigates our animal, our
> vegetable or our mineral kingdoms, the records of his study
> are accepted as true and authoritative. But the study of man
> belongs altogether to a different plane . . . . Here also the eye
> sees, the ear hears, but the real meaning of what is seen or
> heard is supplied not by the senses but by the understanding,
> which interprets what is heard in the light of its own peculiar
> experiences and associations.
>
> (1958: 8–9)

Many years before Said, Frantz Fanon had concluded his indictment of colonialism by pronouncing that it was Europe that
'is literally the creation of the Third World' in the sense that it is
material wealth and labour from the colonies, 'the sweat and the
dead bodies of Negroes, Arabs, Indians and the yellow races' that
have fuelled the 'opulence' of Europe (1963: 76–81). Western intellectuals such as Theodor Adorno, Walter Benjamin and
Hannah Arendt had also explored the connections between the
intellectual production of the colonial world and its growing
global domination (Williams and Chrisman 1994: 7). But although Said's critique is anticipated by others, it was new in its
wide-sweeping range and focus, in its invocation of Foucault's
work to make connections between the production of knowledge
and the exercise of power, and innovative also in its use of literary

materials to discuss historical and epistemological processes. In many ways Said's use of culture and knowledge to interrogate colonial power inaugurated colonial discourse studies.

Discourse analysis, as we have previously discussed, makes it possible to trace connections between the visible and the hidden, the dominant and the marginalised, ideas and institutions. It allows us to see how power works through language, literature, culture and the institutions which regulate our daily lives. Using this expanded definition of power, Said could move away from a narrow and technical understanding of colonial authority and show how it functioned by producing a 'discourse' about the Orient – that is, by generating structures of thinking which were manifest in literary and artistic production, in political and scientific writings and more specifically, in the creation of Oriental studies. Said's basic thesis is that Orientalism, or the 'study' of the Orient, 'was ultimately a political vision of reality whose structure promoted a binary opposition between the familiar (Europe, the West, "us") and the strange (the Orient, the East, "them")'.

Said shows that this opposition is crucial to European self-conception: if colonised people are irrational, Europeans are rational; if the former are barbaric, sensual, and lazy, Europe is civilisation itself, with its sexual appetites under control and its dominant ethic that of hard work; if the Orient as static, Europe can be seen as developing and marching ahead; the Orient has to be feminine so that Europe can be masculine. This dialectic between self and other, derived in part from deconstruction, has been hugely influential in subsequent studies of colonial discourses in other places – critics have traced it as informing colonial attitudes towards Africans, Native Americans, and other non-European peoples. Since *Orientalism*, colonial discourse studies have analysed a wide range of cultural texts and practices such as art works, atlases, cinema, scientific systems, museums, educational institutions, advertisements, psychiatric and other medical practices, geology, patterns of clothing, ideas on beauty. According to one critic, 'colonial discourse analysis . . . forms the point of questioning of Western knowledge's categories and assumptions' (Young 1990: 11).

Said's book denies the claim of objectivity or innocence not only within Oriental studies but on the part of any Western scholarship. It also implicates other human and social sciences as they were traditionally constituted – anthropology, philology, art history, history, economic and cultural studies, and literary studies. All of these disciplines, for various reasons, were inadequate for analysing the colonial construction of knowledge and culture in Said's sense. Anthropological studies rested upon the assumption that non-European peoples were backward, primitive, quaint, sometimes even 'noble', but always different from the products of Western civilisation. Historical scholarship claimed 'objectivity' while being riddled with cultural bias, and its crude separation of 'fact' from fiction had precluded its ability to probe the ideologies that informed Western scholarship's claim to 'truth-telling'. 'Classical' economics was notoriously culture-blind, and even the study of art was premised on cultural generalisations that masqueraded as 'aesthetic taste'. Orthodox literary studies claimed to be 'above' politics altogether, interested only in something called 'the' human condition, and, as Said points out, certainly hostile to any discussion of cultural difference, colonialism and imperialism. Colonial discourse studies entail interdisciplinary work which was only made possible by radical changes within many of these disciplines.

Despite the enormous influence of *Orientalism*, the book has evoked much hostility as well as criticism, especially from Orientalists themselves, but also from others fundamentally sympathetic to Said's project. One recurring critique is that *Orientalism* suggests that a binary opposition between East and West has been a more or less static feature of Western discourses from classical Greece to the present day. Thus Said's book is seen to flatten historical nuances into a fixed East versus West divide (Porter 1983). According to this view, attitudes to non-Europeans fluctuated greatly, not only over time, but also within any given context. Ahmed (1992) also accuses Said of homogenising the West, but the grounds of his criticism are that Said does not sufficiently connect Orientalist knowledge production to colonial history and its connections with the development of capitalism. Instead, it is suggested, he inflates the importance of literary, ideological and discursive aspects at the expense of more institutional or material realities, and hence implies that colonialism was largely an ideological construct. Critics have pointed out too that Said's analysis concentrates, almost exclusively, on canonical Western literary texts. A third, most frequent charge is that Said ignores the self-representations of the colonised and focuses on the imposition of colonial power rather than on the resistances to it. By doing so, he promotes a static model of colonial relations in which 'colonial power and discourse is possessed entirely by the coloniser' and therefore there is no room for negotiation or change (Bhabha 1983: 200).

This last question – that of the nature of colonial power – is and has been a vexed one for postcolonial studies. Some scholars criticise the entire field of 'colonial discourse studies' for adopting a Foucaultian view of colonial power as all pervasive. *Orientalism* is held responsible for this bias in suggesting that Western tests create not only knowledge about the Orient but the very reality they appear to describe and thus implying that

> the historical experiences of colonial peoples themselves have no independent existence outside the texts of Orientalism . . . . At a theoretical level, then, Said appears to have placed himself in the position of denying the possibility of any alternative description of 'the Orient', any alternative forms of knowledge and by extension, any agency on the part of the colonised. The fact that this theoretical position runs counter to Said's

professed political aim of effecting the dissolution of 'Orientalism' could be seen as an ironic validation of his own theory, since even he seems trapped within the frame of Orientalism, unable to move outside it.

(Vaughan 1994: 3)

Foucault, you will recall, suggests that power manifests itself not in a downward flow from the top of the social hierarchy to those below but extends itself in a capillary fashion – it is part of daily action, speech and everyday life. Is such a notion of power useful for re-conceptualising social domination, or does it render it all pervasive and therefore difficult to challenge? Edward Said has himself said he finds such an understanding of power disabling for politically engaged criticism (1984: 245). Some commentators find an irreconcilable contradiction between Said's use of Foucaultian perspectives to critique the operations of colonial discourse, and his political commitment to the possibility of social change. Others have insisted that such contradictions can in fact be productive in dismantling previously secure methods of analysis. In his later work, Foucault began to emphasise the instability and contradictions within discourses, and the possibility of resisting this control. But Foucault also discusses how dominant structures legitimise themselves by allowing a controlled space for dissidence – resistance, in this view, is produced and then inoculated against by those in power. Certain influential bodies of literary and cultural criticism inspired by his work, such as new historicism, emphasise the ways in which, in the final analysis, all manner of oppositional ideologies or resistant groups or individuals are contained by power structures. One can see how such a pessimistic theoretical framework would be criticised by those who are beginning to uncover the histories of women or colonised subjects as histories of resistance and opposition and not just as stories about oppression. But other theorists have appropriated

Foucaultian ideas to conceptualise multiple challenges to authority.

These are matters of ongoing debate. It is true that *Orientalism* is primarily concerned with how the Orient was 'constructed' by Western literature, travel writing and systems of studying the East, and not with how such a construction was received or dismantled by colonial subjects. However, it would, in my opinion, be unfair to conclude that just because Said does not venture into the latter territory, he necessarily suggests that the colonialist's discourse is all pervasive. Those who study modes and ideas of domination cannot necessarily be accused of being complicit with it – Said's own critique, and the work of other scholars before him such as Raymond Schwab, are themselves proof that Orientalist thought can be challenged. Elsewhere Said discusses anti-imperialist theorists such as Fanon in order to think about resistance in the present context (1989). But colonial authority, like any other, is legitimised through a process during which it constantly has to negotiate with the people it seeks to control, and therefore the presence of those people, oppositional or otherwise, is a crucial factor in studying authority itself. Foucault's own work suggests that domination and resistance are inextricably linked. So Said's story about how a body of texts constructed the East is necessarily incomplete without some sense of the specific peoples and cultures it re-wrote, and situations into which it intervened.

Colonial discourse studies today are not restricted to delineating the workings of power – they have tried to locate and theorise oppositions, resistances and revolts (successful and otherwise) on the part of the colonised. Sharp debates continue to be waged over these questions. Critics such as Gayatri Spivak are wary of too easy a 'recovery' of the 'voice' or 'agency' of colonised peoples or 'subaltern' subjects. ('Subaltern' was a military term used for officers under the rank of captain and its origin is somewhat inconsistent with its current usage, borrowed from Gramsci, as a shorthand for any oppressed person.) She argues that to do so would be to undermine the devastating effects of colonial power which was so pervasive that it re-wrote intellectual, legal and cultural systems. Henry Louis Gates suggests that for Spivak, therefore, 'all discourse is colonial discourse' (1991: 466). Others criticise her position by calling attention to nationalist and anti-colonial struggles which did succeed in dismantling formal colonial structures.

Although colonial discourse studies are indebted to the Foucaultian concept of discourse, Foucault himself has been repeatedly criticised for not paying any attention to colonial expansion as a feature of the European civil society or to how colonialism may have affected the power/knowledge systems of the modern European state. Thus Foucault's own theories are Euro-centric in their focus, and of limited use in understanding colonial societies. Their analysis of power is predicated upon a specifically European modernity wherein physical punishment and torture lose their spectacular forms and the state's power over the human body operates far more obliquely through the prison or the asylum. But colonial power did not necessarily operate in that fashion, as Megan Vaughan demonstrates in her analysis of bio-medicine in colonial Africa (1991: 8–10). Vaughan argues that whereas Foucault talks about the 'productive' as opposed to 'repressive' power of the modern state, colonial states were hardly 'modern' in the European sense, and relied on a large measure of repressive power. Secondly, whereas Foucault outlines how modern European states created normative as well as 'abnormal' subjects in order to police both, 'the need to objectify and distance "the Other" in the form of the madman or the leper was less urgent in a situation in which every colonial person was in some sense, already "Other" '. The individuation of subjects that took place in Europe was denied colonised people. Colonial medical discourse conceptualised Africans as members of groups 'and it was these groups, rather than individuals, who were said to possess distinctive psychologies and bodies. In contrast to the

European developments described by Foucault, in colonial Africa group classification was a far more important construction than individualization' (Vaughan 1991: 11). Vaughan concludes that colonial power was different from its European counterpart because of the uneven development of capitalism in Africa and its relation to discourses on 'the African':

> Medical discourses both described and helped create the 'contradictions' of capitalism ('mediated' them, if you like). Africans were expected to move in and out of the market, as conditions dictated. They were to be single-minded cotton producers at one moment, and at another they were prohibited from growing the crop. They were to be 'docile bodies' for mining capital when the conditions of labour supply demanded it, but not for the whole of their lives. They were created as consumers of products for the new, modern bodies at one moment, and at the next they were told to revive their 'traditional' knowledge of soap-producing plants. By relying so heavily on older modes of production for its very success, colonial capitalism also helped create the discourse on the 'traditional', non-individualized and 'unknowing' collective being – the 'African', a discourse to which the idea of difference was central.
>
> (Vaughan 1991: 12)

Jenny Sharpe (1993) offers an analogous critique of Foucault on the basis of her analysis of the 1857 uprisings against the British in India. Sharpe argues that whereas for Foucault modern mechanisms of punishment and control are insidious rather than spectacular, the punishment of Indian rebels by the colonial authorities was excessive, ritualised and ceremonial. It was designed to ' "strike terror" in the rebellious native' and it reduced the rebels 'to the corporeality of their bodies' in a manner 'out of Europe's own "barbaric" past'. Because Foucault 'derives his theory of disciplinary power from a Euro-centric model of prison reforms, it cannot be used to address the colonial situation, in which technologies of discipline are overdetermined by imperial structures of power' (Sharpe 1993: 79). Although they deal with very different colonial situations, and in fact work from different methodological perspectives, Vaughan and Sharpe's overlapping critiques of Foucault serve to demonstrate the complex interaction between post-modern or post-structuralist thought and colonial discourse analysis.

'Colonial discourse', then, is not just a fancy new term for colonialism; it indicates a new way of thinking in which cultural, intellectual, economic or political processes are seen to work together in the formation, perpetuation and dismantling of colonialism. It seeks to widen the scope of studies of colonialism by examining the intersection of ideas and institutions, knowledge and power. Consequently, colonial violence is understood as including an 'epistemic' aspect, i.e. an attack on the culture, ideas and value systems of the colonised peoples. As we have seen, such a perception is not entirely new, and was in circulation among nationalist ideologues. Colonial discourse studies, however, seek to offer in-depth analyses of colonial epistemologies, and also connect them to the history of colonial institutions. For example, Gauri Viswanathan (1990) and David Johnson (1996) situate the institutionalisation of English education, and particularly the study of English literature, within the politics of colonial rule in India and South Africa respectively. In a very different kind of study (mentioned above) Megan Vaughan shows how medicine in colonial Africa constructed 'the African' in particular ways which were intrinsic to the operations of colonial power. David Arnold (1993) has analysed the imperial medical system in British India in an analogous vein. More generally, colonial discourse studies are interested in how stereotypes, images, and 'knowledge' of colonial subjects and cultures tie in with institutions of economic, administrative, judicial, and bio-medical control.

As mentioned above, some critics allege that colonial discourse studies present a distorted picture of colonial rule in which cultural effects are inflated at the expense of economic and political institutions. They claim that 'discourse' in practice comes to mean literary texts and other cultural representations. In other words, colonial discourse studies erase any distinction between the material and the ideological because they simply concentrate on the latter. We have already discussed a version of this problem in relation to revisionist theories of ideology. The concept of 'discourse', as we earlier saw, was meant to uncover the interrelation between the ideological and the material rather than to collapse them into each other. But of course in practice, this ideal does not always work, perhaps because so many of those who work in this area have been trained in literary studies, art history, historical studies, anthropology, film, and media and cultural studies rather than in economics or medicine. Of course, these disciplinary boundaries have been disintegrating over the last two decades, and colonial discourse studies, like feminist studies, are astonishingly inter-disciplinary. Still, the areas from which they have sprung exert their own bias, and mould them in ways that we will examine in subsequent sections.

Recently, however, many critiques of postcolonial studies target not literary scholarship but historical studies for relying on techniques and perspectives developed within linguistics and literary work. Some of the scholars that I have cited as contributing to a study of colonial discourses, such as Megan Vaughan, accuse 'colonial discourse theory' of not paying enough attention to previous analytical methods. For example, she says, much before colonial discourse theorists talked about it, historians of Africa were discussing the ways in which custom and tradition are 'constructed' and 'invented' by both colonialists and their opponents (Vaughan 1994: 1–23). Long before Foucault, they were discussing how the colonisers and the colonised cannot represent neat binaries but are active in constructing each other. Similar arguments have been advanced by feminists with respect to post-modern theory. Judith Newton has rightly suggested that feminist historians had emphasised the centrality of 'representation, role prescription, ideas, values, psychology and the construction of subjectivity', the importance of sexuality and reproduction, and the necessity of inter-disciplinary work long before these ideas were made fashionable as 'new historicism' (Newton 1989: 154).

Certainly, it would be a mistake to detach either 'colonial discourse' analysis, or post-structuralist theoretical innovations from previous intellectual and political histories. Various political movements such as those for decolonisation or for women's equality are as important as earlier modes of analysis in constructing the genealogy of current debates on the subject. At the same time, it would be a caricature of recent theoretical innovations to reduce them to a matter of 'the linguistic turn' and 'textuality' or to claim that they simply re-circulate what historians already knew. The question of the usefulness or otherwise of something called 'post-modern' or post-structuralist theory for 'postcolonial' societies can continue to be debated and we will return to that towards the end of this book. Here I want to emphasise that there is no consensus or homogeneity within 'colonial discourse analysis' which is the site of much debate and controversy precisely because it has drawn from a wide range of intellectual and political histories and affiliations. To pit 'colonial discourse analysts' against 'social historians', or historians against literary critics is to simply resurrect older disciplinary and intellectual divisions, and thus to miss the debates *within* 'colonial discourse analysis', as well as the real innovations within the field. It is far more helpful to engage with different approaches to questions of colonial subjects and power relations, and to see where the real differences of method lie. Viewed this way, the work of someone like Vaughan contributes to and is made possible by current debates on 'discourse' and power. Modern European colonialism has been a historically and geographically nuanced rather than a monolithic phenomenon. How can we be attentive to these nuances, and at the same time find shared attributes and features of power and resistance? Such a task requires an expanded vocabulary, and current debates on colonial discourse are precisely about the nature of that expansion.

COLONIALISM AND KNOWLEDGE

Colonialism reshaped existing structures of human knowledge. No branch of learning was left untouched by the colonial experience. The process was somewhat like the functioning of ideology itself, simultaneously a misrepresentation of reality and its reordering. Like ideology, it arose from 'material circumstances' and was 'material in its effect'. A crucial aspect of this process was the gathering and ordering of information about the lands and peoples visited by, and later subject to, the colonial powers. Fifteenth- and sixteenth-century European ventures to Asia, America and Africa were not the first encounters between Europeans and non-Europeans but writings of this period do mark a new way in thinking about, indeed producing, these two categories of people as binary opposites. Travel writing was an important means of producing 'Europe's differentiated conceptions of itself in relation to something it became possible to call "the rest of the world" ' (Pratt 1992: 5; see also Spurr 1993).

The definition of civilisation and barbarism rests on the production of an irreconcilable difference between 'black' and 'white', self and other. The late medieval European figure of the 'wild man' who lived in forests, on the outer edges of civilisation, and was hairy, nude, violent, lacking in moral sense and excessively sensual, expressed all manner of cultural anxieties. He and his female counterpart were 'others' who existed outside civil society, and yet they constantly threatened to enter and disrupt this society. Such myths intersected with images of foreigners (from

Africa, the Islamic world and India) with whom medieval Europeans (and earlier Greco-Roman societies) had some contact. It is important to remember that images of Africans, Turks, Muslims, barbarians, anthropophagy, 'men of Inde' and other categories had circulated for a long time before colonialism. These images often appear to coincide with the constructions of the 'other' in colonialist discourse. For example, the twelfth- and thirteenth-century image of Muslims as barbaric, degenerate, tyrannical and promiscuous seems identical with the Orientalist images Said identifies in *Orientalism*. Therefore, at times, discussions of 'colonial discourse' treat such images as the static product of a timeless opposition between 'Western' and 'non-Western' peoples and ideas. As a matter of fact, all these images about the other were moulded and remoulded through various histories of contact. Colonialism was perhaps the most important crucible for their affirmation as well as reconstruction.

Colonialism expanded the contact between Europeans and non-Europeans, generating a flood of images and ideas on an unprecedented scale. Europeans who travelled outwards took with them certain previous images of the people they expected to encounter. The actual encounters necessitated both the continuity and a reshaping of these images – continuity because previously held notions about the inferiority of non-Europeans provided a justification for European settlements, trading practices, religious missions and military activities – and reshaping in order to adjust images to specific colonial practices. Thus, for example, the old term 'anthropophagy' (used by the Roman writer Pliny the Elder in his *Natural History* to refer to human beings who ate their own kind) was applied by Columbus to those Indians who were called 'Caribs'. A subsequent linguistic transformation of 'Carib' resulted in the term 'cannibal' which absorbed the connotations of the earlier term 'anthropophagy'. It is interesting to note that Spanish colonists increasingly applied the term 'cannibal' and attributed the practice of cannibalism to those natives within the

Caribbean and Mexico who were *resistant* to colonial rule, and among whom no cannibalism had in fact been witnessed. The idea of anthropophagy was directly applied to justify brutal colonialist practices (Hulme 1986a; Miles 1989: 25).

These new images were also widely circulated for consumption at home. Martin Frobisher even carried an Eskimo and put him on display in England. In Shakespeare's *The Tempest*, Trinculo speculates on the money he could make if he were to do the same with Caliban, since people 'will lay out ten (coins) to see a dead Indian' (II, i, 32–33). Another very different kind of 'Indian' was also viewed by contemporary English people – the American 'princess' Pocahontas, who was presented at court as the wife of the colonist John Rolfe. These two natives of America could not easily be regarded as the same – one was offered as evidence (like Caliban himself) of a people outside of culture altogether, the other as worthy of assimilation into European society. These differences are important for understanding the production of colonial stereotypes. The most extensive pictures of all the different kinds of people of the New World were gathered together in the folios of Theodore de Bry's five volume *America*, issued from the 1590s. But Theodore de Bry also issued another set of volumes that depicted people from the other Indies – *India Orientalis* (1599) documented life in various parts of the East. If we compare these two volumes we shall find an awareness of the differences between various non-European peoples, a difference which was also recorded in the travel narratives collected in the sixteenth and seventeenth centuries by editors such as Richard Hakluyt and Samuel Purchas, or manifest in the growing European collections of objects from different parts of the world. How then can we reconcile increasing knowledge about the diversity of peoples and lands with colonial stereotypes about Europe and its others?

Stereotyping involves a reduction of images and ideas to a simple and manageable form; rather than simple ignorance or lack of 'real' knowledge, it is a method of processing information. The function of stereotypes is to perpetuate an artificial sense of difference between 'self' and 'other' (Gilman 1985b: 18). The travel collections produced in the fifteenth and sixteenth centuries do not actually reproduce non-Europeans as monoliths. They note specific eating habits, religious beliefs, clothing and social organisation in ways that mark the beginning of anthropological studies. This 'noting' includes, in the case of de Bry's pictures in America, the figure of a man whose head is painted between his shoulders as one of the residents of the 'new' continent. Exactly this image is recalled by Othello in Shakespeare's play – on his travels, he says, he has seen 'men whose heads do grow beneath their shoulders'. While, in *Othello*, this image may be considered as the work of a fictional imagination, in de Bry it passes for observed fact. What is even more important, in Shakespeare's play such images function to indicate Othello's *difference* from the monstrous non-Europeans he has seen on his travels. References to Othello's 'thick lips', 'sooty bosom' and animal lust (he's called 'an old black ram') mark him out as both inferior and alien, but he is still distinguished from men whose heads grow beneath their shoulders. European travel accounts and literatures were acutely conscious of these differences. The 'wild man' and the 'barbarian' were not identical – the former lived outside civil society, the latter was part of an alien social system (White 1987: 165). De Bry's volumes graphically portrayed America as a land of cannibalism as well as of noble savages. The point is that both images posited an irreducible difference between Americans and Europeans, and that this difference was reproduced in a wide range of materials, some obviously fictional and some passing as fact.

It is easier to accept such blurring of 'fact' and 'fiction' in older texts, but we often assume that with scientific advances, misrepresentation decreases. As a matter of fact, far from being an objective, ideology-free domain, modern Western science was deeply implicated in the construction of racist ways of thinking about human beings and the differences between them (Stepan 1982; Gould 1996). Mary Louise Pratt has argued that, from the mid-eighteenth century onwards, science 'came to articulate Europe's contacts with the imperial frontier, and to be articulated by them'. Pratt places the emergence of natural history as a structure of knowledge within a 'new planetary consciousness' which emerged in Europe at this time as a result of colonial expansion. Linnaeus's *System of Nature* (1735) which inaugurated a system of classifying plants that is still current, was born of a new totalising conception of the world:

> One by one the planet's life forms were to be drawn out of the tangled threads of their life surroundings and rewoven into European-based patterns of global unity and order. The (lettered, male, European) eye that held the system could familiarize ('naturalize') new sites/sights immediately upon contact, by incorporating them into the language of the system. The differences of distance factored themselves out of the picture: with respect to mimosas, Greece could be the same as Venezuela, West Africa, or Japan; the label 'granite peaks' can apply identically to Eastern Europe, the Andes, or the American West.
>
> (Pratt 1992: 31)

However, Richard H. Grove's *Green Imperialism* points out that Linnaeus's classificatory system, which he thought of as a large map of the world, was also profoundly indebted to the South Indian Ezhava system of classifying plants (1995: 90). Grove's work cautions us against too simplistic a reading of the European will to power: Western science, it points out, developed both as an impulse to master the globe, and by incorporating, learning from, as well as aggressively displacing other knowledge systems. Through the 'objectivity' of observation and science, European penetration into other lands is legitimised. Natural history is

thus as much a form of writing and representation as it is a discovery of something already there in the natural world. But the
power of natural history was also manifested in innovations in
other material practices and in a host of other professions: it demanded

> better means of preserving, transporting, displaying, and doc-
> umenting specimens; artistic specializations in botanical and
> zoological drawing developed; printers were challenged to im-
> prove reproductions of visuals, watchmakers were in demand
> to invent and maintain instruments; jobs came into being for
> scientists on commercial expeditions and colonial outposts;
> patronage networks funded scientific travels and subsequent
> writing; amateur and professional societies of all kinds sprung
> up locally, nationally and internationally; natural history collec-
> tions acquired commercial as well as prestige value; botanical
> gardens became large-scale public spectacles, and the job of
> supervising them a naturalist's dream.
>
> (Pratt 1992: 29)

Thus science and prejudice are not necessarily counter-posed to
one another. On the contrary, the discourse of 'race' was the product of Western science in the eighteenth century. The nature of
and reason for differences in skin colour had been debated for centuries within Europe: was blackness a product of climate and environment, or was it a God-ordained sign of sinfulness? Scientific
discourse suggested that since the skin colour of specific races did
not change when their members moved to a new location (an idea
which had been noted in Hakluyt's late sixteenth-century collection of voyages), therefore it was a biological and natural difference. Thus races were now seen to be the expression of a
biological (and therefore immutable) hierarchy. The important
point is that science did not shed any of the earlier suppositions
about inferior races: thus, race explained not simply people's skin

colour, but also their civilisational and cultural attributes. 'Nature' thus 'explained' and linked black skin, a small brain, and savagery! Darwin's theory of the evolution of the species represented a genuine advance for science and yet it was used to bolster ideas of racial supremacy: in his *Descent of Man* (1871), Darwin wrote: 'Extinction follows chiefly from the competition of tribe with tribe, and race with race .... When civilized nations come into contact with barbarians the struggle is short' (quoted by Young 1995: 18). Hence, races and nations were concepts that developed in connection with one another.

Over time, colour, hair type, skull shape and size, facial angles, or brain size were variously taken up by scientific discourses as the most accurate index of racial differences. As recently as 1994, Charles Murray and Richard J. Herrnstein's *The Bell Curve* suggested that discrepancy between black and white Americans on the standardised IQ tests was due to natural or genetic causes. These authors claimed their 'findings' were objective, scientific and therefore ideologically neutral and did not detract from their own commitment to multiculturalism, but critics pointed out that precisely such arguments about natural inferiority are used to explain away the continuing cycle of poverty in which almost 45 per cent of black children are trapped in the United States (Gates 1994: 10). However, others were swayed precisely because cognitive functioning is regarded as a 'scientific' matter, and thus beyond the realm of ideology. In the debates on women's intelligence and psychology too, we can see how scientific knowledge is refracted through the prism of prejudice, so that age-old ideas about women's instinct as opposed to men's rationality, or about female behavioural patterns, are regularly recycled as 'latest' scientific discoveries.

Dominant scientific ideologies about race and gender have historically propped up each other. In the mid-nineteenth century, the new science of anthropometry pronounced Caucasian women to be closer to Africans than white men were, and supposedly female traits were used to describe 'the lower races' (Stepan 1990: 43). Accordingly African women occupied the lowest rung of the racial ladder. When African men began to be treated for schizophrenia and confined to lunatic asylums, 'African women . . . were said not to have reached the level of self-awareness required to go mad, and in colonial literature on psychology and psychopathology, the African women represented the happy "primitive" state of pre-colonial Africa' (Vaughan 1991: 22) Thus, even madness (here seen an attribute of a 'complex' mind) becomes an index of the ascent of human beings towards modernity, in which African women are seen to lag behind their men who themselves slowly follow Europeans. Scientific language was authoritative and powerful precisely because it presented itself as value-free, neutral and universal (Stepan and Gilman 1991). For this reason, it was extremely difficult to challenge its claims. To some extent, European scientists' own racial and political identities prevented them from radically questioning scientific theories of racial difference, and on the other hand, people who were constructed as inferior by these theories had little access to scientific training, and their objections were dismissed as unscientific. The scientific text was increasingly purged of figurative language and overtly moral and political arguments in order to present itself as purely 'factual'. Thus its biases with respect to both gender and race could aggressively be presented as objective truths. We will revisit the intersection of race, gender and colonialism at greater length a little later in this book.

At a recent lecture at the University of Delhi, the Kenyan novelist Ngũgĩ wa Thiong'o expressed his surprise at the idea that the European 'Renaissance' or 'Enlightenment' could still be taught in some places without reference to colonial history.[6] In fact the growth of modern Western knowledge systems and the histories of most 'disciplines' can be seen to be embedded within and shaped by colonial discourses. Martin Bernal's well-known book *Black Athena* demonstrates this most forcefully in the case of classics.

It argues that the history of black Egypt and its centrality to ancient Greek culture was erased by nineteenth-century scholarship in order to construct a white Hellenic heritage for Europe. Bernal goes further than that: he suggests that the rise of professional scholarship and its bifurcation into 'disciplines' are profoundly connected with the growth of racial theory (1987: 220). Thus he questions the objectivity of not just the writing of history but of all knowledges produced in Europe during the colonial era. The 'complicity' of individuals with ideological and social systems is not entirely a matter of their intentions. Take the case of Roger Williams, the founder of Rhode Island, who wrote *A Key into the Languages of America* (1643) which displays astonishing knowledge of and respect for native languages and even vindicates Indian rights to the land. Gordon Brotherstone discusses how Williams was regularly harassed by the Massachusetts Bay Company for his critique of colonial practices. But he shows how, despite all this, the *Key* betrays loyalty to Puritan attitudes to both wealth and religion. Its deep knowledge of native cultures and languages ultimately works to justify English intrusion into Algonkin life and territory. In this book, familiarity with local languages becomes the key to unlocking their culture and facilitating colonial enterprises in New England (Brotherstone 1986).

Thus, the connections between economic processes, social processes and the reordering of knowledge can be both obvious and oblique. The development or reproduction of even those knowledge systems that appear to be too abstract to have an ideological inflection, such as mathematics, can also be connected to the imperialist project (Bishop 1990). To that extent, we may say that all discourses are colonialist discourses. At one level, such a conclusion simply underlines the Marxist notion that all ideas are inter-dependent with economic and social reality. But at another level, it also alerts us to an aspect of social reality – i.e. colonially honed ideas of cultural and racial difference – which does not sufficiently inflect Marxist history. It in fact highlights how ideas contribute to the creation of (instead of merely replicating) social systems. By pointing out how deeply its knowledge systems were imbricated in racial and colonialist perspectives, scholars such as Bernal, Said or Spivak have contributed to, indeed extended, the discrediting of the project of the European Enlightenment by post-structuralists such as Foucault. The central figure of Western humanist and Enlightenment discourses, the humane, knowing subject, now stands revealed as a white male colonialist. Through its investigations, colonial discourse analysis adds this powerful new dimension to the post-structuralist understanding that meaning is always contextual, always shifting.

Is all this going too far? Does this imply too much ideological closure, or take away from the possibility of alternative intellectual thought, dissident or revolutionary ideas? Despite their belief in the social grounding of ideas, many intellectuals are not willing to abandon the notion of a human subject capable of knowing, acting upon and changing reality. But innocence and objectivity do not necessarily have to be our enabling fictions. The more we work with an awareness of our embeddedness in historical processes, the more possible it becomes to take carefully reasoned oppositional positions, as the work of critical thinkers such as Marx, or Gramsci, or indeed Bernal himself, testifies. Dominant ideologies are never total or monolithic, never totally successful in incorporating all individuals or subjects into their structures. So, to uncover the rootedness of 'modern' knowledge systems in colonial practices is to begin what Raymond Williams called the process of 'unlearning' whereby we begin to question received truths.

It is important to remember that the colonialist production of knowledge was not a simple process. It necessarily included a clash with and a marginalisation of the knowledge and belief systems of those who were conquered, as also with some oppositional views at home. But if the process of conquest highlights brutality and cultural difference, it simultaneously also marks a constant blurring of 'pure' positions of 'self' and 'other' (as we will explore in more detail in the section on colonial identities). Colonialist knowledges were produced also via negotiation with or an incorporation of indigenous ideas. At a very practical level, colonialists were dependent upon natives for their access to the 'new' lands and their secrets. As Caliban reminds Prospero, he showed the latter 'all the qualities o'th'isle,/ The fresh springs, brine-pits, barren place and fertile' (I, ii, 337–339). But historically, Prospero represented his knowledge of the island as 'discovery'. Discovery in the colonial context often consisted of appropriating local knowledges. Colonial landscapes were, after all, penetrated, mapped and annexed literally on the shoulders of local inhabitants. The imperial structure rested on an alien scaffolding. At other times, colonialists' projects made use of local knowledge but also brought Western ideas to bear both upon the nature and the culture of colonised lands: for example, British engineers in India could only complete their bridges and dams by consulting local experts. According to Major Arthur Cotton, called the 'founder' of modern irrigation programmes, when he first arrived in India, the natives spoke 'with contempt' of the English, calling them 'a kind of civilized savages, wonderfully expert about fighting, but so inferior to their great men that we would not even keep in repair the works they had constructed, much less even imitate them in extending the system'. The East India Company was unable to check the rising river bed of the Kaveri Delta: Cotton finally solved the problem by learning from indigenous experts 'how to secure a foundation in loose sand of unmeasured depth . . . . With this lesson about foundations, we built bridges, weirs, aqueducts and every kind of hydraulic works' (Shiva 1988: 187). Richard Grove documents the profound dependence of Western ideas about the natural world upon the knowledges of peoples living in the colonial periphery, showing especially how 'the seeds of modern conservation developed as an integral part of the European encounter with the tropics and with local classifications and interpretations of the natural world and its symbolism' (1995: 3).

Even colonial stereotyping was often based on native images. For example, Mary Louise Pratt tells us that the primal America projected by European travellers such as Alexander von Humboldt was not a pure invention, although it fits in so well with the nature/culture, primeval/developed binaries of colonialist discourses. It already existed within some sectors of American creole culture which, seeking to differentiate itself from Europe, glorified its own country as a vast spectacle of nature:

> In a perfect example of the mirror dance of colonial meaning-making, Humboldt transculturated to Europe knowledges produced by Americans in a process of defining themselves as separate from Europe. Following independence, Euroamerican elites would reimport that knowledge as European knowledge whose authority would legitimate Euroamerican rule.
>
> (Pratt 1992: 137)

Pratt's use of the word 'transculturated' here is important. She points out that ethnographers use it to describe how subordinated groups select and invent from materials transmitted to them by a dominant culture. In her book, she uses 'transculturation' to describe the process of inter-cultural negotiation and selection that is a constant feature of what she calls 'the contact zone' or the social spaces 'where disparate cultures meet, clash, grapple with each other, often in highly asymmetrical relations of domination and subordination'. In thus renaming the arena of colonial conflict as 'the contact zone', Pratt underscores the interaction, the borrowings and lendings, the appropriations in both directions which trouble any binary opposition between Europe and its 'others'.

Concepts like 'contact zone' or its cultural transactions complicate and nuance our understanding of colonial encounters. They underline the fact that although colonialism engendered ideologies of difference, in practice it also brought different peoples into inti-mate contact with one another. Different colonial regimes tried (to varying extents) to maintain cultural and racial segregation precisely because, in practice, the interactions between colonising and colonised peoples constantly challenged any neat division be-tween races and cultures. The result was a mixing, a 'hybridity' which became an important theme within colonial discourse the-ories, and one to which we will return later. However, some crit-ics feel that to present the antagonistic and fraught arena of colonialism in these terms is to downplay colonial violence and the boundaries it enforced. As Aimé Césaire asks, 'has colonialism really *placed civilizations in contact?* . . . I answer no. . . . No hu-man contact, but relations of domination and submission . . . ' (1972: 11, 21). We need to remember that large sections of colonised peoples in many parts of the world had no or little di-rect 'contact' with their foreign oppressors. Yet of course their lives were materially and ideologically reshaped by the latter. Colonialism thus refracted the production of knowledge and structured the conditions for its dissemination and reception. The processes by which it did so testify both to colonial power and to its complex interactions with 'other' epistemologies, ideologies and ways of seeing.

COLONIALISM AND LITERATURE

Objectivity is not the only ground on which claims for ideologi-cal and political innocence can be made. Humanist literary stud-ies have long been resistant to the idea that literature (or at least good literature) has anything to do with politics, on the grounds that the former is either too subjective, individual and personal or else too universal and transcendent to be thus tainted. Accordingly, the relationship between colonialism and literature was not, until recently, dealt with by literary criticism. Today, the situation seems to be rapidly reversing itself, with many, if not a majority, of analysts of colonial discourse coming from a training in, or professional affiliation with, literary studies. This does not mean that the orthodoxies within literary studies have simply evaporated: often analyses of colonialism, or race, like those of gender, are still regarded as 'special interest' topics which do not seriously alter teaching and research in the rest of the discipline. Still, recent attention to the relationship between literature and colonialism has provoked serious reconsiderations of each of these terms.

Firstly, literature's pivotal role in both colonial and anti-colonial discourses has begun to be explored. Ever since Plato, it has been acknowledged that literature mediates between the real and the imaginary. Marxist and post-structuralist debates on ideology increasingly try to define the nature of this mediation. If, as we suggested earlier, language and 'signs' are the sites where different ideologies intersect and clash with one another, then literary texts, being complex clusters of languages and signs, can be identified as extremely fecund sites for such ideological interactions. Moreover, they also show the complex articulation between a single individual, social contexts and the play of language. Literary texts circulate in society not just because of their intrinsic merit, but because they are part of other institutions such as the market, or the education system. Via these institutions, they play a crucial role in constructing a cultural authority for the colonisers, both in the metropolis and in the colonies. However, literary texts do not simply reflect dominant ideologies, but encode the tensions, complexities and nuances within colonial cultures. Literature is an important 'contact zone', to use Mary Louise Pratt's term, where 'transculturation' takes place in all its complexity. Literature written on both sides of the colonial divide often absorbs, appropriates and inscribes aspects of the 'other' culture, creating new genres, ideas and identities in the process. Finally, literature is also an important means of appropriating, inverting or challenging dominant means of representation and colonial ideologies. Let us examine some of these interactions between literature and colonialism.

We have already seen how travellers tales in the European Renaissance were an amalgam of fiction, attitudes received from earlier times, and new observations. Encounters with what lies outside its own boundaries are central to the formation of any culture: the line that separates inside and outside, the 'self' and the 'other' is not fixed but always shifting. The vast new worlds encountered by European travellers were interpreted by them through ideological filters, or ways of seeing, provided by their own cultures and societies. But the impetus to trade, plunder and conquer these new lands also provided a new and crucial framework through which they would interpret other lands and peoples. Hence, black Africans were considered bestial both because of the medieval and religious associations of blackness with filth and dirt, and also because this provided a justification for colonising and enslaving them. This dialectic shaped attitudes to outsiders as well as to 'European' culture itself, for example, the centrality of whiteness to beauty was not an age-old idea that now cast black people as ugly, rather it was the actual contact with black people, based on conquest and exploitation, which also shaped English Renaissance notions of beauty (see Kim Hall 1995). English nationalism relied upon cultural distinctions which demarcated Europeans from blacks, or even the English from Italians or Irish people; conversely, these cultural distinctions rationalised an aggressive nationalism that fuelled England's overseas expansion.

It is not just travel tales which are shaped by cross-cultural encounters but even those pieces of writing which appear to be inward looking, or deal with private rather than public concerns. The lovers in John Donne's poems, for example, explicitly demarcate their private space from the fast expanding outer world. In 'The Sunne Rising', even the sun becomes a peeping Tom, a 'busy olde fool'. Such a retreat both testifies to the growing ideology of coupledom in this period and challenges (via its blatant sexuality and extra-marital connotations) its Protestant version. But the withdrawal into privacy and the celebration of sexuality can only be expressed by images culled from contemporary geographical expansion. The female body is described in terms of the new geography, as in Donne's 'Love's Progress':

> The Nose (like to the first Meridian) runs
> Not 'twixt an East and West, but 'twixt two suns:
> It leaves a Cheek, a rosie Hemisphere
> On either side, and then directs us where
> Upon islands fortunate we fall,
> Not faynte Canaries, but Ambrosiall,
> Her swelling lips . . . and the streight Hellespont betweene
> The Sestos and Abydos of her breasts . . .
> And Sailing towards her India, in that way
> Shall at her fair Atlantick Navell stay . . .
>
> (Donne 1985: 181)

The lovers' relationship is worked out in terms of the colonialists' interaction with the lands they 'discover', as in 'To his Mistris going to Bed':

> Licence my roaving hands, and let them go,
> Before, behind, between, above, below.
> O my America! my new-found-land,
> My kingdome, safeliest when with one man man'd,
> My Myne of precious stones: My Emperie,
> How blest am I in this discovering thee.
>
> (1985: 184)

The colonial contact is not just 'reflected' in the language or imagery of literary texts, it is not just a backdrop or 'context' against which human dramas are enacted, but a central aspect of what these texts have to say about identity, relationships and culture. Moreover, in the second poem by Donne, sexual and colonial relationships become analogous to each other. Donne's male lover is the active discoverer of the female body, and desires to explore it in the same way as the European 'adventurer' who penetrates and takes possession of lands which are seen as passive, or awaiting discovery. Here, the sexual promise of the woman's body indicates the wealth promised by the colonies – hence, in the first poem the lover/colonist traverses her body/the globe to reach her 'India', the seat of riches. But the woman/land analogy also employs a reverse logic as the riches promised by the colonies signify both the joys of the female body as well as its status as a legitimate object for male possession.

Language and literature are together implicated in constructing the binary of a European self and a non-European other, which, as Said's *Orientalism* suggested, is a part of the creation of colonial authority. Peter Hulme's work on the formation of a colonial discourse in sixteenth-century America is extremely illuminating in this regard. Hulme shows how two words – 'cannibal' and 'hurricane' – were lifted from Native American tongues and adopted as new words into all major European languages in order to 'strengthen an ideological discourse' (1986a: 101). Both words came to connote not just the specific natural and social phenomenon they appear to describe but the boundary between Europe and America, civility and wildness. 'Hurricane' began to mean not simply a particular kind of a tempest but something peculiar to the Caribbean. Thus, it indicated the violence and savagery of the place itself. Similarly, 'cannibalism' is not simply the practice of human beings eating their own kind, not just another synonym for the older term anthropophagy. The latter term referred to savages eating their own kind, but cannibalism indicated the threat that these savages could turn against and devour Europeans. Hulme further shows that there was a blurring of boundaries between these two terms, although hurricane supposedly referred to a natural phenomenon and cannibalism to a

cultural practice, they both came to designate whatever lay outside Europe. Moreover, 'cannibal' was etymologically connected
to the Latin word *canis* (dog), reinforcing the view that 'the native
cannibals of the West Indies hunted like dogs and treated their
victims in the ferocious manner of all predators'. Hulme discusses
how a play like Shakespeare's *The Tempest* (far from being a romantic fable removed from the real world) is implicated in these
discursive developments, and in the formation of colonial discourse in general, how its tempests are hurricanes in this new
sense, and why Caliban's name is an anagram for cannibal, and
why also Prospero turns a dog called Fury on to the rebels
(Hulme 1986a: 89–134). Literature, in such a reading, both reflects and creates ways of seeing and modes of articulation that
are central to the colonial process.

Literary texts are crucial to the formation of colonial discourses
precisely because they work imaginatively and upon people as individuals. But literary texts do not simply reflect dominant ideologies; they also militate against them, or contain elements which
cannot be reconciled to them. Such complexity is not necessarily a
matter of authorial intention. Plays such as *Othello* and *The Tempest*
thus evoke contemporary ideas about the bestiality or incivility of
non-Europeans. But we can differ about whether they do so in order to endorse dominant attitudes to 'race' and culture or to question them. Does *Othello* serve as a warning against inter-racial love,
or an indictment of the society which does not allow it? Does *The
Tempest* endorse Prospero's view of Caliban as a bestial savage, or
does it depict the dehumanisation of colonial rule? It is difficult to
establish Shakespeare's intentions, but we can certainly see how
these plays have been read differently by people over time and in
different places. *The Tempest*, for example, has been staged, interpreted and appropriated as a romance that has nothing to do with
colonialism, as an imperial fable depicting the victory of the white
man's knowledge over both nature and the savage, and as an
anti-colonial text that depicts the struggle of the enslaved Caliban.

Literary and cultural practices also embody cultural interactions. Morris dancing, which might be regarded as quintessentially English, evolved from Moorish dances brought back to Europe through the Crusades. In fact, throughout the medieval and early modern periods we can see the European appropriation of non-European texts and traditions, especially Arabic texts, so that European literature is not simply literature written in Europe or by Europeans but is produced in the crucible of a history of interactions going back to antiquity. The syncretic nature of literary texts or their ideological complexities should not lead to the conclusion that they are somehow 'above' historical and political processes. Rather, we can see how literary texts, both through what they say, and in the process of their writing, are central to colonial history, and in fact can help us towards a nuanced analysis of that history. Even a discipline like comparative literature which acknowledged the profound interaction of various literatures and cultures, was hierarchically organised, and its central assumption was that 'Europe and the United States together were the centre of the world, not simply by virtue of their political positions, but also because their literatures were the ones most worth studying'. Instead, Said suggests that Western cultural forms be placed 'in the dynamic global environment created by imperialism' (1995: 22–28).

But what about non-Western forms of writing? These too did not develop in isolation but were shaped by foreign, including colonial, encounters. For example, O. Chandu Menon's *Indulekha* (1889), one of the earliest novels written in Malayalam, was, its author claims, an attempt to fulfil his wife's 'oft-expressed desire to read in her own language a novel written after the English fashion' and to see if he could create a taste for that kind of writing 'among my Malayalam readers not conversant in English' (Pannikar 1996: 97–98). This novel documents the transformation of marital relations in the Malabar region and articulates some of the tensions and desires of the new middle classes in the region through what was initially an alien literary form. In another part of the world, George Lamming, in his famous essay 'The Occasion for Speaking', claimed that there were 'for me, just three important events in British Caribbean history' – Columbus's journey, 'the abolition of slavery and the arrival of the East – India and China – in the Caribbean Sea' and 'the discovery of the novel by West Indians as a way of investigating and projecting the inner experiences of the West Indian community' (1960: 36–37). Published in 1960, Lamming's essay was one of the earlier attempts to understand how important literature can be in devaluing and controlling colonial subjects but also in challenging colonialism.

This may be a good place to ask ourselves how exactly we would demarcate literary texts from other forms of representation. If we go back to a period when European colonial discourse is in its formative stages, we can see the fairly dramatic overlaps between literary texts, visual representations and other writings. Let me begin with a picture that has become, following a seminal essay by Peter Hulme, central to the discussion of the place of women and gender in colonial discourse – it is *Vespucci discovering America*, engraved in the late sixteenth century by Stradanus. In this picture, Vespucci holds a banner with the Southern cross in one hand and a mariner's astrolabe in the other. He stands looking at America, who is a naked woman half rising from a hammock. Hulme analyses this picture to show how it encodes aspects of the colonial drama: America as a naked woman 'lies there, very definitely discovered' (1985: 17). The cannibals in the background signify the supposed savagery and violence of New World natives, which the colonisers used to 'justify' their taking over of American lands. Vespucci is a historical individual, America a whole continent, their 'meeting' enacts a colonial paradigm whereby the European subject achieves individuation precisely in opposition to colonised peoples who represent land (as in this picture), or nature, ideas (commerce, labour, or pain) or a group (Zulu warriors, or Hindu women).

The first of the great sixteenth-century atlases, the *Theatrum Orbis Terrarum*, drawn up by Abraham Ortelius in 1570 (published in English in 1606 as *The Theatre of the Whole World*) encodes the colonial encounter in similar ways. Its frontispiece depicts the figure of America and the accompanying lines tell us:

> The one you see on the lower ground is called AMERICA,
> whom bold Vespucci recently voyaging across the sea
> seized by force, holding the nymph in the embrace of gentle
> love.
> Unmindful of herself, unmindful of her pure chastity,
> she sits with her body all naked, except that a feather
> headdress
> binds her hair, a jewel adorns the forehead,
> and bells are around her shapely calves.
> She has in her right hand a wooden club, with which she
> sacrifices
> fattened and glutted men, prisoners taken in war.
> She cuts them up into quivering pieces, and either
> roasts them over a slow fire or boils them in a steaming
> cauldron,
> or, if ever the rudeness of hunger is more pressing,
> she eats their flesh raw and freshly killed . . .
> a deed horrible to see, and horrible to tell . . .
> At length . . . wearied with hunting men and wanting to lie
> down
> to sleep, she climbs into a bed woven in a wide mesh like a net
> which she ties at either end to a pair of stakes. In its
> weave,
> she lays herself down, head and body, to rest.
>
> (quoted by Gillies 1994: 74–75)

The lines seem virtually a commentary on the Stradanus picture and other visual representations showing America. The birth of a new cartography in the early seventeenth century was made

possible and imperative by travels to the new lands. Maps claim
to be objective and scientific, but in fact they select what they
record and present it in specific ways, which are historically tied
in with colonial enterprises (Harley 1988; Ryan 1994; Rabasa
1985). During the Renaissance, the new artwork and the new geography together promised the 'new' land to European men as if
it were a woman; not to mention the women of the new land who
were regarded as literally up for grabs.

Not surprisingly then, Sir Walter Ralegh who led the first
English voyages to Guiana described the latter as a country that
'hath her maidenhead yet'. America was ready to be deflowered
by Europe. Attached to Ralegh's narrative was a poem by George
Chapman, 'De Guiana' in which Guiana is an enormous
Amazonian female who defers to England, also personified as a
woman:

> *Guiana*, whose rich feet are mines of golde,
> Whose forehead knocks against the roofe of Starres,
> Stands on her tip-toes at fair England looking,
> Kissing her hand, bowing her mightie breast,
> And every signe of all submission making.

But if England is also female, and if the imperial project is carried out in the name of a female monarch (in this case Elizabeth
I), colonial relations cannot be projected always or straightfor-
wardly in terms of patriarchal or heterosexual domination. These
tensions between the female monarch, the male colonists and
colonised people were to be revisited and reworked during the
heyday of British imperialism when Victoria was Empress. These
different kinds of 'texts' – poetry, travelogues, atlases – use different languages and codes to project overlapping images, create a
common vocabulary and construct America as an attractive land
ripe for colonisation.

The interrelatedness of literary with non-literary texts, and the
relation of both to colonial discourses and practices that we have

glimpsed in these early colonial times can be unravelled in later periods too, often even more sharply. We have seen how a wide spectrum of representations encode the rape and plunder of colonised countries by figuring the latter as naked women and placing colonisers as masters/rapists. But the threat of native rebellion produces a very different kind of colonial stereotype which represents the colonised as a (usually dark-skinned) rapist who comes to ravish the white woman who in turn comes to symbolise European culture. One of the earliest such figures is Caliban in *The Tempest*, who, Prospero alleges, threatens to rape his daughter Miranda. This stereotype reverses the trope of colonialism-as-rape and thus, it can be argued, deflects the violence of the colonial encounter from the coloniser to the colonised. Understood variously as either a native reaction to imperial rape, or as a pathology of the darker races, or even as a European effort to rationalise colonial guilt, the figure of the 'black' rapist is commonplace enough to be seen as a necessary/permanent feature of the colonial landscape.

In the very different context of nineteenth-century colonial India, Jenny Sharpe (1993) demonstrates that the dark-skinned rapist is not an essential feature at all but discursively produced within a set of historically specific conditions. Sharpe shows that though such a figure comes to be a commonplace during and after what the British called 'The Mutiny' of 1857 (a revolt which spread from the Sepoys of the army and involved local rulers as well as peasants, and which nationalist historiography was to call the First War of Indian Independence). This event inaugurated the transformation of an existing colonial stereotype, that of the 'mild Hindoo', into another, that of the savage rapist of British women. Before the revolt, there were no stories of rape. The imperialists had for long scripted Indians as mild and ripe for colonial education. Through a reading of various reports, memoirs and other Mutiny narratives written by men as well as women, Sharpe suggests that the rebellion shook the British and left them 'without a script on which they could rely'. Sharpe demonstrates what she calls 'the truth effects' of stories about white women's violation and mutilation. Even though there was no evidence of systematic violence of this sort, she suggests that the 'fear-provoking stories have the same effect as an actual rape, which is to say, they violently reproduce gender roles in the demonstration that women's bodies can be sexually appropriated' (1993: 67). This idea of 'truth-effects' where discourses can produce the same effects as actual events is Foucaultian in origin and it is useful in expressing the material effects of ideology without conflating the two. Sharpe discusses how these rape stories allowed a shaken British administration not only to consolidate its authority but to project itself as part of a civilising mission. Thus 'a crisis in British authority is managed through the circulation of the violated bodies of English women as a sign for the violation of colonialism' (1993: 4).

A whole range of English novels about India play with this history: E.M. Forster's *A Passage to India*, in which an Indian man is wrongly accused of raping a British woman, evokes the same 'racial memory that echoes across the Mutiny novels as a horrific nightmare' (Sharpe 1993: 123). But the book was written much later in the 1920s during a period haunted by the massacre by the British of hundreds of defenseless Indians who had assembled for a non-violent public meeting at Jallianwallah Bagh at Amritsar in March 1919, an event which challenged the usual British claim to a civilising presence. Similarly Paul Scott's *The Jewel in the Crown*, most explicitly offers rape as a metaphor for imperialism by depicting how an Indian man accused of raping a British woman is in turn violated by the colonial machinery. This novel too was written during the height of the nationalist struggles, at which time there was no threat of inter-racial rape analogous to that which was evoked and circulated during the Mutiny. Thus, at a time when the crisis of colonial authority is at a fever pitch, both these books evoke an earlier discourse which had tried to establish the moral value of colonisation. According to Sharpe, this harking back in *The Jewel in the Crown* works to suggest that 'imperialism is a violation only at the moment of an organized opposition to British rule' (1993: 141). Thus, while 'exposing the British abuse of power in India, the novel also consolidates a colonial discourse of rape' (1993: 146). In this reading, specific texts are not always simply pro- or anti-colonial, but can be both at the same time.

Sharpe's book is part of the growing body of work that not only warns us against abstracting literary from other writings, but conversely, reminds us that non-literary texts such as newspaper stories, government records and reports, memoirs, journals, historical tracts or political writings are also open to an analysis of their rhetorical strategies, their narrative devices. They are not necessarily 'objective' but represent their version of reality for specific readers. So it is not just that literary texts are useful for analysing colonial discourse, but that the tools we use for their analysis can also be used for understanding the other 'texts' of empire. Gayatri Spivak endorses Foucault's suggestion that 'to make visible the unseen can also mean a change of level, addressing oneself to a layer of material which hitherto had no pertinence for history and which had not been recognized as having any moral, aesthetic or historical value' (Spivak 1988: 285). In this sense, literary texts have become more widely recognised as materials that are essential for historical study.

Today, even those works where the imperial theme appears to be marginal are being reinterpreted in the context of European expansion. As Spivak pointed out in an early essay, 'It should not be possible to read nineteenth-century British literature without remembering that imperialism, understood as England's social mission, was a crucial part of the cultural representation of England to the English' (1985a: 243). Thus, no work of fiction written during that period, no matter how inward-looking, esoteric or apolitical it announces itself to be, can remain uninflected by colonial cadences. Although 'the Victorian novel turned its face from . . . unpalatable colonial details', such details cannot be excluded from our readings of these novels. In Jane Austen's *Mansfield Park*, Sir Thomas Bertram's estate which seems so sheltered in its English provincialism is propped up by Antiguan sugar plantations which were run by slave labour (Boehmer 1995: 25). Of course, the colonies are not marginal in all European literature; on the contrary, English fiction becomes fairly obsessed with colonial travel, an obsession which resulted in bestsellers such as G.A. Henty's novels for young adults (*With Clive in India*, or *With Wolfe in Canada*), Rider Haggard's adventure stories or Kipling's fictions. But here let us examine, via recent discussions of Charlotte Brontë's *Jane Eyre*, how attention to the colonial dimension alters our understanding of European literature and culture.

Marxist critics such as Terry Eagleton read Jane's passage from an impoverished orphan and governess to the wife of wealthy Mr Rochester in terms of social mobility and the ambiguous class position of the governess; feminist critics such as Sandra Gilbert and Susan Gubar appropriated the novel as a landmark text about the birth of a female individualism and the rise of the female subject in English fiction. But this reading had already been disturbed in 1966 by Jean Rhys's novel *Wide Sargasso Sea*, which amplified a figure that is hauntingly marginal to *Jane Eyre* – that of Bertha Mason, Mr Rochester's 'mad' first wife who is burnt to death, clearing the way for Jane's marriage to Mr Rochester. Rhys rewrote Bertha's 'madness' as the misery and oppression of a white Creole woman married for her plantation wealth, then dislocated from her island home in the Caribbean and locked up in an English manor. Going back to Rhys, Gayatri Spivak (1985a) criticised feminist critics for reading 'Bertha Mason only in psychological terms, as Jane's dark double'; she suggested instead that nineteenth-century feminist individualism was necessarily inflected by the drama of imperialism, and that it marginalised and dehumanised the native woman even as it strove to assert the white woman as speaking and acting subject.

This position was criticised by Benita Parry (1987), who pointed out that Bertha Mason, tormented Caribbean woman as she is, is not the real 'woman from the colonies' in Rhys's novel. Bertha, first called Antoinette, is the white mistress of Christophine, a black plantation slave who is exploited but not silenced or reduced to the margins as she articulates her critique of Rochester, and of race and class relations on the island. Of course Christophine is not present in *Jane Eyre*, but we can see how the world she occupies is necessary to the construction of English domestic peace and prosperity. However, in a fine essay on *Wide Sargasso Sea*, Peter Hulme suggests that while such a move is enormously useful in re-reading the European canon, we need to pay simultaneous attention to the historical and political nuances of texts produced in the erstwhile colonies. Thus Jean Rhys's novel cannot be read simply alongside, and in opposition to *Jane Eyre*, and celebrated as 'postcolonial' in opposition to 'colonial'. For *Wide Sargasso Sea* was 'written by, in West Indian terms, a member of the white colonial elite, yet somebody who always defined herself in opposition to the norms of metropolitan "Englishness"; a novel which deals with issues of race and slavery, yet is fundamentally sympathetic to the planter class ruined by Emancipation' (Hulme 1994: 72). Hulme makes the important point that returning this novel to its local context complicates the term 'postcolonial' which is in some danger of being ho-mogenised and flattened if simply pitted against the 'colonial'. Instead, he suggests, 'postcolonial theory, if it is to develop, must produce "native" terminology', by which he means terms of refer-ence that are local, rooted in specific histories. In this particular case, it would mean returning Rhys's novel not just to a gener-alised 'West Indian' context but teasing out its Dominican and Jamaican strands as well. In this series of critical exchanges, we can see that a focus on colonialism productively re-opens Marxist

and feminist readings of canonical English fiction to a new debate, but also demands that we widen our understanding of the
terms colonial and postcolonial.

This brings us to yet another aspect of the relation between
literature and colonialism which has to do not with what texts
mean but what they are made to mean by dominant critical
views, which are then enshrined within educational systems. We
can easily grasp this from a play such as Shakespeare's *Othello*, a
standard text in schools and colleges in many parts of the world.
For years critics refused to acknowledge that Othello is meant to
be black – they argued endlessly that he was actually some shade
of brown, not really 'Negroid', or was 'white' inside. The play
could then be read as making a statement about masculine jealousy as a 'universal' attribute, provoked by the real or potential
transgression of women. If Othello's blackness was acknowledged,
it was to suggest that his 'race' explained his jealousy, his emotional outbursts and his irrationality. These readings may be contradictory, but they can and were reconciled within racist
readings of the play which needed to argue that Shakespeare's
hero was white, and simultaneously read blackness in terms of
certain stereotypes. But if we seriously consider the race relations
in the play, the theme of sexual jealousy cannot be seen as a universal statement about human relations in general, but is a crucial
aspect of the racist context in which Othello and Desdemona live
and love. Iago's machinations then are not 'motiveless malignity'
(Samuel Taylor Coleridge's phrase endorsed by generations of literary critics) but born out of racial hatred and insecurity. Of
course, we can read Shakespeare's play either as a passionate defence of, or as a warning against, inter-racial love, but the crucial
point is that on the stage, in critical evaluations and within class-
rooms all over the world, its racial theme was read to *bolster* racist
ideologies existing in different contexts – in Britain, in South
Africa and in India among other places (see Cowhig 1985; Orkin
1987; Loomba 1989; Johnson 1996). In all these places,

Shakespeare's play worked to reinforce the cultural authority of not just Shakespeare, but 'Englishness'.

Even those literary texts that are, arguably, distant from or even critical of colonial ideologies can be made to serve colonial interests through educational systems that devalue native literatures, and by Euro-centric critical practices which insist on certain Western texts being the markers of superior culture and value. The rise of literary studies as a 'discipline' of study in British universities was in fact linked to the perceived needs of colonial administrators: English literature was instituted as a formal discipline in London and Oxford only after the Indian Civil Service examination began to include a 1000 mark paper in it, on the assumption that knowledge of English literature was necessary for those who would be administering British interests. Soon after, it was also deemed important that the natives themselves be instructed in Western literatures. Thomas Babington Macaulay, the architect of English education in India put the case succinctly in his famous 'Minute on Indian Education' written in 1835: English education, he suggested, would train natives who were 'Indian in blood and colour' to become 'English in taste, in opinions, in morals, and in intellect'. These people would constitute a class who would in fact protect British interests and help them rule a vast and potentially unruly land (Macaulay 1972: 249).

Literary studies were to play a key role in attempting to impart Western values to the natives, constructing European culture as superior and as a measure of human values, and thereby in maintaining colonial rule. Gauri Viswanathan's book, *Masks of Conquest,* argues this by examining British parliamentary papers and debates on English education in India. The book (like its title) suggests that English literary studies became a mask for economic and material exploitation, and were an effective form of political control. Not only was the colonial classroom one of the testing grounds for developing attitudes and strategies which became a fundamental part of the discipline itself, but

certain humanistic functions traditionally associated with literature – for example, the shaping of character or the development of the aesthetic sense or the disciplines of ethical
thinking – were considered essential to the processes of sociopolitical control by the guardians of the same tradition.

(Viswanathan 1990: 3)

Far from being antithetical to the political sphere, then, literature and culture are central to it. Like Said, Viswanathan has been
criticised on the grounds that she does not take into account the
role of Indians in either resisting or facilitating such literary
studies. In fact, many Indians themselves *demanded* English education, including reformers and nationalists who were opposed to
British rule in India. The making of British colonial policy thus
played upon and was moulded by indigenous politics, and was
not simply exported from England.

One of the ideologies underpinning literary education was the
assumption that there was an insurmountable cultural gap between those who had 'natural' access to literary culture, and these
others who needed to be taught it. Far from bridging this gap,
literary education would reinforce inferiority; in the words of one
H.G. Robinson

As a clown will instinctively tread lightly and feel ashamed of
his hob-nailed shoes in a lady's boudoir, so a vulgar mind may,
by converse with minds of high culture, be brought to see and
deplore the contrast between itself and them.

(quoted Baldick 1983: 66)

Such cultural control necessarily meant a suppression of the
creativity and intellectual traditions of those who were to be
schooled in English literature. Macaulay's remark that a single
shelf of European literature was worth all the books of India and
Arabia is notorious but not unique. It is true of course that

Orientalists defended some indigenous works, such as the ancient cultural artefacts and literary texts of India, but they too did so at the explicit expense of contemporary works of art – thus indigenous intellectual production was either completely disparaged (as in Africa) or seen as an attribute of a hoary past (as in India). Whether or not they were granted a cultural heritage of their own, colonised societies were seen as unworthy of developing on independent lines.

What *was* this culture that was constructed as the authoritative measure of human values? As the Scottish writer James Kelman puts it:

> when we talk about the hegemony of English culture we aren't referring to the culture you find down the Old Kent Road in London, we aren't talking about the literary or oral traditions of Yorkshire or Somerset: we are speaking about the dominant culture within England; the culture that dominates all other English-language based cultures, the one that obtains within the tiny elite community that has total control of the social, economic and political power-bases of Great Britain.... There is simply no question that by the criteria of the ruling elite of Great Britain so-called Scottish culture, for example, is inferior, just as *ipso facto* the Scottish people are also inferior. The logic of this argument cannot work in any other way. And the people who hold the highest positions in Scotland do so on that assumption. Who cares what their background is, whether they were born and bred in Scotland or not, that's irrelevant, they still assume its inferiority. If they are native Scottish then they've assimilated the criteria of English ruling authority ....
>
> (1992: 71–72)

Kelman is here making the important point that neither the colonisers nor the colonised are homogeneous categories. The process of devaluation was not confined to colonies far away but also drew upon and attempted to calcify divisions of gender, class and ethnicity at or nearer home: thus, for example, as Robert Crawford has shown, the marginalisation of the Scottish language and literatures was an important feature of the 'invention of English literature' (1992: 16–44). And although racial and cultural boundaries were drawn with different degrees of rigidity in various parts of the world, and in Africa it may not have been so easy to forget the 'background' or race even of those natives who were co-opted by their colonial masters, still we do need to acknowledge that colonial domination implicated sections of the local population.

Various accounts of the colonial ideologies of English literary studies extend Althusser's point that educational systems are important means for the dissemination of dominant ideologies. But did such a process of control work? Countless colonial intellectuals certainly parroted the lines of their masters; here is an extract from a prize winning essay written in 1841 by an Indian student at Hindu College, Calcutta titled 'The Influence of Sound General Knowledge on Hinduism':

> With the Hindus everything and all things are incorporated in their religion. Their sciences, their arts are all revealed from heaven. If, therefore, their science is overthrown, their religion is also overthrown with it . . . . The citadel of Hinduism is the religion of the country. Attack, capture that citadel, the system of Hinduism lies a conquered territory. And it is the science and religion of Christendom which have now encompassed round about that citadel. Several of its walls are beaten down, but still it is not surrendered: but we hope ere long the faith and science of Christendom shall fully be established in India . . . . But, alas, alas our countrymen are still asleep – still sleeping the sleep of death. Rise up, ye sons of India, arise, see the glory of the Sun of Righteousness! . . . And we who

have drunk in that beauty, we who have seen that life – shall
we not awake our poor countrymen?

                                        (quoted Majumdar 1973: 201)

I have quoted at some length from this essay because it closely
echoes Macaulay's opinion that in India, literature, science and religion were intermixed (while each was distinct in the West) and
also because the author explicitly takes on the role of Macaulay's
English educated Indian who acts as a surrogate Englishman and
awakens the native masses.

But is mimicry an act of straightforward homage? In a series of
essays, Homi Bhabha suggests that it is possible to think of it as
a way of eluding control (1994: 125–133). He draws upon recent
theories of language, enunciation and subjectivity which point
out that communication is a process that is never perfectly
achieved and that there is always a slippage, a gap, between what
is said and what is heard. As we have been discussing, in the colonial context 'the English book' (the Western text, whether religious like the Bible, or literary like Shakespeare) is made to
symbolise English authority itself. But this process whereby a
text or a book stands in for an entire culture is a complex, and ultimately fraught exercise. The process of replication is never complete or perfect, and what it produces is not simply a perfect
image of the original but something changed because of the context in which it is being reproduced. Bhabha suggests that colonial authority is rendered 'hybrid' and 'ambivalent' by this
process of replication, thus opening up spaces for the colonised to
subvert the master-discourse. This is a complex argument, and
one that we will return to when we discuss colonial identities and
anti-colonial rebellion. For now, let us look at mimicry and the
study of literature in the colonies.

The process by which Christianity is made available to heathens, or indeed Shakespeare made available to the uncultured, is
designed to assert the authority of these books, and through these

books, the authority of European (or English) culture and to make the latter feel like clowns in the boudoir. Thus the intention is to assert an unbridgeable gap or difference between colonisers and colonised peoples. But the effort to convert the natives also assumes that the latter can be transformed by the religious or cultural truths enshrined in the colonial texts. Here the assumption is that the gap between cultures and people can be bridged. Thus there is a fundamental contradiction at the heart of the attempt to educate, 'civilise' or co-opt the colonial 'other'. We can certainly see how such a contradiction is seized upon and used by colonised peoples. Lala Hardayal, a founder of the anti-colonial Ghadder Association, used Shylock's speech in *The Merchant of Venice*, which begins 'I am a Jew. Hath not a Jew eyes?' (III, i, 51–57) to argue that Shakespeare stood for human equality and that we should remember Shylock if we are 'ever tempted to scorn or wrong a brother man of another race or creed' (Hardayal 1934: 238). Now, at one level, such an invocation of Shakespeare might be seen to prop up the authority of the Bard. But at another level, it certainly challenges rather than accepts colonialist views of racial difference. Thus Hardayal mimics the English uses of Shakespeare in order to contest the legitimacy of English rule in India.

We can also trace a wider pattern here. Hindu College, to take the very institution which produced the essay quoted above, was also the hotbed of Indian nationalism, and many of the early nationalists were English educated, and even used English literature to argue for independence. One form of this argument had been put forward by imperial historians who claimed that English literature (especially Shakespeare) and English education in general, had fostered ideas of liberty and freedom in native populations. It took Western Enlightenment notions of democracy and fraternity to make Indians or Africans demand equality for themselves! This dynamic is perhaps best symbolised by Shakespeare's Caliban, who tells Prospero and Miranda:

> You gave me language, and my profit on't
> Is, I know how to curse. The red-plague rid you
> For learning me your language!
>
> (I, ii, 363–365)

Caliban can curse because he has been given language by his captors. But one problem with such a line of reasoning is that subversion, or rebellion, is seen to be produced entirely by the malfunctioning of colonial authority itself. In Bhabha's view, too, it is the *failure* of colonial authority to reproduce itself that allows for anti-colonial subversion. As a result, he does not consider the indigenous sources of anti-colonial intellectual and political activity.

This question, whether the dominant language, literature, culture and philosophic ideas can be turned around and used for subversive purposes, has been central to postcolonial, feminist, and other oppositional discourses. Within literary studies, one of the best known exchanges on the subject is the one between Ngũgĩ wa Thiong'o and Chinua Achebe. Achebe suggests that given the multilingual nature of most African states as well as the colonially generated presence of the English language there, 'the national literature of Nigeria and of many other countries of Africa is, or will be, written in English'. Achebe invokes the creative hybridity of African writers who moulded English to their experience rather than the other way round, and concludes that

> for me there is no other choice. I have been given this language and I intend to use it .... I feel that the English language will be able to carry the weight of my African experience. But it will have to be a new English, still in full communion with its ancestral home but altered to suit its new African surroundings.
>
> (Achebe 1975: 103)

A similar position has been taken by writers and critics of

African origin or ancestry who live within metropolitan cultures such as James Baldwin or David Dabydeen. In reply to Achebe, and explaining his own decision to write in Gikuyu rather than English, Ngũgĩ wa Thiong'o invokes the multiple connections between language and culture, and argues that colonialism made inroads into the latter through control of the former. For him, the 'literature by Africans in European languages was specifically that of the nationalistic bourgeoisie in its creators, its thematic concerns and its consumption' (1986: 20) . This literature was part of the 'great anti-colonial and anti-imperialist upheaval' all over the globe, but became increasingly cynical and disillusioned with those who came to power in once-colonised countries, and then bedevilled by its own contradictions because it wanted to address 'the people' who were not schooled in European languages (1986: 21). Ngũgĩ casts a division between writers who were part of these people and wrote in indigenous languages, and those who clung to foreign languages, thus suggesting an organic overlap between political and cultural identities and the medium of literary expression.

How can we unravel these issues? Powerful anti-colonial writings have adopted both these perspectives. Further, choice of language does not always neatly represent ideological or political positions. Solomon T. Plaatje, founder member of the ANC wrote a novel in English called *Mhudi* (1930) which he said would be 'just like the style of Rider Haggard when he writes about the Zulus'. Plaatje raises his voice against colonial dispossession of Africans in vocabularies inspired by Shakespeare, African oral forms, and the Bible. Similarly George Lamming's writing of a novel seizes a colonial form of writing and uses it to challenge the coloniser's claim to culture. On the other hand, writers who express themselves in indigenous tongues are not necessarily anti-colonial or revolutionary, and they may be 'contaminated' by Western forms and ideas in any case, as is the case with the writer of the Malayalam novel *Indulekha*, discussed earlier. Nevertheless, turning away from colonial culture is often a necessary precondition

for paying serious attention to the literatures and cultures devalued under colonialism.

Literary studies also evoke a range of strategies. Historically,
Shakespeare was used in South Africa to contest as well as foster
racism. The contestations took place both from within and outside the education system, with African political leaders and intellectuals often using Shakespeare either to express their own
psychological and political conflicts, or to challenge divisive ideologies. But how effective is such a strategy – do we need to use
Joseph Conrad, whom Achebe called a 'bloody racist', to challenge colonialism? To the extent that Shakespeare and Conrad are
still taught and still read in the postcolonial world, why not?
Thus, Martin Orkin argues that Shakespeare can be used progressively within the South African context. But at the same time, it
is also necessary to challenge the Euro-centric canons that are still
taught in many parts of the once-colonised world (and schools
and universities within Europe and the United States). So for
David Johnson, the effort to appropriate Shakespeare will only re-
tard the move towards a fresh, more meaningful curriculum. Of
course, simply reshuffling texts does not entail a shift of political
or theoretical perspective, and decolonisation will demand more
than teaching African or Asian or Latin American texts. These
texts are also written across a huge political spectrum and can be
taught from a variety of perspectives. Still, it is significant that
many recent books on 'postcolonial literature' only consider literatures written in English, or widely available in translation, or
those that have made the best-seller lists in Europe and the
United States. We certainly need to widen our perspective on
postcoloniality. For Edward Said, it is as crucial to read outside
Western culture, to become comparative in a new sense: 'to read
Austen without also reading Fanon and Cabral . . . is to disaffili-
ate modern culture from its engagements and attachments'
(1995: 38). For many third world intellectuals and artists, however, such an exercise is not enough. Non-Western literatures

need to be recovered, celebrated, re-circulated, reinterpreted not just in order to revise our view of European culture but as part of the process of decolonisation.

The study of colonialism in relation to literature and of literature in relation to colonialism has thus opened up important new ways of looking at both. Even more important perhaps is the way in which recent literary and critical theory has influenced social analysis. Developments in literary and cultural criticism have not only demanded that literary texts be read in fuller, more contextualised ways, but conversely, have also suggested that social and historical processes are textual because they can only be recuperated through their representation, and these representations involve ideological and rhetorical strategies as much as do fictional texts. The analogy of text and textile may be useful here: critical analysis teases out the warp and woof of any text, literary or historical, in order to see how it was put together in the first place. Colonialism, according to these ways of reading, should be analysed as if it were a text, composed of representational as well as material practices and available to us via a range of discourses such as scientific, economic, literary and historical writings, official papers, art and music, cultural traditions, popular narratives, and even rumours.[7]

TEXTUALITY, DISCOURSE AND MATERIAL PROCESSES

If literary and cultural theory has widened the scope of studies on colonialism, it also poses real problems for a historically specific materialist critical practice. The idea that historical processes and practices can be analysed by looking at them as 'texts' has proved to be both enabling and problematic. In recent postcolonial theory and criticism, some critics allege, literary texts begin to stand in for all social processes; analysis of representation and discourse replaces all discussion of events and material reality. It has been suggested that this tendency emanates from *Orientalism*, which situates literary texts as a colonial battlefield. However, *Orientalism* analyses texts and discourses as they relate to a specific institutional field. In later studies, a different notion of discourse as 'text' emerges as can be seen in the following statement by two leading scholars of the field:

> Imperial relations may have been established initially by guns, guile and disease, but they were maintained in their interpellative phase largely by textuality, both institutionally . . . and informally. Colonialism (like its counterpart racism), then, is a formation of discourse, and as an operation of discourse it interpellates colonial subjects by incorporating them in a system of representation.
>
> (Tiffin and Lawson 1994: 3)

The counterpoising of 'guns, guile and disease' to 'textuality' is precisely what disturbs some scholars: Sumit Sarkar, for example, finds Gauri Viswanathan's assertion that English studies 'became the core of colonial hegemony whereas "the exercise of direct force [was] discarded as a means of maintaining social control" ' untenable in the face of continuing English brutality in India (1994: 218, 223). By the 1890s aesthetic display was central to the operations of imperialism (Morris 1982). But, as Elleke Boehmer suggests, 'discussions of text and image mask this reality of empire: the numbers who died in colonial wars and in labour gangs, or as a result of disease, starvation, and transportation' (1995: 20). Many writings on colonial or postcolonial discourse may not expressly privilege the textual, but they implicitly do so by interpreting colonial relations through literary texts alone. Others do not necessarily concentrate on literature alone but their analysis of colonial discourse blurs the relationship between the material and the ideological, leading one critic to warn that 'in calling for the study of the aesthetics of colonialism, we might end up aestheticizing colonialism, producing a radical chic version of raj nostalgia' (Dirks 1992: 5).

Abdul JanMohamed (1985), Benita Parry (1987) and other critics have accused postcolonial theorists like Homi Bhabha and Gayatri Spivak of an 'exhorbitation of discourse' – of neglecting material conditions of colonial rule by concentrating on colonial representations. I want to suggest that this tendency has to do with the fact that what is circulated as 'postcolonial theory' has largely emerged from within English literary studies. The meaning of 'discourse' shrinks to 'text', and from there to 'literary text', and from there to texts written in English because that is the corpus most familiar to the critics. The recent *Post-colonial Studies Reader*, for example, aims 'to assist in the revision of teaching practice within literary studies in English' and therefore it is primarily interested in 'the impact of postcolonial literatures and criticism on the current shape of English studies' (Ashcroft *et al*. 1995: 4). The first problem with this approach is that it limits 'postcolonial literatures' to texts written in various Englishes. Secondly, postcolonial studies are located entirely within English studies, a location that not only seriously circumscribes the scope of the former, but also has serious implications for its methodology. The isolation of text from context is an old and continuing problem in literary studies. The liberal-humanist orthodoxy placed great literature 'above' politics and society; new criticism privileged words-on-the-page, and even some recent approaches such as deconstruction can continue to think about literary texts in isolation from their contexts. Revisionary English studies, although more inter-disciplinary and contextual, are not automatically rid of the isolationist tendency, partly because it is indeed very difficult to work out the connections between representation and reality. And so we have a somewhat paradoxical situation: on the one hand, we can see the power of texts, and read power as a text; on the other hand, colonialism-as-text can be shrunk to a sphere away from the economic and the historical, thus repeating the conservative and humanist isolation of the literary text from the contexts in which it was produced and circulated.

It has become commonplace to reject the empiricist divisions between something called 'the real' and something else called 'the ideological', and of course the two cannot be bifurcated in any neat fashion. But it is important to keep thinking about the over-laps as well as distinctions between social and literary texts, and about what we mean by 'textual' and 'discursive'. It is useful too to remind ourselves that discourse is not simply another word for representation. Rather, discourse analysis involves examining the social and historical conditions within which specific representa-tions are generated. The study of colonial discourse ought to lead us towards a fuller understanding of colonial institutions rather than direct us away from them.

In any colonial context, economic plunder, the production of knowledge and strategies of representation depended heavily upon one another. Specific ways of seeing and representing racial, cultural and social difference were essential to the setting up of colonial institutions of control, and they also transformed every aspect of European civil society. Guns and disease, as a matter of fact, cannot be isolated from ideological processes of 'othering' colonial peoples. The gathering of 'information' about non-European lands and peoples and 'classifying' them in various ways determined strategies for their control. The different stereotypes of the 'mild Hindoo', the 'warlike Zulu', the 'barbarous Turk', the 'New World cannibal', or the 'black rapist' were all generated through particular colonial situations and were tailored to differ-ent colonial policies. In Africa and India, by attributing particu-lar characteristics to specific tribes and groups, colonial authorities not only entrenched divisions between the native pop-ulation, but also used particular 'races' to fill specific occupations such as agricultural workers, soldiers, miners, or domestic ser-vants. In Bulawayo, Tonga, people were forced into a critical de-pendence on wage labour because they were far away from mines and other markets. Thus they became associated with the dirtiest, most physically exacting and lowliest paid kinds of labour, and after a while Europeans maintained that 'the Tonga had an "inborn" affinity to manual labour' (Ranger 1982: 129).

Of course, stereotypes of races or groups were not consistent over time: following the 1857 rebellion, as discussed earlier, the 'mild Hindoo' figure gave way to an image of the Hindu rapist which came much closer to the stereotype of the brute black man generated in the African context. The so-called Cape Boys were initially used by whites in military actions against the Shona and the Ndebele peoples, but once they began to compete with whites as market-gardeners, artisans or transport-drivers, they were stereotyped as uncontrollable drunks (Ranger 1982: 127–128). Stereotypes also work in tandem with pre-colonial power relations. In India they carried strong underpinnings of caste divisions, for instance, wiliness and cunning were attributed to upper caste Brahmins, traditionally the keepers of education and learning. Various tribal peoples, historically repressed by the upper-castes and already relegated to the margins of Hindu society, were also regarded by the British authorities as less sophisticated, more warlike, child-like and gullible.

Colonial ethnographies and catalogues of colonial peoples codified some of these divisions and fed into policy making at various levels. Various institutions and practices were implicated in such a process. For example, photography was pressed into the service of colonial ethnography in the famous *The People of India*, an eight volume series published in 1868–1875 by the Politics and Secrets Department of the India Office in London which became fundamental reading for colonial administrators. Pre-existing notions of difference were now freshly articulated through nearly 500 photographs supplied by amateurs employed by either the military or the civil government, each accompanied by a brief 'descriptive letterpress'. These volumes attempt to squeeze the bewildering varieties of Indian peoples into categories of caste, race, religion, and occupation seen not as dynamic and evolving but as a more or less static inheritance from the distant past. *The People of India* reveals the attempt both to master colonial subjects and to represent them as unalterably alien; it thus represents both the intrusiveness of the colonial gaze and an inability to comprehend what it seeks to codify. These ways of codification were not, however, confined to the British and colonial and native ways of representation played upon and against each other: the Jodhpur census of 1891, commissioned by the Maharajah of Marwar was also organised upon similar caste and tribal divisions and illustrated by black and white photographs.

The linkage between photographic images, ethnographic and quasi-scientific data gathering, census taking and colonial policy underlines the intricate, subtle, and even contradictory, connections between colonial representations, institutions and policies. Recent research has established such connections with respect to scientific knowledge and establishments, theatre and cinema, art, cartography, city planning, museums, educational, legal, and medical institutions, prisons and military establishments, to mention just a few areas. Such studies underline that the cultural, discursive or representational aspects of colonialism need not be thought of at all as functioning at a remove from its economic, political or even military aspects. From the very beginning, the use of arms was closely connected to the use of images: English violence in colonial Virginia, for example, was justified by representing the Native Americans as a violent and rebellious people. Hence from the beginning there was what Abdul JanMohamed calls 'a profoundly symbiotic relationship between the discursive and the material practices of imperialism' (1985: 64).

In Brian Friel's play *Translations*, the colonial struggle in Ireland is represented as a contest over words and language. Set in a hedge-school in Donegal in 1833, it shows how British cartographers, with Irish help, attempted to transliterate and Anglicise

Gaelic names for various places in Ireland. At the same time, the hedge-school's days are numbered for a national educational system in English is in the offing. In this powerful play, the linguistic mutilation of Ireland overlaps with the penetration and 'mapping' of the land. At the same time, English incomprehension of Gaelic is a measure of the distances between the colonisers and the colonised, and their dependence upon Irish subordinates a comment both on the nature of colonial authority and on the complex positioning of the colonial subject. The English Yolland needs the Irish Owen's help to rename Irish place-names, but cannot get even the latter's name right:

Owen: I suppose we could Anglicise it [Bun na hAbbann] to Bunowen; but somehow that's neither fish nor flesh.
(*Yolland closes his eyes again*)
Yolland: Give up.
Owen: (at map) Back to first principles. What are we trying to do?
Yolland: Good question.
Owen: We are trying to denominate and at the same time describe that tiny area of soggy, rocky, sandy ground where that little stream enters the sea, an area known locally as Bun na hAbhann . . . Burnfoot! What about Burnfoot?
Yolland: (Indifferently) Good, Roland, Burnfoot's good.
Owen: George, my name isn't . . .
Yolland: B-u-r-n-f-o-o-t?

(Friel 1984: 410)

Friel was accused by some critics of dissolving economic issues into the politics of language, but says Declan Kiberd in his monumental book on Irish colonialism,

> The struggle for the power to name oneself and one's state is enacted fundamentally within words, most especially in colo-

nial situations. So a concern with language, far from indicating a retreat, may be an investigation into the depths of the political unconscious.

(1995: 615)

Gaelic was virtually wiped out as a language, and this play, even though it is imagined as taking place in Gaelic, was written and enacted in English. This is a clever way of making the 'postcolonial' audience critique its own lack of Irish, and reflect upon the legacy of colonisation.

Kiberd reminds us too that 'A root meaning of "translate" was "conquer"' (1995: 624). This is a crucial point for colonial attempts to classify, record, represent and process non-European societies, as we have already seen, were attempts to re-order worlds that were often incomprehensible to the masters and make them more manageable, comprehensible for imperial consumption. These attempts restructured, often violently, the world of the colonised, and birthed new concepts, images, words and practices that bear testimony to the complexity of colonial 'translations', a process which is brilliantly illustrated by Gananath Obeyesekere's fascinating account of the contact between James Cook and his men and the Pacific islanders. Obeyesekere shows how 'statements about cannibalism' in the diaries and writings of Cook and his companions, some of whom were ethnographers of the Royal Society, 'reveal more about the relations between Europeans and Savages during early and late contact than, as ethnographic statements, about the nature of Savage anthropophagy' (1992: 630). On all the South Sea islands that they visited, the British sailors obsessively inquired about the cannibalism of the natives because:

cannibalism is what the English reading public wanted to hear. It was their definition of the Savage. Thus in the many places Cook visited, the inevitable question he asked was about cannibalism, and the replies for the most part convinced Cook of its universal prevalence . . . .

(1992: 635)

But this confirmation came both from those people who did eat human flesh, and those who did not. Probing this Obeyesekere suggests that the native responses were based on their counter-assumption that the British inquiries stemmed from the fact that the British themselves were cannibals and wanted to eat the islanders:

> The Hawaiians' hypothesis was based on the pragmatics of common sense. Here were a ragged, filthy, half-starved bunch of people arriving on their island, gorging themselves on food, and asking questions about cannibalism. Since Hawaiians did not know that the British inquiry was a scientific hypothesis, they made the pragmatic inference that these half-starved people were asking questions about cannibalism because they were cannibals themselves and might actually eat the Hawaiians. If the British could ask what seemed to the Hawaiians an absurd question – whether they ate their enemies slain in battle – it is not unreasonable for the Hawaiians to have made a further inference: that since the British had slaughtered so many Hawaiians, it is they who ate their slain enemies.

(1992: 634)

Obeyesekere further suggests that the British presence was a 'new and traumatic event' in the history of the region, and it 'produced a new discourse on cannibalism'. Whereas those people who did not eat human flesh (like the Hawaiians) feigned cannibalism, those who did (like the Maoris) exaggerated it in order to 'terrify [the Europeans] in the context of unequal power, where their real weapons were nothing in comparison to European guns' (1992: 646).

Thus cannibalism is 'constructed out of an extremely complex dialogue between Europeans and Polynesians which affects both 'the British practice of ethnological science and the late Maori practice of cannibalism'. The Maoris, Obeyesekere speculates, once ate human flesh simply as part of human sacrifice rituals, but in response to the colonial presence, it became a method of counter-attack and became 'conspicuous anthropophagy' where their enemies were consumed in large numbers. Thus, 'large-scale anthropophagy was a reaction to the European presence'. Older beliefs that consuming one's enemy was empowering for the victor are reworked and become a testimony to colonial struggle for power. In this account, representations, images and stereotypes are shown to be an integral part of colonial violence. As Obeyesekere reminds us, a

> discourse is not just speech; it is imbedded in a historical and cultural context and expressed often in the frame of a scenario or cultural performance. It is about practice: the practice of science, the practice of cannibalism. Insofar as the discourse evolves it begins to effect the practice.
>
> (1992: 650)

2

COLONIAL AND POSTCOLONIAL IDENTITIES

CONSTRUCTING RACIAL AND CULTURAL DIFFERENCE

Are human beings essentially the same or different? Is difference defined primarily by racial attributes? Colonial and racial discourses and their attendant fictions and sciences, as well as anti-colonial thought, have been preoccupied with these questions. The 'othering' of vast numbers of people, and their construction as backward and inferior depended upon what Abdul JanMohamed calls the 'Manichean allegory', in which a binary and implacable discursive opposition between races is produced (1985: 60). Such oppositions, as we have earlier discussed, are crucial not only for creating images of the outsider but equally essential for constructing the insider, the (usually white European male) 'self'. Therefore many anti-colonial and postcolonial critiques are preoccupied with uncovering the way in which such oppositions work in colonialist representations. But now, many critics are beginning to ask whether, in the process of exposing the ideological and historical functioning of such binaries, we are in danger of reproducing them. In other words, are we now reiterating the importance of cultural/racial difference and alterity, albeit from a different ideological standpoint than those of colonialist discourses?

Of course, in reality any simple binary opposition between 'colonisers' and 'colonised' or between races is undercut by the fact that there are enormous cultural and racial differences within each of these categories as well as cross-overs between them. What should be our strategy in dismantling the legacies of such beliefs? Several critics, and most notably Homi K. Bhabha, have emphasised the failure of colonial discourses to produce stable and fixed identities, and suggested that cross-overs of various sorts or 'hybridity' and 'ambivalence' more adequately describe the dynamics of the colonial encounter. But JanMohamed argues that ambivalence is itself a product of 'imperial duplicity' and that underneath it all, a Manichean dichotomy between coloniser and colonised is what really structures colonial relations. These are tricky questions and we will approach them by examining various discourses about racial difference and how they work in relation to class, gender, sexuality and other social hierarchies.

First of all, racial stereotyping is not the product of modern colonialism alone, but goes back to the Greek and Roman periods which provide some abiding templates for subsequent European images of 'barbarians' and outsiders. These were reworked in medieval and early modern Europe, where Christianity became 'the prism through which all knowledge of the world was refracted' (Miles 1989: 16). But, since the Bible held that all human beings were brothers descended from the same parents, the presence of 'savages' and 'monsters' was not easy to explain. One response was to locate them as creatures who had incurred God's wrath – hence the Biblical association of blackness with the descendants of Ham, Noah's bad son, and with the forces of evil. However, such an explanation created more conceptual problems than it solved. If there was a single origin for all humanity then presumably these fallen people could be brought back into the fold, and converted to Christian ways. But could racial difference be so easily shed? In early modern times, aphorisms such as the impossibility of 'washing the Ethiope white' were commonly used to indicate the biological basis and hence the immutability of race and colour. For example, Thomas Palmer's *Two Hundred Posies*, England's earliest known emblem book (first published 1565), depicts, under the title 'Impossible things', two white men washing a black man. The accompanying lines read:

Why washeste thou the man of Inde? . . .
Indurate heart of heretics
Much blacker than the mole;
With word or writte who seeks to purge
Starke dead he blows the coal.

(1988: 56)

This image was extremely common throughout the sixteenth and seventeenth centuries. In medieval and early modern Europe, Christian identities were constructed in opposition to Islam, Judaism or heathenism (which loosely incorporated all other religions, nature worship, paganism and animism). Above all, it was Islam that functioned as the predominant binary opposite of and threat to Christianity (Chew 1937). Religious difference thus became (often rather confusedly) an index of and metaphor for racial, cultural and ethnic differences. Shylock's reference to his 'tribe' thus includes all these shades of meaning. The term 'Moors' at first referred to Arab Muslims, but although not all Muslims were dark-skinned (and travelogues as well as literary texts abound with references to white Moors), over time Moors came overwhelmingly to be associated with blackness, as is evident from the term 'blackamoors'. Religious and cultural prejudice against both blackness and Islam, each of which was seen to be the handiwork of the Devil, intensified the connection between them.

With European colonial expansion, and nation-building, these earlier ideas (and their contradictions) were intensified, expanded and reworked. Despite the enormous differences between the colonial enterprises of various European nations, they seem to generate fairly similar stereotypes of 'outsiders' – both those outsiders who roamed far away on the edges of the world, and those who (like the Irish) lurked uncomfortably nearer home. Thus laziness, aggression, violence, greed, sexual promiscuity, bestiality, primitivism, innocence and irrationality are attributed (often contradictorily and inconsistently) by the English, French, Dutch, Spanish and Portuguese colonists to Turks, Africans, Native Americans, Jews, Indians, the Irish, and others. It is also worth noting that some of these descriptions were used for working-class populations or women within Europe. But, at the same time, travel collections like *Principall Navigations* or *Hakluytus Posthumus* do not simply project some generalised 'other', but also begin to shape particular groups of 'Indians': Americans as opposed to 'Turks' or Africans as opposed to the people of 'Indoostan'. While these are rather confused categories ('Moors' for example being a term that applies vaguely to all non-American 'Indians') these collections are early ethnographies that simultaneously note, blur and produce the specific features of different non-European peoples. Note the contradiction here: the subtleties of each encounter recorded by collectors of early travel narratives like Richard Eden, Ramusio, Richard Hakluyt and Samuel Purchas contributed to the consolidation of various European national cultures, a pan-European 'Western' culture and a central division between Europe and its 'others'.

Columbus's 'mistake' about the location of India swelled to become a metaphor for this division. As Samuel Purchas noted in 1614 the 'name of India is now applied to all farre-distant Countries, not in the extreme limits of Asia alone; but even to whole America, through the error . . . in the Western world' (1614: 451). In unravelling the histories of 'race', the real difficulty lies in walking the tightrope between highlighting the specificity of various images and recognising the flexibility of colonial ideologies.

Contact with racial others was structured by the imperatives of different colonial practices, and the nature of pre-colonial societies. Early colonial discourses distinguished between people regarded as barbarous infidels (such as the inhabitants of Russia, Central Asia, Turkey) and those who were constructed as savage (such as the inhabitants of the Americas and Africa). Peter Hulme identifies a central division between colonial 'discursive practices which relate to occupied territory where the native population has been, or is to be, dispossessed of its land by whatever means' and 'those pertaining to territory where the colonial form is based primarily on the control of trade . . . . America and India', he says, 'can exemplify very roughly this division' which also manifests itself as 'a discursive divide between those native peoples perceived as being in some sense "civilized" and those not . . . ' (1986a: 2–3). With respect to the Americas, Columbus's arrival functions as an 'originary moment' that diminishes native histories and cultures which precede it and that is endlessly revisited by subsequent encounters (Greenblatt 1991: 52–53). In the East, however, each journey only adds another layer to a thick and confused pre-history: not only had other Europeans always gone before, but before Europeans other foreigners had trodden so that no one could say of India, as Ralegh did of Guiana, that she still had her 'maidenhead'. No one encounter could be discursively enshrined as primary.

These differences feed into colonial stereotyping. 'New World natives' have been projected as birthed by the European encounter with them; accordingly, a discourse of primitivism surrounds them. On the other hand, 'the East' is constructed as barbaric or degenerate. Europeans travelled in both directions in search of wealth. But if, in the New World, to use Stephen Greenblatt's words, 'the European dream, endlessly reiterated in the literature of exploration, is of the grossly unequal gift exchange: I give you a glass bead and you give me a pearl worth half your tribe' (1991: 110), in the Ottoman or Mughal territories, that dream turned into an endless nightmare in which the

European pearls were treated as baubles by Eastern emperors. In a letter to his employers, the East India Company, Sir Thomas Roe, who was resident for many years at the court of the Mughal Emperor Jahangir, complained that the presents sent by the Company 'are extremely despised by those [who] have seen them; the lyning of the coach and cover of the virginalls scorned . . . . Here are nothing esteemed but of the best sorts: good cloth and fine, rich pictures . . . soe that they laugh at us for such as wee bring' (1926: 76–77). In 1605 James I allocated £5,332 to the Levant Company for a present to the Turkish Sultan, who was, like the Mughal Emperor Jahangir, always unimpressed. The English turned their feeling of inadequacy into an account of Oriental greed or lack of manners. Edward Terry described the Mughul Jahangir's heart as 'covetous' and 'so unsatiable, as that it never knows when it hath enough; being like a bottomless purse, that can never be fill'd' (1655: 378–379). Medieval notions of wealth, despotism, and power attaching to the East (and especially to the Islamic East) were thus reworked to create an alternative version of savagery understood not as lack of civilisation but as an excess of it, as decadence rather than primitivism.

Differences were 'noted' *within* each group as well. Columbus distinguished between 'canibales' and 'indios' – the former were represented as violent and brutish, the latter as gentle and civil. Both however, were regarded as inferior to the white people. In some cases, colour was the most important signifier of cultural and racial difference (as in the representations of Africans) and in other cases it was less remarked upon (as in the case of the Irish). In fact the lack of colour difference *intensified* the horror of the colonial vis-à-vis the Irish. Thus Charles Kingsley observed after his first trip to Ireland: 'I am haunted by the human chimpanzees I saw along that hundred miles of horrible country . . . . But to see white chimpanzees is dreadful; if they were black, one would not feel it so much, but their skins, except where tanned by exposure, are as white as ours' (quoted by Gibbons 1991: 96). The construction of racial differences had to do both with the nature of the societies which Europeans visited, the class of people who were being observed, as well as whether trade or settlement was the objective of the visitors. The crucial point is that such constructions were based on certain observed features, the imperatives of the colonists, and preconceptions about the natives. Moreover, they were filtered through the dynamics of actual encounters. 'Construction' should not thus be understood as a process which totally excludes the responses and reactions of those who were being represented. This does not mean that the vast populations that were stereotyped in colonial discourses were responsible for their own images; rather, the very process of misrepresentation worked upon certain specific features of the situation at hand. Thus misrepresentations or constructions need to be unravelled rather than simply attributed to some timeless, unchanging notion of racism or Orientalism. Obeyesekere's analysis of cannibalism in the Pacific islands (discussed above) is a good example of such unravelling.

Colonisers differed in their modes of interacting with the local populations, and these differences had a profound impact on racial discourses and identities. For example, the Spanish in America and the Portuguese in India settled down in the lands they colonised, adopted local manners and inter-married in a way that the English derided. Eventually, inter-marriages and concubinage blurred racial distinctions and created a population which acted as a strong base for colonial rule. According to some commentators, this showed a 'lack of racial feeling' on the part of the Portuguese or the Spanish. But in fact colour and race consciousness marked even the policy of cohabitation, and racial distinctions continued to inform the subsequent 'mixed' social order. Albuquerque invited his men to marry 'the white and beautiful' widows and daughters of the defenders of Goa, making a distinction between them and the darker South Indian women whom he called 'Negresses'. The Jesuit priest Francis Xavier, who worked in both India and the Spice Islands, drew sharp colour lines even as he urged the casados to marry their local concubines, encouraging the men to abandon the dark ones and even offering to find substitutes for them. Class was also an important factor in interracial marriages, with poorer casados marrying locally and the elite keeping mistresses, but also maintaining their marriages in Portugal. Similar fine-tuning is evident in Latin America where the hybrid population resulting from Spanish and Indian sexual contact encoded a complex hierarchy of colour, class and gender.

British colonialism, on the other hand, did not allow for easy social or sexual contact with local peoples. Although of course this policy was hardly watertight or successful, in India it also reflected the nature of colonial administration, which functioned to a large extent through local authorities and existing power structures. Thus it often incorporated rather than disturbed native hierarchies: in Bengal, for example, taxes were collected through hereditary Indian collectors who were liable for a fixed sum as laid down in the 'Permanent Settlement' of 1793. Millions of Indians never saw an English person throughout the term of the Raj, although that did not mean their lives had not been woven into the fabric of empire. This kind of 'shallow penetration' can be seen as a prototype for modern imperialism, which functions largely through remote control. But in countries like Namibia and South Africa there was yet another pattern where racial divisions were maintained along with direct and powerful intervention, and with less spinoffs of power and wealth among the indigenous population.

Heterogeneity, variety and diversity are sometimes understood as lack of purpose or ideology: Jan Morris contends that the British Empire 'never really possessed an ideology – was temperamentally opposed, indeed, to political rules, theories and generalizations. It was the most important political organism of its time, yet it was seldom altogether sure of itself or its cause' (1994: 2). Analyses of colonial discourses are most useful in deconstructing precisely this assumption that only a tightly controlled operation could be ideologically motivated. Certainly, colonialism had not one but several ideologies, and these ideologies were manifest in hundreds of different institutional and cultural practices. But we also cannot forget that they all fed into a global imbalance. Colonialism did have an economic as well as philosophic imperative, although it did not always succeed in either making money or entirely suppressing the peoples it exploited. Moreover, military violence was used almost everywhere, although to different degrees, to secure both occupation and trading 'rights': the colonial genocide in North America and South Africa was spectacular. In the 'scramble for Africa', only Ethiopia held out because of her technological and military superiority. The fact that Asian armies had been equipped with firearms prior to the coming of the Europeans was undoubtedly a crucial factor in shaping the relationship of coloniser and colonised. Gunpowder had been invented in China, and used by the Mughals and the Ottoman Empire. But, even in the East, 'present profit' was not divorced from the use of arms: Irfan Habib has suggested that the 'European triumph' over Asian merchants was 'a matter of men-of-war and gun and shot, to which arithmetic and brokerage could provide no answer ... ' (1990: 399). The point is that violence was readily resorted to wherever necessary, and the enormous differences of strategy in different places indicate the flexibility of colonial ideologies and practices, rather than the absence of the desire for conquest in some colonial ventures.

Moreover, colonial discourses fluctuated in tandem with changes in political situations within the same place over time. In December 1783, Edmund Burke delivered an angry speech on the humiliating and unjust treatment meted out to the Mughal Emperor by officials of the honourable East India Company. At one point, he interrupted himself to observe:

It is impossible, Mr Speaker, not to pause here for a moment to reflect on the inconsistency of human greatness and the stupendous revolutions that have happened in our age of wonders. Could it be believed, when I entered into existence or when you, a younger man, were born, that on this day, in this House, we should be employed in discussing the conduct of those British subjects who had disposed of the power and person of the Grand Mogul?

(Parker 1990: 162)

The reversal in the relations of power between the English and the Mughals was indeed so swift as to be conceptually bewildering for both parties; my purpose in recalling it is to remind us that if the history of America moved from colonisation to trade, that of India moved the other way around. Constructions of the 'other' shifted in response to these changes, in Australia, for example, images of the Aboriginal population changed drastically (from meekness, savagery became its supposed attribute) as the colonists encountered Aboriginal resistance to working as manual labourers.

I have been suggesting that representations of the 'other' vary according to the exigencies of colonial rule. But such an explanation is somewhat functional in that it posits racial ideologies as simply *reflecting* economic and material factors. European discourses about Africans make it clear that such functionalism is inadequate because even before the actual enslavement and colonial plunder of Africans began, racist stereotypes which were obsessed with colour and nakedness were well in place. In fact in several colonial situations these stereotypes provided an ideological *justification* for different kinds of exploitation. Therefore the relationship between racial ideologies and exploitation is better understood as dialectical, with racial assumptions both arising out of and structuring economic exploitation (Miles 1989: 27).

During colonial expansion and consolidation, the contradiction between universalism and racist thought intensified as

Europeans seemed bent on the supposedly impossible task of washing black people white. The efforts to convert natives accompanied most colonial endeavours, even though they were often unsuccessful. From the earliest ventures, the fantasy of conversion was rampant, and sixteenth- and seventeenth-century plays, travelogues and pamphlets all showed 'good' Turks, Moroccans, 'Indians' and others willingly embracing Christianity. In fact religious conversion begins to figure as a justification for economic plunder: for example, in *The Triumphs of Honour and Virtue*, a pageant written by the well-known dramatist Thomas Middleton for the Lord Mayor of London's inaugural ceremonies in 1622, an Indian Queen celebrates her own conversion to Christianity which, she says, 'settles such happiness' on her that the 'gums and fragrant spices' which the English traders take away with them, indeed all 'the riches and the sweetness of the east' are only fair exchange for the 'celestial knowledge' that is now hers. She also asks the viewer to observe her 'with an intellectual eye', to see beyond her blackness and its associations with depravity, sin and filth, and to perceive her inner goodness, which, she suggests, is made possible by her new faith.

The Indian Queen's speech here, like other writings of the period, intricately mixes the language of religion with that of commerce: it is 'blest commerce' that becomes a crusader for Christianity. Two points are important here. Firstly, what was once impossible – washing the Ethiope white – is now rendered feasible by Christianity. But in the process, skin colour is unyoked from moral qualities. The black queen must now be recognised as good. Secondly, colonial plunder of goods is justified by the gift of Christianity. But if blackness can be washed white, that means whiteness is also vulnerable to pollution. The recurrent images of black people, Moors and heathens and other outsiders converting to Christianity try to keep at bay another set of anxieties, those generated by the possibility of Christians 'turning Turk' (a phrase that also enters the English language during the Renaissance and begins to stand in for all betrayals and desertions) and Europeans 'going native'. As Peter Hulme reminds us,

> the boundaries of civility proved extraordinarily permeable in the other direction. Just as Othello was a single, fictional counterexample to the thousands of Christians who 'turned Turk' in the ports of Southern Europe and North Africa in the sixteenth and seventeenth centuries, so Pocahontas was a unique convert, uniquely remembered.
>
> (1985: 26)

As colonialism advanced, missionary activities expanded, but so did European fears of contamination.

Ideologies of racial difference were intensified by their incorporation into the discourse of science. Science claimed to demonstrate that the biological features of each group determined its psychological and social attributes. Linnaeus had drawn a distinction between *Homo sapiens* and *homo monstrous*; by 1758, the first category had been further bifurcated in John Burke's *The Wild Man's Pedigree* into the following:

a.   Wild Man. Four footed, mute hairy.
b.   American. Copper coloured, choleric, erect. Hair black, straight, thick; nostrils wide; face harsh; beard scanty; obstinate, content, free. Paints himself with fine red lines. Regulated by customs.
c.   European. Fair, sanguine, brawny; hair yellow, brown, flowing; eyes blue; gentle, acute, inventive. Covered with close vestments. Governed by laws.
d.   Asiatic. Sooty, melancholy, rigid. Hair black; eyes dark; severe, haughty, covetous. Covered with loose garments. Governed by opinions.
e.   African. Black, phlegmatic, relaxed. Hair black, frizzled; skin silky; nose flat, lips tumid; crafty, indolent, negligent. Annoints himself with grease. Governed by caprice.

The pseudo-scientific format here simply enforces the ideology of European superiority. And as Mary Louise Pratt comments, 'Except for monsters and wild men, the classification exists barely modified in some of today's schoolbooks' (1992: 32).

Three points about scientific theories of race (which are actually fairly diverse and not always in agreement with one another) should be noted. Firstly, the idea of biologically-constituted races intensified the contradiction we found earlier between racial difference and the Biblical notion of the human species as a unitary creation of God. Many scientists attempted to erase this contradiction by suggesting that environmental factors such as climate had mutated the single originary species. However, science itself revived an older objection to this argument by pointing out that when people were moved to new locations their racial attributes did not change. The movement of African slaves to the Americas and elsewhere was cited as an example (Miles 1989: 33). Robert Young discusses how the question 'Are human beings a single species or not' was the central issue at the heart of anthropological, cultural and scientific debates throughout the nineteenth century. Different species were supposed to be unable to sexually reproduce with each other. Thus the interpretation of 'race' as 'species' tries to deny the possibility of inter-mixing between races, and the inevitable dissolution of racial difference. But the mixed populations of places like the West Indies and parts of the United States obviously gave the lie to any notion of black and white as distinct species. One response was to argue that intermixtures between races led to diminishing fertility. Another was to suggest that racial difference indicated variety *within* a single species, rather than different species altogether. Young traces some of the tensions between Enlightenment ideals of universality and equality and theories of racial difference, pointing out that

> debates about theories of race in the nineteenth century, by settling on the possibility or impossibility of hybridity, focused

explicitly on the issue of sexuality and the issue of sexual unions between whites and blacks. Theories of race were thus also covert theories of desire.

(Young 1995: 9)

Secondly, scientific discussions of race, rather than challenging earlier negative stereotypes of savagery, barbarism, and excessive sexuality, extended and developed these. By attributing racial characteristics to biological differences such as skull and brain sizes, or facial angles, or genes, and by insisting on the connection between these factors and social and cultural attributes, science turned 'savagery' and 'civilisation' into fixed and permanent conditions. Again, such fixity seems to contradict the imperial claim of civilising the natives: if savagery is a biological condition then improvement by social means seems pointless. Thus, in 1859, the German anthropologist Theodor Waitz's *Introduction to Anthropology* pronounced:

If there be various species of mankind, there must be a natural aristocracy among them, a dominant white species as opposed to the lower races who by their origin are destined to serve the nobility of mankind, and may be tamed, trained, and used like domestic animals, or . . . fattened or used for physiological or other experiments without any compunction. To endeavour to lead them to a higher morality and intellectual development would be as foolish as to expect that lime trees would, by cultivation, bear peaches, or the monkey would learn to speak by training. Wherever the lower races prove useless for the service of the white man, they must be abandoned to their savage state, it being their fate and natural destination. All wars of extermination, whenever the lower species are in the way of the white man, are fully justifiable.

(quoted Young 1995: 7)

Thirdly, science extended the association of 'race' and 'nation'. From the sixteenth to eighteenth centuries, the word 'race' was often read as synonymous with various forms of social collectivities such as 'kinsfolk', 'lineage', 'home' and 'family'. Montaigne, for example, uses it interchangeably with 'household'. At other times, 'race' and 'caste' were used as interchangeable terms. 'Race' thus became a marker of an 'imagined community', a phrase that Benedict Anderson has used (in a book we will discuss later) in relation to the nation. Both nations and races are imagined as communities which bind fellow human beings and demarcate them from others. Both speak to members of all classes and genders (although this does not mean that all classes and genders are treated as equal within them). From the sixteenth century on, we can trace the connections between the formation of the English nation (for example) and the articulation of the superiorities of the Anglo-Saxon race. Scientific racism from the eighteenth century calcified the assumption that race is responsible for cultural formation and historical development. Nations are often regarded as the expression of biological and racial attributes. The yoking of race and nation was especially powerful in the writings of Gobineau and others who articulated fascist doctrines. Sometimes of course, nations were (and are) imagined as composed of many races, but at other times, as in the case of Australia, the very idea of nationhood was developed by excluding certain racial others, such as the Aboriginal peoples (Miles 1989: 89, 91).

As we have seen, the connection between the outer manifestation of racial difference and the moral and social differences they were supposed to signify hardened over time. According to Hayden White, the ideological effect of the term 'noble savage' is 'to draw a distinction between presumed types of humanity on manifestly qualitative grounds, rather than such superficial bases as skin color, physiognomy, or social status' (1987: 17). The noble savage idea therefore represents a rupture, a contradiction, a point at which the seamless connections between interiority and external characteristics are disturbed. Similarly, the converted heathen and the educated native are images that cannot entirely or easily be reconciled to the idea of absolute difference. While at one level they represent colonial achievements, at another they stand for impurity and the possibility of mixing, or to use a term that has become central to postcolonial theory, 'hybridity'.

Theories of race, and racial classifications were often attempts to deal with the 'hybridisation' that was a feature of contact zones everywhere. A table from W.B. Stevenson's *Narrative of Twenty Years' Residence in South America* (1825) detailing 'the mixture of the different castes, under their common or distinguishing names' that is worth reproducing here (see p. 120).

Notice how the category 'European' in relation to other Europeans or Creoles becomes 'white' when put in relation to 'Indian' or 'Negro'. The chart also suggests that paternity is genetically dominant (the child born to a white father and an Indian mother will be 6/8 white and 'very fair') as is the white race (the offspring of a white father and Negro mother is 7/8 white, but that of a Negro father and white mother is 4/8 white). The need for detailed classification is testimony to the constant transgression of racial boundaries in colonial America. Such transgressions did not diminish the effort to maintain the racial purity of whites. There is a wonderful anecdote about an American journalist's interview with Haiti's Papa Doc Duvalier which indicates the connections between theories of racial purity and social dominance. The journalist wanted to know what percentage of Haiti's population was white. Ninety-eight per cent, was the response. Struggling to make sense of this incredible piece of information, the American finally asked Duvalier: 'How do you define white?' Duvalier answered the question with a question: 'How do you define black in your country?' Receiving the explanation that in the United States anyone with black blood was considered black, Duvalier nodded and said, 'Well, that's the way we define white in my country' (Fields 1982: 146).

Table 1   W.B. Stevenson's chart of different 'castes' and their mixtures

FATHER	MOTHER	CHILDREN	COLOUR
European	European	Creole	White
Creole	Creole	Creole	White
White	Indian	Mestiso	6/8 White, 2/8 Indian – Fair
Indian	White	Mestiso	4/8 White, 4/8 Indian
White	Mestiso	Creole	White – Often Very Fair
Mestiso	White	Creole	White – But Rather Sallow
Mestiso	Mestiso	Creole	Sallow – Often Light Hair
White	Negro	Mulatto	7/8 White, 1/8 Negro – Often Fair
Negro	White	Zambo	4/8 White, 4/8 Negro – Dark Copper
White	Mulatto	Quarteron	6/8 White, 4/8 Negro – Fair
Mulatto	White	Mulatto	5/8 White, 3/8 Negro – Tawny
White	Quateron	Quinteron	7/8 White, 1/8 Negro – Very Fair
Quarteron	White	Quarteron	6/8 White, 2/8 Negro – Tawny
White	Quinteron	Creole	White – Light Eyes, Fair Hair
Negro	Indian	Chino	4/8 Negro, 4/8 Indian
Indian	Negro	Chino	2/8 Negro, 6/8 Indian
Negro	Mulatto	Zambo	5/8 Negro, 3/8 White
Mulatto	Negro	Zambo	4/8 Negro, 4/8 White
Negro	Zambo	Zambo	15/16 Negro, 1/16 White – Dark
Zambo	Negro	Zambo	7/8 Negro, 1/8 White
Negro	Chino	Zambo-Chino	15/16 Negro, 1/16 Indian
Chino	Negro	Zambo-Chino	7/8 Negro, 1/8 Indian
Negro	Negro	Negro	

Source: Reproduced from Pratt 1992: 152

If miscegenation was a nightmare, colonial administrators nevertheless dreamt of racial mixings that would produce the ideal colonial subject. Here is what Sir Harry Johnson, the first commissioner of British Central Africa visualised in 1894:

> On the whole, I think the admixture of yellow that the Negro requires should come from India, and that eastern Africa and British central Africa should become the America of the Hindu. The mixture of the two races would give the Indian the physical development which he lacks, and he in turn would transmit to his half-Negro offspring the industry, ambition, and aspiration towards civilized life which the Negro so markedly lacks.
>
> (quoted Robinson 1983: 131)

Race has thus functioned as one of the most powerful and yet the most fragile markers of human identity, hard to explain and identify and even harder to maintain. Today, skin colour has become the privileged marker of races which are, as Miles points out, thought of as

> either 'black' or 'white' but never 'big-eared' and 'small-eared'. The fact that only certain physical characteristics are signified to define 'races' in specific circumstances indicates that we are investigating not a given, natural division of the world's population, but the application of historically and culturally specific meanings to the totality of human physiological variation. . . . 'races' are socially imagined rather than biological realities.
>
> (1989: 71)

While colour is taken to be the prime signifier of racial identity, the latter is actually shaped by perceptions of religious, ethnic, linguistic, national, sexual and class differences. 'Race' as a concept receives its meanings contextually, and in relation to other social groupings and hierarchies, such as gender and class. For example, Paul Gilroy has explored how:

> the idea of the city as a jungle where bestial, predatory values prevail preceded the large-scale settlement of Britain by blacks in the post-war period. It has contributed significantly to contemporary definitions of 'race', particularly those which highlight the supposed primitivism and violence of black residents in inner-city areas. This is the context in which 'race' and racism come to connote the urban crisis as a whole . . . . This connection between contemporary British racism and the city is an important reminder that 'race' is a relational concept which does not have fixed referents. The naturalization of social phenomena and the suppression of the historical process which are introduced by its appeal to the biological realm can articulate a variety of different political antagonisms. They change, and bear with them no intrinsic or constant political effects.
>
> (1994: 409)

In order to signal the mutability and constructedness of race, many writers frame the word within quote marks and others substitute it with 'ethnicity'. But despite the fact that racial classification may be at several levels a 'delusion' and a myth, we need to remember that it is all too real in its pernicious social effects. Ethnic, tribal and other community groupings are social constructions and identities that have served to both oppress people and radicalise them. In southern Africa, pre-colonial tribal groupings were transformed by white differentiation and the assignment of particular kinds of jobs to different groups of people. Colonial regimes manipulated as well as created ethnic and racial identities. But Africans also participated in the process of tribal creation. Later the same tribalism also fed into the creation of anti-colonial movements (Ranger 1982). Similarly, the discourse of race has also been appropriated and inverted by anti-colonial and black resistance struggles, such as the Negritude or Black power movements. But equally, many resistance movements have had to struggle to *transform*, and not simply invert, existing discourses about race. In his remarkable autobiography, *Long Walk to Freedom*, Nelson Mandela describes how the hardest, most complex task for the African National Congress was to build solidarity across the racial and tribal divides that had been calcified and institutionalised by the apartheid state.

To sum up then, perceived or constructed racial differences were transformed into very real inequalities by colonialist and/or racist regimes and ideologies. Accordingly, the analysis of race must take cognisance of both the reality of racial discriminations and oppressions, as well as call attention to the constructedness of the concept itself. Having established that racial constructions are shaped within particular historical contexts and alongside other social hierarchies, we can examine, more specifically, the relationship between race and class.

RACE, CLASS AND COLONIALISM

In Charlotte Brontë's novel *Jane Eyre*, the young orphan Jane is to be sent away from the house of her rich relatives who think of her as a badly behaved burden. Jane chooses to go to a boarding house rather than to her poorer relations because, she says, 'I was not heroic enough to purchase liberty at the price of caste' (1981: 19). Caste was of course a concept that became familiar in England from colonial experiences in India, and it marked a social, economic and religious hierarchy overlaid with connotations of purity and pollution, similar to those that shape the idea of race. For the young Jane a movement down the class ladder is understood as a transgression of caste, a virtual crossing of racial divides. Robert Young points out that 'If, according to Marxism, race should be properly understood as class, it is clear that for the British upper classes class was increasingly thought of in terms of race'. He cites the first version of D.H. Lawrence's *Lady Chatterley's Lover* as an instance: when Connie thinks of her lover Parkin at home in his shirt sleeves, eating bloaters for tea and saying 'thaese' for 'these', she gives up the idea of moving in with him, for 'culturally he was another race' (Young 1995: 96). Precisely the opposite sort of movement is registered by Hanif Kureishi's film *My Beautiful Launderette* (1985) in which a white working-class lad suggests to his Pakistani employer that as non-white person he should not evict his Caribbean tenant. The landlord replies: 'I am a professional businessman, not a professional Pakistani'. As an upwardly mobile immigrant, the landlord refuses to overlook the class distinctions that fracture racially oppressed communities as much as racially dominant ones. In this section we will examine the intersection of race and class in the colonial context.

There have been two broad tendencies in analyses of race and ethnicity: the first, which stems from Marxist analysis, can be referred to as the 'economic' because it regards social groupings, including racial ones, as largely determined and explained by economic structures and processes.[1] Colonialism was the means through which capitalism achieved its global expansion. Racism simply facilitated this process, and was the conduit through which the labour of colonised people was appropriated. The second approach, which has been called 'sociological', and derives partly from the work of Max Weber, argues that economic explanations are insufficient for understanding the racial features of colonised societies. While the first approach tends to be functionalist in its understanding of race, the second tends to ignore economic questions and is often descriptive rather than analytical. Of course, we should not reduce these approaches to watertight compartments, because each includes complex and nuanced debates, but on the whole, the former privileges class, and the latter race in understanding colonial social formations. The differences between them are, however, not merely theoretical but have direct consequences for political struggles. If racial relations are largely the offshoot of economic structures, then clearly the effort should be to transform the latter; on the other hand, if this is not the case, racial oppression needs to be accorded a different political weightage and specificity.

Recently, a sophisticated dialogue between these two tendencies, exemplified by the work of sociologist John Rex, has helped develop a more dialectical approach to this question. Rex (1980) suggests that in South Africa, capitalism was installed through the enforced labour of the Bantu peoples. Thus race relations were crucial in making available a labour force. In *Capital*, Marx had suggested that capitalism depends upon 'the free labourer selling his labour power' to the owner of the means of production (1961: 170). But in South Africa, as in a variety of other colonial situations, the labour of colonised peoples was commissioned through a variety of coercive measures. It was not free labour at all. Rex quotes an East African settler to make his point: 'We have stolen his land. Now we must steal his limbs . . . . Compulsory labour is the corollary of our occupation of the country' (1980: 129). 'Classical' Marxism attributes capitalism's efficiency to its having replaced slavery and crude forms of coercion with the 'free' labour market in which the force is exerted through economic pressure. But under colonialism, according to Rex, these other supposedly outdated features of control carry on, *not as remnants of the past but as integral features of the capitalist present*. Race and racism are the basis on which unfree labour is pressed into colonialist service.

Racist ideologies identified different sections of people as intrinsically or biologically suited for particular tasks. Aimé Césaire angrily quotes Ernst Renan on this point:

> Nature has made a race of workers, the Chinese race, who have wonderful manual dexterity and almost no sense of honour;

govern them with justice, levying from them, in return for the blessing of such a government, an ample allowance for the conquering race, and they will be satisfied; a race of tillers of the soil, the Negro ... ; a race of masters and soldiers, the European race. Reduce this noble race to working in the ergastulum like Negroes and Chinese, and they rebel .... But the life at which our workers rebel would make a Chinese or a fellah happy, as they are not military creatures in the least. *Let each one do what he is made for, and all will be well.*

(1972: 16)

The ideology of racial superiority translated easily into class terms. The superiority of the white races, one colonist argued, clearly implied that 'the black men must forever remain cheap labour and slaves'. Certain sections of people were thus racially identified as the natural working classes. The problem was now how to organise the social world according to this belief, or to force 'the population into its "natural" class position: in other words, reality had to be brought into line with that representation in order to ensure the material objective of production' (Miles 1989: 105).

Miles illustrates this process by examining how the racial ideologies with which British colonisers arrived in Kenya structured capitalist development there. First of all, Africans were dispossessed from the best lands, and settled in adjacent reserves. Such a process was facilitated by the creation of African chiefs, contrary to the custom hitherto prevailing in most Kenyan communities. Land that was considered unused by Africans was appropriated after being defined as 'waste'. Local populations were often nomadic, so lands that lay unused at a particular time were potentially available for future use, but the new order curbed their movements and confined them to specific areas. After acquiring land, colonists needed to recruit labour. The different methods employed all required the intervention of the colonial state. The new 'chiefs' were commissioned to supply men to construct roads, railways and docks and act as porters, away from their place of residence. The fees paid were low, and refusal was treated with harsh punishment. The colonists also developed a 'squatter system' whereby African communities were encouraged to live on European lands in return for a certain quantum of labour power. Finally cash taxes were imposed, which Africans were forced to raise by selling their labour for a wage. 'Chiefs' were also used to 'persuade' Africans to enter the labour force, and these measures were defended on the grounds that they would eliminate 'idleness and vice' among the local population. Thus the imperial mission, based on a hierarchy of races, coincided perfectly with the economic needs of the colonists. In the process, as we have already noted, divisions between different African groups and tribes were also emphasised by creating particular sub-divisions and attributing particular kinds of skills and shortcomings to them. Thus the process of 'class formation was shaped by racialization' (Miles 1989: 111).

Capitalism therefore does not override and liquidate racial hierarchies but continues to depend upon, and intensify, them. Ideologies of race and the social structures created by them facilitate capitalist production, so that, Rex argues, 'the South African labour system is the most efficient system for the capitalist exploitation of labour yet devised, resting as it does on the three institutions of the rural reserve, the mining compound and the controlled urban "location" ' (1980: 129). While Rex's critics argued that even in 'classic' capitalism, labour is hardly 'free' in any real sense, his essential point is that in the colonial situation, capitalism works differently, and that this difference needs to be accounted for by thinking more concretely about race and ethnicity.

In colonial situations the state and its various institutions (such as educational establishments) are especially crucial in maintaining these racial and class distinctions and ideologies necessary for creating capitalism. We noted that the state made possible the acquisition of both land and labour in Kenya. Race relations are not determined by economic distinctions alone, rather economic disparities are maintained by ideologies of race. In the previous section we noted that racism helps to structure capitalist expansion. It is especially crucial in maintaining certain hierarchies when the state and legal systems can no longer be blatantly partisan:

> when the social order could no longer be buttressed by legal sanctions it had to depend upon the inculcation in the minds of both exploiters and exploited of a belief in the superiority of the exploiters and the inferiority of the exploited. Thus it can be argued that the doctrine of equality of economic opportunity and that of racial superiority and inferiority are complements of one another. Racism serves to bridge the gap between theory and practice.
>
> This is not of course to say that the use of force ceases with slave emancipation. In some countries like South Africa it is systematically mobilized on a political level to ensure continued white supremacy. But it is to say that when inequality, exploitation and oppression are challenged by economic liberalism, they have to be opposed by doctrines which explain the exceptions to the rule. While it is admitted that all men are equal, some men are deemed to be more equal than others.
>
> (Rex 1980: 131)

That is why some critics have suggested that racial hierarchies are the 'magic formula' which allow capitalism to expand and find all the labour power it needs, and yet pay even lower wages, and allow even fewer freedoms than are given to the white working classes (Wallerstein 1988: 33). Racial difference, in such an analysis, is more than a by-product of class relations, although it is firmly connected to economic structures. Also important to Rex's analysis is the question of internalisation of racial ideologies, to which we will turn in the next section. Thus Rex's approach, says Stuart Hall, 'yields a "Marx plus Fanon" sort of argument' (1980: 315).

The precise intersection of racial ideologies with the process of class formation depended both upon the kinds of societies which colonial powers penetrated and the specific racial ideologies that emerged there. A dialectical perspective helps us understand not just colonial history but the postcolonial world as well. The race relations that are put into place during colonialism survive long after many of the economic structures underlying them have changed. The devaluation of African slaves still haunts their descendants in metropolitan societies, the inequities of colonial rule still structure wages and opportunities for migrants from once-colonised countries or communities, the racial stereotypes that we identified earlier still circulate, and contemporary global imbalances are built upon those inequities that were consolidated during the colonial era. A complex amalgam of economic and racial factors operates in anchoring the present to the colonial past.

According to Stuart Hall, one of the most valuable aspects of emergent theories is to show more precisely how this anchoring works, and how it structures contemporary relations between the once colonised countries and their erstwhile masters. The classical Marxist view that capitalism will eventually erase pre-capitalist economic systems does not seem to work either with regard to colonial societies or in the postcolonial world. In *The Communist Manifesto* Marx and Engels suggested that 'the bourgeoisie . . . draws all, even the most barbarian nations into civilization, it compels them to introduce what it calls civilization into their midst, i.e. to become bourgeois themselves. In one word, it creates a world after its own image' (1976, vol. 6: 488). All over the world capitalism replaces all previous social formations. Rex pointed out that the South African social system displayed no such inevitable tendencies. Within the colonies, pre-capitalist economic forms of exploitation such as plantation slavery persisted, indeed flourished and expanded for a long time. In the postcolonial world also, capitalist economies coexist with, or are 'hampered' by pre-capitalist forms. Why do these social formations resist full-fledged capitalist development?

In one influential analysis, A. Gunder Frank (1969) argued that under the aegis of colonialism, capitalism *had* in fact penetrated everywhere. Latin America, he claimed, has been capitalist since the sixteenth century. According to this view, plantation slavery is nothing but one kind of capitalism, where the slave functions like capital, or like property. 'Underdevelopment' is the result of the manner in which countries around the globe were incorporated into the world system. Imperialism had divided the world into metropoles and satellites, and their relationship was marked by the unequal development of capitalism itself, and the dependency of the latter upon the former. Hence we live in a single world capitalist system that structures both the development of some countries and the underdevelopment, or dependency of others. Today's world is divided into 'advanced' capitalist countries and 'underdeveloped' ones because of the manner in which each of them became capitalist.

There are several obvious problems with this thesis. Ernesto Laclau (1977) points out that it regards 'capitalism' as only a system of production for the market, without taking into account how it structures human relationships. That is why it cannot distinguish between West Indian plantations and English textile mills. Enormously varied exploitative practices are all understood within a single rubric, differentiated only by varying degrees of 'development'. Rex also argues that such a view implies that the third world will have to continue to be exploited as capitalism advances, till it is overthrown by the working class in the advanced countries. Thus it locks advanced and underdeveloped countries into a relation of near-perpetual inequity. Is there a less restrictive way of conceptualising the role of colonialism in the development of capitalism?

An alternative perspective is explained by Stuart Hall (1980) via current debates on plantation slavery. The slave, unlike the worker under capitalism, does not own his or her labour power. Thus she/he is not a worker in the same way as the free wage labourer. The slave's relations with the master are markedly different than those between the worker and the capitalist. However, the slave (via the slave trade) as well as the fruits of the slave's labour enters and circulates within the global capitalist market. Mercantile capital funded the slave trade as well as the trade in plantation goods. Hence plantation slavery was made possible via colonial, agrarian as well as capitalist practices and relations. The non-capitalist practice of slavery coexists with, feeds into, and aids, the development of capitalism. Thus pre-capitalist modes do not simply give way to capitalist ones in any simple teleological sense, but persist precisely because they contribute to the growth of the latter. The relation between them is not simple coexistence but what Hall describes as 'an articulation between different modes of production, structured in some relation of dominance' (1980: 320). This analysis is extremely useful in understanding why capitalism does not simply erase pre-capitalist formations and relations. It is in the interest of capitalism that certain older social structures *not* be totally transformed, and certain older forms of exploitation based on racial and ethnic hierarchies continue to make available cheap labour. If plantation slavery once provided cheaper labour than would otherwise have been available, today the non-capitalist sector continues to play an analogous role. Capitalism coexists with, or is 'articulated' with these other modes of production, but this coexistence is structured by the dominance of capitalism, which therefore benefits from it.

In this section, we have considered only the general framework within which class and race may be articulated together. One of the areas we have not touched is how, from the early days of colonial contact, racial ideologies and images also shaped class relations and perceptions in the metropolis. For example, in early modern Europe, travelling salesmen (who were usually poor peddlers) were routinely perceived as foreign and black. In eighteenth-century Europe, the image of the noble savage fuelled bourgeois critiques of the nobility:

> the concept of Noble Savage stands over against, and under-cuts, the notion, not of the Wild Man, but rather of 'noble man' . . . . The very notion of 'man' is comprehensible only as it stands in opposition to 'wild' and that term's various synonyms and cognates. There is no contradiction in 'wild savage' since these are in fact the same words . . . . But given the theory of the classes prevailing at the time, Noble Savage is an anomaly, since the idea of nobility (or aristocracy) stands opposed to the presumed wildness and savagery of other social orders as 'civility' stands to 'barbarism'. As thus envisaged, the Noble Savage idea represents not so much an elevation of the idea of the native as a demotion of the idea of nobility. That this is so can be seen by its usage, on the one side, and by its effects, on the other. It appears everywhere that nobility is under attack; it has no effect whatsoever on the treatment of the natives or on the way natives are viewed by their oppressors. Moreover, the idea of the Noble Savage brings to the fore (or calls up) its opposite: that is to say, the notion of the ignoble savage, which has as much currency in literate circles in Europe as its opposite.
>
> (White 1987: 191)

Peter Hulme suggests that the development of 'the discourse of the plantation, which recognized only two locations, inside and outside, white and black . . . was itself to provide a central image for the class struggle of industrial Europe' (1986b: 75).

In recent years, there has been considerable work around the dynamic intersection of race and class in specific contemporary situations, and especially postwar Britain. Race is fundamental to the formation of the working classes in general, and to the experiences of black labour in particular. A pioneering study pointed out that the class relations within which black working-class people exist 'function as *race relations*. The two are inseparable. Race is the modality in which class is lived. It is also the medium in which class relations are experienced. This . . . has consequences for the *whole class*, whose relation to their conditions of existence is now systematically transformed by race' (Hall *et al.* 1978: 394). Many anti-colonial intellectuals had previously grappled with this connection between race and class, which is why even the Marxists among them found Negritude so compelling. They needed to foreground the question of race because, as Aimé Césaire put it, 'Marx is all right, but we need to complete Marx' (1972: 70). Césaire writes the colonial encounter as an equation: 'colonisation = "thingification" ' (1972: 21). This 'thingification', or the reduction of the colonised person into an object was achieved not only by turning her/him into 'an instrument of production', but also, by Western accounts (including some radical or socially progressive accounts) of subject-formation. If Marx needed to be 'completed', Freud and his legacy also needed to be re-written, for reasons that we will now examine.

PSYCHOANALYSIS AND COLONIAL SUBJECTS

In *The Deceivers*, John Masters's not very well-known novel, written in 1952 and set in the colonial India of 1825, William Savage, an East India Company official finds himself impersonating Gopal, a local weaver who has disappeared and whose wife, thinking him dead, is about to immolate herself and become a sati. William soon discovers that Gopal is alive and part of a flourishing band of Thugs (Deceivers) or highway robbers who strangle their victims with scarves and supposedly owe allegiance to the goddess Kali. Kali, a single goddess whose worship has been associated with Tantric Hinduism, carries connotations of female power, energy, sexuality, death, magic and rebelliousness. Savage infiltrates the Thugs in order to determine the extent and nature of their operations and to wipe them out. In the process, he finds that he possesses their skills of strangulation as well the ability to interpret certain omens, believed to be signs from Kali, which dictate Thugee operations. Through the novel, William becomes increasingly alienated from his Western self, and finds himself intoxicated by the thrill of murder and the power of Kali. He participates in Thugee rituals, including the eating of a certain consecrated sugar, 'the sweetness of Kali' which marks the allegiance of the bandit to the goddess and her protection in return: 'You are hers and she is yours' (1952: 179–180). Hussein, an ex-Thug turned informer for the British, had previously warned him that none who partake of the sacred sugar can escape Kali's seductive power. After William has eaten the sugar, Hussein laments:

> you are a Deceiver, from this dawn on for ever. A strangler . . . . It doesn't matter what a man *thinks* he is. When he eats consecrated sugar, on the blanket, in front of the pick-axe, he is a strangler, because Kali enters into him . . . . Now you will never return to your office . . . . Kali wills it, so it is.
>
> (1952: 185–186)

As a British official dedicated to the 'civilising mission' but wanting to respect Indians, Savage had started out with a 'battle within himself' with regard to sati. Was sati a barbaric custom against women or a 'beautiful' idea, besides being 'the people's custom and religion'? He

> tried to understand, tried in the Western fashion to separate the good from the evil, to balance the beauty of sacrifice against the ugliness of waste . . . . But to these Hindus there

was no conflict between God, who is all-powerful, and Satan, who yet flouts and perverts His intentions. Here creation and destruction were the opposite faces of the same medal . . . . He had to understand it if he could. Men and women who thought and acted in those beliefs were his charge. If he failed to understand, he could work only from a single, sweeping generalization: that Indians were fatalistic, brutal and loveless.

(1952: 25)

Now, his empathy turns into potential deculturation – he is seduced by Kali into abandoning Western civilisation, and becoming a real Deceiver. At the Thugs feast, he eats goat meat and drinks arrack and is maddened by his dual identities: 'He was William Savage, taking ritual part in a decorous, blood-bathed fantasy. He was Gopal the weaver, eating contentedly, with respect . . . ' (1952: 192). Then Kali possesses him, and 'blown by the fumes of the arrack' he becomes 'not a person but a place, cloudy with red blood and white rice'. In a charged sequence Masters describes his possession by Kali as a kind of madness, where his Christian self is torn asunder by a frenzied desire for Kali, who becomes identified both with a dancing girl present at the feast and India herself:

Father, I have sinned and am no more worthy to be called Thy son. He had eaten the sugar, Kali was Death. Kali was a woman. The zither urged him to spend desire. The girl's hands demanded him and crept over him. He put down the beaker, and touched her, and found her full, warm and waiting . . . . He went to her and strove with her. Suddenly she looked at him, and her eyes sprang wide open, as wide as his. The rumal (scarf) was in his hands, it circled her neck. The muscles were taut in his wrists. Death and love surged up together in him, ready to flood over together, and together engulf her.

(1952: 201–202)

William is possessed by Kali's 'infinite power', but Hussein pulls him away in the nick of time. Hussein's own salvation lies in the small wooden cross gifted him by William's wife Mary, and *his* desire is also to cross boundaries, and wear a 'red coat' as a loyal servant of the East India Company. At the end, Kali's 'blood-wet mouth and lascivious tongue' proves to be no match for a combination of Christ and 'Mary and the baby' which pulls William back to his reality. Thus the loyal native servant of the Empire guides William back to his true British colonial official identity away from the madness of native India.

Both in novels and in non-fictional narratives, the crossing of boundaries appears as a dangerous business, especially for those who are attracted to or sympathise with the alien space or people. 'Going native' is potentially unhinging. The colonised land seduces European men into madness. *The Deceivers* has not received much critical attention, but Conrad's *Heart of Darkness* is a well-known example of this pattern. There Africa is a primeval jungle and a source of power and wealth which fascinates and maddens the colonialist hero Kurtz. Marlow, the narrator of the story tells us that while Kurtz's 'intelligence was perfectly clear . . . his soul was mad. Being alone in the wilderness, it had looked within itself, and by heavens! I tell you it had gone mad' (Conrad 1975: 95). Marlow journeys down the river Congo, into 'the heart of darkness,' in search of Kurtz, whose experiences are recreated as simultaneously a journey into childhood, madness and Africa. Although several critics regard Kurtz's dislocation as a product of colonialist greed, and the novel as a critique of imperialism, it can be seen to rehearse the primitivism of classical psychoanalysis. Chinua Achebe (1989) called it 'a story in which the very humanity of black people is called into question'. In this novel as in much colonialist fiction, Africa is a place where the European mind disintegrates and regresses into a primitive state. Africa, India, China and other alien lands induce madness, they *are* madness itself.

John Barrell opens his study of the imperial roots of Thomas De Quincey's neurotic visions with an extended quotation from De Quincey's *Confessions of an English Opium-Eater*:

> May 1818. The Malay has been a fearful enemy for months. Every night, through his means, I have been transported into Asiatic scenery. . . . I have often thought that, if I were compelled to forgo England, and to live in China, among Chinese manners and modes of life and scenery, I should go mad. . . . In China, over and above what it has in common with the rest of Southern Asia, I am terrified by the modes of life, by the manners, by the barrier of utter abhorrence placed between myself and *them*, by counter-sympathies deeper than I can analyse. I could sooner live with lunatics, with vermin, with crocodiles or snakes . . . .
>
> (Barrell 1991: xi)

Barrell discusses how these traumas are impelled by a fear of 'society in the mass', 'the monstrous aggregations of human beings' (1991: 6), both swarming Orientals and working-class hordes, and also shaped by sexual guilt. His book compellingly illustrates Roy Porter's suggestion that madness is not 'an individual atom' but is culturally shaped and determined.

The three instances of the maddening colonial encounter I have mentioned are all very different from one another, but in all of them, only the European subject is individuated. The 'mark of the plural', Albert Memmi tells us, is a 'sign of the colonised's depersonalization': 'The colonised is never characterized in an individual manner; he is entitled only to drown in an anonymous collectivity ("They are this"; "They are all the same")' (1967: 88). The individual European faces the alien hordes, and if he identifies with them, if he transgresses the boundary between 'self' and 'other', he regresses into primitive behaviour, into madness. These associations between European male adulthood, civilisation and rationality on the one hand, and non-Europeans, children, primitivism and madness on the other are also present in Freudian and subsequent accounts of the human psyche. In Freud's writings, especially *Totem and Taboo* (1913) and *Civilization and its Discontents* (1930), historical and cultural development was visualised as akin to individual, psychic and biological growth (see Seshadri-Crooks 1994). A child's growth towards adulthood and social progress from savagery towards monotheism and patriarchy (Freud's criteria for human civilisation) are mapped on to one another. 'Primitives' are thus akin to children, and to the civilised 'neurotic', having not achieved the psychological growth of the adult European. In the primitive mind, 'the deed . . . is a substitute for thought', and pleasure is primary. Thought and reflection are not available to 'primitive men'. This division between instinctive and reflective human beings has informed the practice of ethnopsychology wherein cultural difference is pathologised and psychic growth understood in terms of cultural/racial difference.

But where does this leave the mad 'primitive'? Michel Foucault describes the creation of mental illness in European society as a process of 'othering', where the madman is confined and silenced in order to define the normative, rational self. But, as Megan Vaughan points out, in colonised societies, 'the need to objectify and distance the "other" in the form of the madman or the leper, was less urgent in a situation in which every colonial person was in some sense, already "Other"' (1991: 10). Therefore, in Africa there was no 'great confinement' akin to what Foucault describes for nineteenth-century Europe. Instead, there was a great concern to describe and pathologise Africans in general in order to then define the European as inherently different. By and large therefore, 'the literature on madness in colonial Africa was more concerned with a definition of "Africanness" than with a definition of madness' (1991: 119). How could African madness be slotted into this framework? Vaughan shows that the mad

African is understood as one who is insufficiently 'other', as one who crosses cultural boundaries and becomes European. Madness, as in the case of the European who goes native, is a transgression of supposed group identities.

The most widespread understanding was that 'deculturation' was the cause of rising insanity. The breakdown of traditional structures and the strains of 'modern' society had literally unhinged Africans who were unable to cope with change: an influential report on cases of insanity in Nyasaland suggested that 'Native schizophrenics with their sexual disturbances and European type of delusions, and their fondness for offense against property, seem to manifest a more European attitude of mind than the members of other groups' (quoted by Vaughan 1991: 108). Extensive studies of how modernisation was eroding traditional social structures were impelled by colonial fears of loss of control; the solution suggested was indirect rule, whereby Africans would be controlled through their 'traditional' leaders and customary practices. We have already discussed how a reinforcement of tradition also served colonial economic and political needs. Writings on African psychology and psychiatry served the need to define the other as firmly other, as incapable of crossing the colonial boundary lines that demarcated her/him from the European male self. Therefore it is hardly surprising that within the frameworks of psychoanalytic discourse, anti-colonial resistance is coded as madness, dependency or infantile regression (see Cooppan 1996).

Frantz Fanon pointed out that resistance to colonial rule is routinely 'attributed to religious, magical, fanatical behavior' (1965: 41). Octavio Mannoni's notorious study *Prospero and Caliban: The Psychology of Colonisation* employed these theories of the African mind to 'explain' the Malagasy revolt of 1947. Mannoni argued that particular ('backward') peoples are colonised because they suffer from an unresolved 'dependence complex', which leads them to revere their ancestors, and to transfer this

reverence to their colonial masters. Thus he accounted for colonisation by suggesting that it is the result of psychic differences between those who show such dependency and some others, who
become colonisers, who fear their own inferiority and seek out
ways of proving themselves: 'To my mind there is no doubting
that colonisation has always required the existence of the need for
dependence. Not all peoples can be colonised: only those who experience this need' (Mannoni 1956: 85). Mannoni explained the
revolt of 1947 as the result of the granting of some concessions
by the French which had left the islanders half free, half unfree
and created a sense of desolation and of being abandoned by their
colonial masters. Thus it is not colonial repression but the lifting
of adequate controls that triggered off native rebellion. In J.C.
Carothers' studies of the Mau Mau rebellion in Kenya (in
1952–1954), resistance is similarly pathologised as an aspect of
underdeveloped individualism. In Rudyard Kipling's novel *Kim*,
the 'Mutiny' or Rebellion of 1857 sparked off by Hindu and
Muslim soldiers of the Indian Army against the British is represented (by an Indian soldier loyal to the British) as a 'madness
[that] ate into all the Army'. In his discussion of the novel,
Edward Said suggests that Kipling simply did not conceive of
any conflict in India, which is why his hero Kim sees no contradiction between serving the Empire and remaining loyal to his
Indian companions (1994: 146–147). But it is possible to read
the conflation of madness and rebellion in the novel as Kipling's
repression of his own awareness of the colonial conflict.

There were of course those who challenged such absolute notions of psychic difference between races. The South African psychoanalyst and doctor Wulf Sachs, for example, argued that there
was no fundamental difference between his black and white patients. In *Black Hamlet: The Mind of an African Negro Revealed by
Psychoanalysis* (first published in 1937) Sachs suggested that his
patient, a black man called John Chavafambira was suffering
from 'Hamletism'. Shakespeare's Hamlet, Sachs follows Freud in

suggesting, is unable to act because of an unresolved Oedipus complex. 'Hamletism' is, accordingly, a 'universal phenomenon symbolizing indecision and hesitancy when action is required' (1947: 176). Given the context in which 'the African mind' was slotted into a permanent and fixed difference from the European, Sachs' suggestion that Chavafambira's mental processes are part of a universally applicable framework, can be seen as a progressive move. However, Sachs was not entirely free of the influence of the 'deculturation' school of thought, and he too regarded his subject's problems as a manifestation of his inability to cope with the demands of modern life. Sachs recognised that Chavafambira's life and his own work were structured by the political and economic realities of South Africa, where black Africans were constantly subject to political harassment and relentlessly pushed into urban proletarianisation. But he did not adequately confront the implications of his own material and argued instead for a fundamental sameness between black and white psychic structures – thus suggesting that Freudian categories such as the Oedipus complex are universally valid (see Dubow 1993).

The discourse of colonial psychology and psychiatry pathologised difference. It was 'unable to contain any notion of difference that was not directly tied to the question of inferiority and the necessity of subordination' (Vaughan 1991: 115). Sachs tried to counter this by erasing the notion of difference altogether. We have already considered how notions of the 'universal' can also be deeply ethnocentric because they are formulated in the image of the dominant culture. Thus, a highly specific image of culture, or in this case, the psyche, is projected as globally applicable. Such a projection works to dehistoricise or depoliticise the notion of the psychic because, as happened in Sachs's case, it does not adequately confront the relation between social structures and the inner lives of human beings. Thus, both in the ways it has projected racial and cultural differences and in the ways it has erased them, psychoanalysis as an institution and as a theory has served colonial interests in Africa and elsewhere (Gilman 1993). Therefore Gayatri Spivak rightly points out that 'institutional psychoanalysis can be a latter-day support of what I have earlier called epistemic violence' (1990: 226).

Freud wrote: 'Every new arrival on this planet is faced by the task of mastering the Oedipal complex; anyone who fails to do so falls a victim to neurosis' (1953: 226, n.1). But to universalise the Oedipal drama is to suggest that it accounts definitively for the development of identities everywhere, as if there were no differences in the ways subjectivities are formed or sexual dramas played out around the world, or as if no other differences of class or culture shape their performance. In *Anti-Oedipus: Capitalism and Schizophrenia*, Gilles Deleuze and Félix Guattari condemn 'the analytic imperialism of the Oedipus complex' which inflates an unhistorical notion of the family as the site for human conflicts whereas in reality the family itself is not immune from political and historical reshaping. For Deleuze and Guattari, the idea of Oedipus is not only inadequate to the task of social analysis, it is itself 'colonialism pursued by other means' (1977: 170). Frederic Jameson argues for the need to 'radically historicize' psychoanalysis, to locate its account of Oedipal conflicts within a specific history of the family and to recognise that 'the structure of the psyche is historical, and has a history' (1981: 62).

Today, the critique of an 'African Oedipus' as nothing but a 'European Oedipal Phantasy' is not uncommon (Hitchcott 1993: 62). But given the history of the psychoanalytic institution, suggestions to this effect by the Martiniquan psychoanalyst Frantz Fanon in *Black Skin, White Masks* and *The Wretched of the Earth* were explosive. Fanon's work directly intervened in the legacy of racist theories of biological and psychological development. It pushed to its logical conclusion the view that 'modernisation' led to native madness by suggesting that it was not modernisation *per se* but colonialism that dislocated and distorted the colonised's psyche. The colonised could not 'cope' with what was happening because colonialism eroded his very being, his very subjectivity. Thus, Fanon announced at the beginning of *Black Skin, White Masks:* 'At the risk of arousing the resentment of my coloured brothers, I will say that the black man is not a man' (1967: 8). The colonial experience annihilates the colonised's sense of self, 'seals' him into 'a crushing objecthood', which is why he is 'not a man'. Fanon thus does not entirely depart from the then current paradigms about the black mind, but he extends them to the point where their political meaning is inverted. Now, it is colonialism that is regarded as psychopathological, a disease that distorts human relations and renders everyone within it 'sick'. Conversely, traits that had been characterised within ethnopsychiatry as forms of native hysteria and evidence of atavistic brain structures are interpreted by Fanon as signs of resistance; laziness, for example, is 'the conscious sabotage of the colonial machine' on the part of the colonised: 'The Algerian's criminality, his impulsivity, and the violence of his murders are therefore not the consequences of the organization of his nervous system or of the characterial originality, but the direct product of the colonial situation' (1963: 239, 250). Whereas Mannoni had suggested that colonialism is the *result* of certain psychic differences between races (which lead some people to dependency or the need to be ruled) Fanon argued that in fact colonialism was the *cause* which engendered psychic difference along racial lines and annihilated the black subject into nothingness.

In recent years, Fanon has been treated (often to the exclusion of other important figures) as the most important anti-colonial writer-activist; he has become, in the words of his comrade and critic Albert Memmi, 'a prophet of the Third World, a romantic hero of decolonization' (1973: 39). Within postcolonial studies, his status as 'a global theorist' may derive from the fact that in Fanon's writings, as in recent critical work, subject formation converges with the colonial and postcolonial question (Gates 1991: 457–458). Let us examine how this convergence works in Fanon's own writings. First of all, Fanon reworks the Lacanian schema of the 'mirror stage', regarded as the crucial stage in the formation of the subject. According to Lacan, when the infant first contemplates itself in a mirror, it sees a reflection smoother, more co-ordinated and stable than itself. The subject constructs itself in the imitation of as well as opposition to this image. Fanon writes:

> When one has grasped the mechanism described by Lacan, one can have no further doubt that the real Other for the white man is and will continue to be the black man. And conversely. Only for the white man the Other is perceived on the level of the body image, absolutely as the not-self – that is, the unidentifiable, the unassimilable. For the black man . . . historical and economic realities come into the picture.
>
> (1967: 161)

For the white man (and woman) the black man is marked by his colour and his supposedly limitless sexuality. 'Negrophobia' turns on the fear and desire of rampant black sexuality. For the white subject, the black other is everything that lies outside the self. For the black subject however, the white other serves to define everything that is desirable, everything that the self desires. This desire is embedded within a power structure, therefore 'the white man is not only the Other but also the master, real or imaginary' (1967: 138). Therefore, blackness confirms the white self, but whiteness empties the black subject. He cannot identify with that which is so persistently negated by the racist/colonialist structure. Thus Fanon's Antillean patients reported that in their delirium, they had 'no color'.

For the 'Negro', racial identity overrides every other aspect of existence. Fanon recalls that when a child on the streets of Paris pointed to him, calling out 'Look! A Negro', he felt 'responsible at the same time for my body, for my race, for my ancestors . . . I was battered down by tom-toms, cannibalism, intellectual deficiency, fetishism, racial defects, slave-ships, and above all else, above all: "Sho' good eatin" ' (1967: 112). The black person attempts to cope by adopting white masks that will somehow make the fact of his blackness vanish. This is a precarious process. Fanon records his shock at realising, at the screening of a film in France, that he was expected to identify with a 'negro' instead of, as he had always done, with Tarzan (1967: 152). Thus black skin/white masks reflects the miserable schizophrenia of the colonised's identity.

Secondly, Fanon suggests that the Oedipal complex and the family structures within which it is housed are incapable of describing the psychic structures of the Antillean subject:

> Like it or not, the Oedipus complex is far from coming into being among Negroes ... in the French Antilles 97 per cent of the families cannot produce one Oedipal neurosis .... With the exception of a few misfits within the closed environment, we can say that every neurosis, every abnormal manifestation ... in an Antillean is the product of his cultural situation. ... In the Antilles that view of the world is white because no black voice exists.
>
> (1967: 151–153)

Whereas for the European child, the nation is an extension of the family, for the Antillean child the family is not reflected at all in the colonial nation. His/her father is subject to colonial authority, hence the law of the father becomes the law of the white man. The colonial subject occupies the place of the transgressive child. This reinscription disrupts the universalism of psychoanalytic categories which Fanon says have always struck him as very far from 'the reality that the Negro presents' (1967: 151). Nevertheless, as we can see, Fanon does not entirely break away from the Oedipal framework, but rewrites it in racial terms.

Instead of the Oedipal scenario where the male child desires its mother, the fantasy of possession of white women by black men is offered by him as the primal scene of colonialism: 'When my restless hands caress those white breasts, they grasp white civilization and dignity and make them mine'. Thus, colonialism is described as an Oedipal scene of forbidden desire.

Fanon was not just a radical psychoanalyst, but also an anticolonial activist. Some critics suggest that there is a tension between these two aspects of Fanon: the first Fanon is the Fanon of *Black Skin, White Masks* who is concerned with the psychologies of the oppressed. The second Fanon is the Fanon of *The Wretched of the Earth*, who turns his attention to the revolt of the oppressed, espouses the cause of Algerian resistance and projects, in his writings, a unified people who have overcome the debilitating effects of colonialism. Of course, these twin concerns – the psychological ill-effects of colonialism and anti-colonial liberation – are interrelated throughout Fanon's work, but critics are sharply divided about how such an interrelation might work. Homi Bhabha, for example, appropriates Fanon as 'a premature post-structuralist' (Parry 1987: 31). Bhabha's Fanon indicates that colonial identities are always oscillating, never perfectly achieved. The divide between black skin and white mask is not, Bhabha explains, 'a neat division' but

> a doubling, dissembling image of being in at least two places at once . . . . It is not the Colonialist Self or the Colonised Other, but the disturbing distance in between that constitutes the figure of colonial otherness – the White man's artifice inscribed on the Black man's body. It is in relation to this impossible object that emerges the liminal problem of colonial identity and its vicissitudes.
>
> (1994: 117)

On the other hand, Benita Parry reads Fanon (and his fellow Martiniquan Aimé Césaire) as

authors of liberation theories . . . [who] affirmed the intervention of an insurgent, unified black self, acknowledged the revolutionary energies released by valorising the cultures denigrated
by colonialism and, rather than construing the colonialist relationship in terms of negotiations with the structures of imperialism, privileged coercion over hegemony to project it as a
struggle between implacably opposed forces . . . .

(1994a: 179)

Both these Fanons – the one who embodies post-structuralist
angst, and the one who embodies revolutionary fervour – are cast
in the very images that the critics would like to project of themselves; thus, says Gates, 'it's hard to avoid a sort of tableau of nar-
cissism, with Fanon himself as the Other that can only reflect and
consolidate the critical self' (1991: 465). Both are hard to sustain
in absolute terms. The post-structuralist Fanon is wrested by
Bhabha against the obvious evidence of some of his own writing.
Fanon the revolutionary remained 'a European interloper' in the
causes he espoused, never learning the language or participating
in the daily life of the people he championed. Albert Memmi
(1973) astutely suggests that Fanon's revolutionary romanticism
has much to do with his own rootlessness: because he was alienated from the French culture that he was brought up to revere,
the Martiniquan culture that he was brought up to reject, and the
Algerian culture he espoused but was never familiar with, Fanon
adopted a universalist humanism, speaking for all colonised peoples and indeed all humanity in a Messianic tone (Memmi 1973).

There are other problems in trying to appropriate Fanon for
our own ends today. Fanon's split subject should not be read as
the paradigmatic colonised subject: the psychic dislocations
Fanon discusses are more likely to be felt by native elites or those
colonised individuals who were educated within, and to some extent invited to be mobile within, the colonial system than by
those who existed on its margins. And in the next section, when

we examine the place of gender in Fanon's schema, we will see how his subject is also resolutely male, and reinforces existing gender hierarchies even as it challenges racial ones. We'll return to Fanon in the section on hybridity, but the fundamental question posed by these debates over Fanon's real legacy is: how do we interrelate the question of psychic oppression and trauma to the material, economic aspects of colonialism? Or, to use Memmi's terse formulation: 'Does psychoanalysis win out over Marxism? Does all depend on the individual or on society?' (1967: xiii; see also Gates 1991: 467).

In some ways this is not a helpful way of posing the question. Some of Marxism's fundamental concepts, such as those of alienation or ideology have psychological as well as social dimensions. Gramsci's crucial contribution was to recognise the importance of subjectivity in the study of domination. On the other hand, psychoanalytic accounts of subject formation are also, as we have seen, theories of socialisation, or of how an individual enters the world of sexuality, language and power. And psychoanalysis has had much to say about groups of people and the relations between them. There have been intense and complex dialogues between Marxism and psychoanalysis both because of their differences and their shared terrain. But in practice it *has* been notoriously difficult for contemporary cultural theorists to pay equally nuanced attention to both socio-political and psycho-sexual aspects of human existence. Feminism, for example, has most insistently and radically questioned as well as appropriated psychoanalysis to question both its constitution of female sexuality and to interrogate the very divisions between 'inside' and 'outside', personal and political, biology and culture, individual and society.[2] But Jacqueline Rose points out that feminism has been 'so successful . . . in insisting on the political nature of the sexual and the psychic, that the sexual and psychic nature of the political in the other sense had become correspondingly neglected' (1993: 244). How does what Rose calls the 'two-way process between the field of psychoanalysis and politics' (1993: 243) work in relation to colonial difference? Even feminist psychoanalysis has not yet cleared the ground for thinking about issues of race and ethnicity. In fact, Kalpana Seshadri-Crooks accuses feminism of reproducing the existing problems of mainstream psychoanalytic discourse by 'not raising the question of racial difference with regard to irrational and mysterious "others" (Africans and Orientals) in theories of subject formation'. She rightly points out that when questions of cultural as opposed to sexual difference come up, 'we mark a moment of departure for postcolonials from the political and theoretical intentions of First World feminism' (1994: 175, 189).

Is it at all possible, then, to use psychoanalysis to think productively about colonial relations? If psychoanalytic theory and practice have been moulded by the histories of colonialism and imperialism, is it possible to appropriate their paradigms or are they too bound up with colonialist ways of ordering culture and biology? Can we use the master's tools to dismantle the master's house? Despite the problems outlined above, psychoanalytical theories of subject-formation have been widely deployed within postcolonial studies, even by those who otherwise strongly disagree such as Abdul JanMohamed who emphasises the 'Manichean' opposition between colonised and colonisers and Homi Bhabha who suggests the fuzziness and ambiguity of this divide. The work of Ashis Nandy on colonialism and its legacy in India, and of Gananath Obeyesekere on colonial encounters in the Pacific testify to the widespread use of psychoanalytic vocabularies in this field. As Seshadri-Crooks says, psychoanalysis does provide 'our most elaborate language of subject-constitution'. Therefore it remains a potentially useful tool for the analysis of colonial identities, the psychic effects of colonial rule, and the dynamics of resistance.

Perhaps the answer lies in a *selective* use of psychoanalytic insights, as suggested by Jacqueline Rose who does not 'want to give psychoanalysis the status of a meta-discourse. The point is to use psychoanalysis selectively and not as a fixed body of 'truth" ' (1993: 243). However, within postcolonial studies, some influential deployments of psychoanalytic concepts and vocabularies, as in the work of Homi Bhabha, may have made them more, rather than less difficult, to interrelate with nuanced social critique. Freud had mapped individual development on to civilisational growth; Fanon answered by reading individual neuroses in social terms. Moreover, Fanon traced patterns through various individual neurosis in order to generalise about his colonised subject, 'the black man', 'the Negro'. But such a figure ought not to become a paradigm for the colonial condition, as it does for Bhabha (whose work we will consider in greater detail in the section on hybridity). Colonised subjects are, after all, simultaneously moulded by class and gender considerations. Also, the split between 'black skin' and 'white masks' is differentially experienced in various colonial and postcolonial societies. We cannot forge a template of *a* split colonised subject and then apply it to *all* colonised subjects.

By pointing to the slippery process of subject-formation, psychoanalysis can be very useful for critiquing colonialism's constructions of self and other as fixed binaries. But the processes of individual subject-formation cannot endlessly be expanded to account for social collectivities. Even as we insist that madness can be understood in political terms, and political structures analysed in psychic terms, should we completely collapse the distinction between 'political repression and individual neurosis?' (Gates 1991: 467). Fanon may not have satisfactorily resolved the tension between psychoanalysis and Marxism, but he remains a vital figure for us precisely because of his attempts to combine a sociopolitical critique and activism with an analysis of colonial and anti-colonial subjectivities. This doubleness is the most useful legacy of Fanon for postcolonial studies, reminding us of the need as well as the difficulties of using psychoanalytical concepts to talk about the political realities of colonial encounters.

GENDER, SEXUALITY AND COLONIAL DISCOURSE

In an earlier section, we discussed the famous picture by Stradanus in which a naked America half rising from her hammock looks back at a clothed Vespucci who has awakened her: she has been literally 'dis-covered' (Hulme 1985: 17). We also noted that, in various kinds of sixteenth-century representations such as pictures, atlases, poetry and travel writing, sexual and colonial relationships become analogous to each other. Stradanus's picture typifies Renaissance representations of that continent, which usually show America naked or scantily clad in a feather skirt or head-dress, with either a club or bow and arrow, and accompanied by crocodiles and other beasts. The long pictorial tradition in which the four continents were represented as women now generated images of America or Africa that positioned these continents as available for plunder, possession, discovery and conquest. Conversely, native women and their bodies are described in terms of the promise and the fear of the colonial land, as in the much later description of 'a wild and gorgeous apparition of a woman' whom the narrator in Conrad's *Heart of Darkness* encounters on the shores of Congo river:

> She walked with measured steps, draped in striped and fringed cloths, treading the earth proudly, with a slight jingle and flash of barbarous ornaments. She carried her head high; her hair was done in the shape of a helmet; she had brass leggings to her knees, brass wire gauntlets to the elbow, a crimson spot on her tawny neck; bizarre things, charms, gifts of witch-men, that hung about her, glittered and trembled at every step. She must have had the value of several elephant tusks upon her. She was savage and superb, wild-eyed and magnificent; there was something ominous and stately in her

deliberate progress. And in the hush that had fallen suddenly upon the whole sorrowful land, the immense wilderness, the colossal body of the fecund and mysterious life seemed to look at her, pensive, as though it had been looking at the image of its own tenebrous and passionate soul.

(1975: 87)

Thus, from the beginning of the colonial period till its end (and beyond), female bodies symbolise the conquered land. This metaphoric use of the female body varies in accordance with the exigencies and histories of particular colonial situations. For example, in comparison with the nakedness of America or Africa in early modern iconographic representations, Asia is always sumptuously clothed, usually riding on a camel and carrying an incense burner. On her head she wears either a wreath of flowers and fruit (symbolising plenty) or a turban. These discursive divisions also spill over to depictions of ordinary women – in Cesare Vecellio's well-known sixteenth-century costume book, for example, women from India, Turkey and Persia are heavily draped in comparison with their naked African or American sisters.

Such distinctions did not mean that Eastern women and lands were not represented as interchangeable terrain on which colonial power could be deployed. But at that time, Europeans were often supplicants in front of powerful rulers in Asia and could hardly encode themselves as the male deflowerers of a feminised land. Alternate discursive strategies thus came into play. The Oriental male was effeminised, portrayed as homosexual, or else depicted as a lusty villain from whom the virile but courteous European could rescue the native (or the European) woman. After the middle of the eighteenth century, Asia is often personified as a turbaned potentate. If America and Africa, then, are usually represented as savage women, images of 'the Orient' cluster around riches, splendour and plenty. As we might expect, women attached to the royalty – either queens or harem girls – become symbols of this world (see Kabbani 1986). The veiled Asian woman becomes a recurrent colonial fantasy, as does the recurrent figure of the Eastern Queen, whose wealth testifies to the riches of 'the Orient' and whose gender renders those riches vulnerable to the European self. The Biblical story of Sheba arriving laden with gold at Solomon's court and willingly surrendering her enormous wealth in return for sexual gratification initiated a long tradition of stories in which the desire of the native woman for the European man coded for the submission of the colonised people. In early modern English literature, well before the English had established themselves as a colonial power, an 'Indian queen' who converts to Christianity and marries the coloniser became a recurrent figure. Of course the most famous instance of an 'Indian Queen' who abandons her own people for a white man came from other side of the world – the Pocahontas story was to receive recurrent reinscription as a colonial fantasy, the latest being at the hands of Disney films.

Another favourite figure in colonial inscriptions was that of the burning widow or sati: almost every European commentator of the sixteenth and seventeenth centuries stops to savour that picture of Oriental barbarity and female helplessness and devotion (Teltscher 1995). Eastern royal or upper class/caste women being watched by, consorting with, and being saved by, European men is a feature of colonial narratives from the seventeenth century to the present. Job Charnock, the 'founder' of Calcutta, is supposed to have rescued a young widow with whose beauty he was 'smitten' from the flames. In Jules Verne's *Around the World in Eighty Days* (1873), Phileas Fogg also saves a beautiful young Parsi woman and then marries her (even though Parsis never practised widow immolation). In John Masters's *The Deceivers* (1952) William Savage sets out to rescue a beautiful young widow and is seduced, not by her but by the goddess Kali. And in M.M. Kaye's *The Far Pavilions* (1978, made into a popular television serial in the 1980s) the young hero sets out to save yet another young royal widow, and ends up marrying her half-sister! This pattern is not confined to literary texts. The barbarity of native men becomes a major justification for imperial rule, impels colonial policy, and shapes and directs colonial confrontations. On the other hand, such interference by white men into 'their' culture catalyses native opposition. Gayatri Spivak telescopes this dynamic into a pithy sentence: 'White men are saving brown women from brown men'. This, she suggests, is for her as fundamental for an investigation of colonial dynamics as Freud's formulation 'a child is being beaten' was for his inquiry into sexuality (1988: 296).

Before we pursue this further, we should note that not all 'brown' or 'black' women are represented as victims, or as desirable or passive. The non-European woman also appears in an intractable version, as 'Amazonian' or deviant femininity. The Amazons are located by early colonial writings in virtually every part of the non-European world, and provide images of insatiable sexuality and brutality. Thus female volition, desire and agency are literally pushed to the margins of the civilised world. But not all margins are equally removed from the centre: skin colour and female behaviour come together in establishing a cultural hierarchy with white Europe at the apex and black Africa at the bottom. Thus, in seventeenth-century English drama, for example, sexual liaisons between aggressive black African women and white men never culminate in marriage and evoke far more horror than between the same men and the more 'subtle' and 'wily women' from the East.

Renaissance travel writings and plays repeatedly connect deviant sexuality with racial and cultural outsiders and far away places, which, as Anne McClintock puts it, 'had become what can be called a porno-tropics for the European imagination – a fantastic magic lantern of the mind onto which Europe projected its forbidden sexual desires and fears'. Thus non-Europeans, especially women, are repeatedly constructed as libidinally excessive, and sexually uncontrolled. Francis Bacon imagined the spirit of fornication as a 'little foule, ugly Ethiope' (MClintock 1995: 22). Non-European peoples were imagined as more easily given to same-sex relationships. Harem stories, in particular, fanned fantasies of lesbianism. In his account of early seventeenth-century Turkey, for example, George Sandys contemplates what happens when women are cloistered with each other, engaged in long hours of massaging and pampering their bodies: 'Much unnaturall and filthie lust is said to be committed daily in the remote closets of these darksome [bathhouses]: yea, women with women; a thing incredible, if former times had not given thereunto both detection, and punishment' (1627: 69). Another traveller to Turkey claims that the men too 'are extremely inclined to all sorts of lascivious luxury; and generally addicted, besides all their sensual and incestuous lusts, to Sodomy, which they account as a dainty to digest all their other libidinous pleasures'. For this writer, Constantinople becomes 'A Painted Whore, the mask of deadly sin' (Lithgow 1928: 102, 85). Renaissance writings on Islam always emphasise that it encourages licentiousness because it promises 'marvelous beautiful women, with their Breastes wantonly swelling' as well as 'fair Boyes' in paradise (Warmistry 1658: 145).

Leo Africanus, a converted African Moor whose real name was Al Hassan Ibn Mohammed Al Wezaz Al Fazi (and on whom Shakespeare's *Othello* is sometimes supposed to be modelled) fuelled such imaginings in his *A Geographical History of Africa* (translated into English in 1600) which became the most influential early account of Africa. Africanus repeatedly attributes 'venerie', 'lecherie', homosexuality, drugs and cross-dressing to Africans. Thus, for example, the 'Inne-keepers of Fez . . . goe apparalled like Women, and shave their Beards, and are so delighted to imitate women, that they will not only counterfeite their speech, but will sometimes also sit downe and spin' (1905: 413); in Tunis they 'have here a Compound, called Lhasis, whereof whosoever eateth but one Ounce, falleth a laughing, disporting, and dallying, as if he were halfe drunken, and is by the said confection marvellously provoked into lust' (1905: 498), and in Fez there are witches who

> have a damnable custome to commit unlawful Venerie among themselves, which I cannot expresse in any modester termes. If faire women come unto them at any time, these abominable Witches will burne in lust towards them, . . . yea, some there are, which being allured with the delight of this abominable vice, will desire the company of these Witches, and faining themselves to be sicke, will either call one of the Witches home to them or will send their husbands for the same purpose . . . .
>
> (1905: 435)

The point about such accounts is that they do not exist in isolation simply as stories about 'the other' but serve also to define deviant and normative behaviour at home. This very story of the witches of Fez is cited by the French surgeon Ambroise Paré first to 'verify' his descriptions of female parts that 'grow erect like the male rod' enabling the women to 'disport themselves . . . with other women' and then to defend the excision of such parts (Parker 1994: 84). At the same time, these stories also circulate as fantasies that can work both to legitimate the *status quo* and to subvert it. In contemporary travel writings, the Turkish patriarchy is censored for its barbaric attitudes to women, but at the same time it becomes a model for English life as in *The Travels of Foure Englishmen* (first published in 1608):

> If their husbands have been abroad, at his entrance into the house, if any one of their women be sitting on a stool, she riseth up, and boweth herself to her husband, and kisseth his hand, and . . . (standeth) so long as he is in presence . . . . If

the like order were in England, women would be more dutiful and faithful to their husbands than they are: and especially, if there were the like punishment for whores, there would be less whoredom: for there if a man have a hundred women, if any one of them prostitute herself to any man but her own husband, he hath authority to bind her, hands and feet, and cast her unto the river, with a stone about her neck, and drown her . . . .

(Osborne 1745: 792)

The figure of the 'other woman' haunts the colonial imagination in ambivalent, often contradictory ways. She is an example of barbarism, but also encodes colonial fantasies of the perfect feminine behaviour: the burning widow, for example, is an awesome sign of wifely devotion, in many ways worthy of emulation by English women. Thus, for example, Richard Head writes as early as 1666:

For my part, I could wish for the like custom (*sati*) enjoyn'd on all married English females (for the love I bear to my own Country) which I am confident would prevent the destruction of thousands of well-meaning Christians, which receive a full stop in the full career of their lives, either by corrupting their bodies by venemous medicaments administred by some pretended Doctors hand (it may be here Stallion) unto which he is easily perswaded, by the good opinion he hath of his wifes great care and affection for him: or else his body is poysoned by sucking or drawing contagious fumes which proceed from her contaminated body, occasion'd by using pluralities for her venereal satisfaction, and so dies of the new consumption.

(1666: 92)

Early connections between foreign lands and deviant sexualities only deepened in the colonialist imagination. Richard

Burton, translator of the *Thousand and One Nights* claimed that there was a 'Sotadic Zone' in which sodomy was 'popular and endemic', and such a stereotype of 'Eastern perversity . . . [is] firmly wedged in the dominant Western imaginary' (Boone 1995: 115, 91). According to Ronald Hyam (1990), colonial frontiers offered Europeans the possibility of transgressing their rigid sexual mores. Foreign lands and peoples certainly spelt the possibility of new sexual experiences, which is why they became both exciting and monstrous for the European imagination. Sexual relations in non-European cultures were certainly different and sometimes less repressive than in Christian Europe. For most European travellers and colonialists, however, the promise of sexual pleasure rested on the assumption that the darker races or non-Europeans were immoral, promiscuous, libidinous and always desired white people. And while cross-cultural sexual contact was certainly transgressive (and is celebrated as such in contemporary commentary on European sexual practices), we should not forget that colonial sexual encounters, both heterosexual and homosexual, often exploited inequities of class, age, gender, race and power. In colonial fictions and travelogues, however, they are often embedded within a myth of reciprocity. I have earlier referred to one early version of this myth – the dark queen who gives her body and her self to the white man. Other versions place the black woman as slave, nurtured and even liberated by the European male. Peter Hulme shows how such love plots articulate 'the ideal of cultural harmony through romance' (1986a: 141). Colonial trade too is projected as a transaction desired by both parties, an enterprise mutually beneficial and entered into via the exercise of free will.

Not surprisingly, the romance is less sustainable in the case of white women who couple with black men. The fear is that such contact will 'people the isle with Calibans' (to use the words of Shakespeare's savage when he is charged with attempting to rape Prospero's daughter Miranda). The spectre of miscegenation most graphically brings together anxieties about female sexuality and racial purity, and, as colonial contacts widen and deepen, it increasingly haunts European and Euro-American culture. Here is the eighteenth-century historian Edward Long on the question of letting blacks into England:

> The lower class of women in England are remarkably fond of the blacks, for reasons too brutal to mention; they would connect themselves with horses and asses if the laws permitted them. By these ladies they generally have numerous brood. Thus, in the course of a few generations more, the English blood will become so contaminated with this mixture ... as even to reach the middle, and then the higher orders of people.
>
> (quoted Lawrence 1982: 57)

The fear of cultural and racial pollution prompts the most hysterical dogmas about racial difference and sexual behaviours because it suggests the instability of 'race' as a category. Sexuality is thus a means for the maintenance or erosion of racial difference. Women on both sides of the colonial divide demarcate both the innermost sanctums of race, culture and nation, as well as the porous frontiers through which these are penetrated. Their relationship to colonial discourses is mediated through this double positioning.

These various ways of positioning and erasing women in colonial writings indicate the intricate overlaps between colonial and sexual domination. According to Helen Carr,

> in the language of colonialism, non-Europeans occupy the same symbolic space as women. Both are seen as part of nature, not culture, and with the same ambivalence: either they are ripe for government, passive, child-like, unsophisticated, needing leadership and guidance, described always in terms of

> lack – no initiative, no intellectual powers, no perseverance; or
> on the other hand, they are outside society, dangerous, treach-
> erous, emotional, inconstant, wild, threatening, fickle, sexually
> aberrant, irrational, near animal, lascivious, disruptive, evil,
> unpredictable.
>
> (1985: 50)

These connections exist both as part of the 'common sense'
about race and gender, and, in a more codified form, within scientific discourse. Sander Gilman (1985a; 1985b) shows how
nineteenth-century medical and popular discourses progressively
intensified the linkages between 'blackness', sexuality and femininity by using one to describe the other. The sexuality of black
men and especially that of black women 'becomes an icon for
deviant sexuality in general'. Thus black women are constructed
in terms of animals, lesbians and prostitutes; conversely the deviant sexuality of white women is understood by analogies with
blackness: 'The primitive is black, and the qualities of blackness, or at least of the black female, are those of the prostitute'
(1985a: 248).

The equivalencies suggested between women, blacks, the
lower classes, animals, madness and homosexuality calcify and
harden with the growth of science. In an extremely thought-
provoking essay, Nancy Leys Stepan argues that 'So fundamental
was the analogy between race and gender (in scientific writings)
that the major modes of explanation of racial traits were used to
explain sexual traits'. In the nineteenth century, she writes,

> it was claimed that women's low brain weights and deficient
> brain structures were analogous to those of the lower races,
> and their inferior intellectualities explained on this basis.
> Women, it was observed, shared with Negroes a narrow, child-
> like, and delicate skull, so different from the more robust and
> rounded heads characteristic of males of 'superior' races . . . .

> In short, lower races represented the 'female' type of the human species, and females the 'lower race' of gender.
>
> (1990: 40)

Science did not proceed through empirical observation 'but by and through a metaphorical system that structured the experience and understanding of difference and that in essence created the objects of difference'. Science elaborated familiar analogies, which could then be extended in new ways. Thus the jaws of Irish people were described by one scientist to have become 'more like the negro' after the potato famine. Initially, women were described in terms taken from racial discourse, and then gender differences were used in turn to explain racial difference (Stepan 1990: 41–43).

It is, then, no accident that, in a famous formulation, Freud expresses his incomprehension of the sexual life of women by calling it a 'dark continent':

> We know less of the sexual life of little girls than of little boys; the sexual life of grown-up women, too, is still a 'dark continent' for psychology. But we have learnt that the small girl feels sensitive over the lack of a sexual organ equal to the boy's and holds herself to be inferior on that account; and that this 'penis-envy' gives rise to a whole series of characteristic feminine reactions.
>
> (1947: 34–35)

Both femininity and Africa, the analogy suggests, defy rational understanding and signify a lack. Do patriarchal relations provide a model for colonial domination? Since the terms used by psychoanalysis are sexual, psychoanalytically inflected accounts of the construction of race (even by those who seek to dismantle existing hierarchies) rest on the question of sexual difference. Thus, Gilman's account of the production of stereotypes explains that racial as well as sexual 'others' derive from 'the same deep structure' (1985b: 25). Fanon's schema also indicates some congruence in the position of women and colonised subjects. In patriarchal society, women are split subjects who watch themselves being watched by men. They turn themselves into objects because femininity itself is defined by being gazed upon by men (Berger 1972: 47). Fanon describes the objectification of blacks and their internalisation of this process in the same way: 'I cannot go to a film without seeing myself . . . . The people in the theater are watching me, waiting for me'. As one critic has noted, 'racial and gender privilege are so intertwined that Fanon evokes castration to describe racial disempowerment: "What else could it be for me but an amputation, an excision, a hemorrhage that spattered my whole body with black blood?" ' (Bergner 1995: 79; Fanon 1967: 112).

But while Fanon's use of the schema of sexual difference to understand the production of racial difference challenges the colour-blindness of psychoanalytic categories, it only confirms, and indeed depends upon, their gender asymmetry. While the black man's desire for white women is contextualised and historicised, the white woman's fantasy of being raped by a black man is 'in some way the fulfillment of a private dream, of an inner wish'. His colonised subject is exclusively male and he abruptly dismisses the psychosexuality of the 'woman of colour': 'I know nothing about her' (1967: 180). In his account the male colonial subject moves from disempowerment and objectification to revolt. But he does not use the analogies between race and gender to reconfigure female subjectivity: both black and white women remain, in his account, the terrain on which men move and enact their battles with each other. In other words, women remain as much of a 'dark continent' for Fanon as they were for Freud. Fanon's work thus illustrates both the utility and the limits of a theory of Western sexuality to account for the production of racial difference. Above all, it reminds us how 'race' and 'colonial difference' are both produced and split by gender differences. Many of those who invoke and use Fanon to discuss colonial identities simply extend his gender blindness. Robert Young points out that Homi Bhabha, for example, does not address questions of gender: he 'seems to regard the troubled structures of sexuality as a metaphor for colonial ambivalence' and his discussions of colonial desires 'invoke the structures of desire without addressing the structures of sexuality' (1990: 119). Fanon's appropriation of psychoanalysis to account for the production of racial difference needs to be brought together with feminist critiques of the subject before it can serve as a useful paradigm for colonial identity.

The analogy between the subordination of women and colonial subjects runs the risk of erasing the specificity of colonialist and patriarchal ideologies, besides tending to homogenise both 'women' and 'non-Europeans'. The 'colonial subject' is usually conceptualised as male and the 'female subject' as 'white'. When parallels are drawn between them, the colonised, especially black, woman's situation is glossed over. Historically, analogies between the oppression of white women and black men often 'pitted white women against Black men in a competition for privileges that erased Black women altogether' (Hurtado 1989: 840). Moreover, such comparisons erase the fact that black women suffer from both racial and gendered forms of oppression simultaneously.

The analogy exercise is sometimes promoted by women and non-Europeans themselves. Sandra Harding draws our attention to the fact that there is a 'curious coincidence of African and feminine "world views" . . . . What they call the African view is suspiciously similar to what in feminist literature is identified as a distinctively feminine world view. What they label European and Eurocentric shares significant similarity with what feminists label masculine or androcentric' (1986: 165). Thus, both Africans and women are regarded as more community-minded in their outlook than Europeans or men. As Harding points out women of colour 'totally disappear from both analyses, conceptualized out of existence because African men and white women are taken as the paradigms of the two groups' (1986: 178).

In order to draw attention to their own complex positioning, black and postcolonial feminists and women's activists have had to challenge both the colour prejudices within white feminism and the gender-blindness of anti-racist or anti-colonial movements. Colonising as well as anti-colonial men, while being otherwise opposed, have often shared certain attitudes to women. In colonialist as well as nationalist writings, racial and sexual violence are yoked together by images of rape, which in different forms, becomes an abiding and recurrent metaphor for colonial relations. If colonial power is repeatedly expressed as a white man's possession of black women and men, colonial fears centre around the rape of white women by black men. Certain anti-colonial or anti-racist activists have also problematically appropriated such a possession as an act of insurgency. Machismo has been manifest in many nationalist movements, as we will discuss in greater detail later.

Women of colour have also had to challenge the colour-blindness of Euro-American feminist theory and movements. Gayatri Spivak (1985a) alleged that feminist criticism 'reproduces the axioms of imperialism' in valorising the emergence of the articulate Western female subject and her entry into individualism without marking how such a process is inflected, indeed made possible, by the expansion of imperialism. We have noted how this works in a novel such as *Jane Eyre*. Aphra Behn's novella *Oroonoko* (first published in 1688) provides an even earlier instance of how a consolidation of Western female selfhood is predicated upon an 'othering' of black woman. Oroonoko is a royal slave, much like Othello, and his wife Imoinda, a 'beautiful black Venus' (1986: 34). They are taken from their native Coramantein and brought to Surinam, and the story turns on their romance, their troubles as slaves, and their suicide pact which is designed to save their honour and that of their unborn child. While Behn's tale critiques existing patriarchal as well as colonial relations, it also places the white female narrator, Imoinda and Oroonoko in a strangely triangulated relationship. The author is enamoured of both Oroonoko's beauty and Imoinda's. At the same time, there is a competitive relation between the narrator and Imoinda. While one woman will tell Oroonoko's story, the other carries his child. Imoinda's pregnancy is thus set against Behn's construction of her own self as a woman writer. Even though Behn is in sympathy with Imoinda's plight, the differentiation between the narrator and Imoinda is essential to the construction of a white female authority. Thus, as Ferguson (1991) argues, one has to constantly 'juggle the categories of race and gender'.

Many scholars and activists have critiqued the Western feminist project for its neglect of racial and colonialist politics. To take just a few examples of a huge body of work: in an important essay, Hazel Carby (1982) marked the 'boundaries of sisterhood' as demarcated by differential understanding of the role played by race in defining women's experience and as an analytical category in feminist thought. Ann Jones (1981) showed that notions of female identity and pleasure in French feminist theory are deeply ethnocentric. Pratibha Parmar and Valerie Amos (1984) have described Euro-American feminism's drive to establish itself as the only legitimate feminism as 'imperial' because it erases the experience of non-white and third world women. Chandra Mohanty (1988) has accused Western feminist scholarship of constructing a monolithic 'third world' woman as an object of knowledge. Nonwhite feminists have written alternative histories of women's oppression, and also offered alternative blueprints for action. Angela Davis (1982) pointed out that although black as well as white women are oppressed within the family, the family as an institution carries different meanings for them – American blacks, and other immigrants of colour, have historically been denied the privilege of forming family units and the family for them has been forged in the crucible of racial oppression. Ideologies of black female sexuality thus do not arise primarily from the family, as Carby also argues. Hortense Spillers (1987) drew out the implications of this difference for ideologies of the family and sexuality. Within once colonised countries, where women's activism has been proliferating in this century, some activists have rejected the term 'feminist' as too tainted by its white antecedents.

But although these critiques of white feminism and patriarchal anti-colonialisms together cleared the conceptual space for more sophisticated understandings of how racist and sexist discourses are related, they often did not go beyond asserting that black and/or colonised women were doubly oppressed. In this view of a 'double colonisation', race and gender categories are not analogous but they remain mutually intensifying: Gwen Bergner concludes her critique of Fanon by suggesting that 'the most important effect of conjoining postcolonial and feminist psychoanalysis may well be to clear a space for black women as subjects in both discourses' (1995: 85). Combining postcolonial and feminist perspectives can perhaps achieve more than that. For one, it would alert us to the ways in which the category 'black woman' itself does not take into account the enormous range of cultural, racial or locational differences internal to it, all of which would complicate the relationship between black women and colonial or racist ideologies. This is not to suggest that we endlessly bifurcate our categories of analysis to the point where no grouping makes any sense. But is 'the black' or 'the postcolonial' woman the same thing? The social or the sexual identities of African-American women have at least as much in common with white American women as they do with women in Morocco or Pakistan. The veil, segregation, or the institution of the extended family, structure sexuality and gender relations in highly specific ways, and they also shaped the impact of colonial rule upon existing gender relations. Finally, class is extremely important in analysing how race and gender have historically shaped one another: colonial practices were nothing if not conscious of indigenous class, gender, caste or regional hierarchies, which they manipulated, altered or entrenched.

Colonialism eroded many matrilineal or woman-friendly cultures and practices, or intensified women's subordination in colonised lands. In rural Africa, the control of women over farming and the crops they produced declined with the advent of the slave trade. As village agriculture declined, and male labour migrated to urban centres, women became increasingly dependent economically upon men's incomes. Christianity profoundly altered family structures and sexual patterns. Colonial law restructured customs by taking the texts and practices of the elites as the basis on which changes should be made. For example, in India, the colonial administration consulted only pundits (Hindu priests) resident at the courts in order to decide the status of widow immolation:

> The question posed to the pundit was whether sati was enjoined by the scriptural texts. The pundit responded that the texts did not enjoin but merely permitted sati in certain instances . . . . Nevertheless based on this response the Nizamat Adalat concluded that 'The practice, generally speaking, being thus recognized and *encouraged* by the doctrines of the Hindoo religion, it appears evident that the course which the British government should follow, according to the principle of religious tolerance . . . is to allow the practice in those cases in which it is countenanced by their religion; and to prevent it in others in which it is by the same authority prohibited'.
>
> (Mani 1989: 99)

In the process, a scriptural sanction and a religion tradition were constructed for a practice which had been diverse, variable and uneven. Pundits became the spokesmen for a vast and heterogeneous Hindu population, and facilitated the replacement of multiple local non-scriptural laws and procedures by a standardised, inflexible 'brahminical' (and more patriarchal) version of Hinduism, which received ideological sanction by Orientalist scholarship. The existing hierarchies of Hindu society were thereby calcified in new and dangerous ways. Similarly, in Kerala, the colonial state recast matrilineal extended Nair households, which allowed women some sexual and economic freedoms, into a Western patriarchal family mould. The previous norm of *sambandhan* relationships which women could enter at will was legislated as illegal and the monogamous, co-residential unit recognised as the only permissible form of marriage (Mies 1980: 84–90; Arunima 1996). These changes affected both sexual and property relations. In both these cases, the authority of the upper castes (which in India usually corresponded to the upper classes) was legitimised by colonial intervention. But in both cases, colonial intervention often coincided with internal desire for reform and change.

Colonialism intensified patriarchal relations in colonised lands, often because native men, increasingly disenfranchised and excluded from the public sphere, became more tyrannical at home. They seized upon the home and the woman as emblems of their culture and nationality. The outside world could be Westernised but all was not lost if the domestic space retained its cultural purity. The example of widow immolation will again serve to illustrate this process. Following the 1813 legislation banning of widow immolation, most commentators agree, there was a sharp increase in the number of satis. Ashis Nandy interprets this as a form of anti-colonial disobedience: 'the rite', he suggests, 'became popular in groups made psychologically marginal by their exposure to Western impact . . . the opposition to sati constituted . . . a threat to them. In their desperate defence of the rite they were also trying to defend their traditional self-esteem' (1980: 7). If defence of sati is a form of 'native resistance', we must recognise that the natives in question are men, and that the form of this 'resistance' deeply oppressive of women. Of course, the process whereby women became the metaphor for indigenous culture was reinforced by colonial law, which sought to mold the public sphere according to European ideals but emphasised religion and custom as the basis for personal law in colonised countries.

Although men on both sides of the colonial divide engaged in bitter strife, they also often collaborated when it came to the domination of women. When, for example, in 1910 the distinguished courtesan and woman of letters Bangalore Nagaratnamma reprinted an epic poem *Radhika Santwanam*, written in the late eighteenth century by another courtesan Muddupalani, there was a furore. Indian men of letters protested the publication, saying that the poem was too sexual in tone and the British courts upheld this objection (despite protests to the contrary) by banning the poem. Although the ban was lifted after Independence in 1947, it continued to be 'decreed out of existence ideologically' (Tharu and Lalita 1991: 6). Such collaboration across the colonial divide spans individual cases as well as aspects of law and tradition. For example, in 1887, Rakhamabai, an educated daughter of a Bombay doctor refused to cohabit with the much older man to whom she had been married as a child. Her husband sued her on the grounds that she was his rightful property, but lost the case under civil law. However, the Chief Justice bowed to the conservative demand that she be tried under Hindu law, and finally Rakhamabai was ordered to go and live with her husband. In a book called *The High Caste-Hindu Woman* (1888), Pandita Ramabai, scholar, educationist and reformer, charged that the case revealed an alliance between the colonial government and Indian men in questions involving women.

Often new forms of patriarchal domination were introduced in colonised lands. In Peru, for example, Spanish rule constricted women's participation in public life. It grafted Christian notions of female purity and pollution encoded in the opposition between virgin and witch upon the gender divisions of Andean culture (which had also devalued women, but not in the same ways as were imported from Europe):

> As opposed to long-standing Andean traditions, Spanish law presumed women were innately unsuited to public offices. Coming from the climate of European witch hunts, Spanish theology targeted native women as the most likely consorts of God's enemies – Peru's devil/huacas .... The gendered institutions of Spanish colonialism systematically eroded the life possibilities of most Andean women ....
>
> (Silverblatt 1995: 288–289)

Of course, the irony here was that women were able to use precisely these impositions to challenge colonial rule, but we will discuss that later.

A great deal of writing has begun to explore European women's relation to colonial discourses as fraught with these contradictions – they participated in the imperial mission, and were tangential to or at odds with it as well. The English 'memsahib' is routinely portrayed in fiction as well as historical criticism as more racist and parochial than the British administrator himself – she becomes the main reason why he cannot develop a working comradeship with his subordinates. Recent feminist criticism has emphasised the patriarchal structures within which the memsahib was trapped at home and abroad, and has highlighted the differences between female and male fictions, travelogues and memoirs in various parts of the colonial world. However, not all imperial women were alike: their writings demonstrate an enormous range of attitudes and ideologies: at the one end of the spectrum, we have the outpourings of a Katherine Mayo, whose *Mother India* was a virulent attack on Indian culture, and, at the other, there were women like Annie Besant who became part of the Indian nationalist struggle. More difficult to assess is someone like the Irishwoman Margaret Noble, who became a disciple of Swami Vivekananda, adopted the name Sister Nivedita and defended Indian culture by romanticising some of its most patriarchal practices.

European colonialism often justified its 'civilizing mission' by claiming that it was rescuing native women from oppressive patriarchal domination. Katherine Mayo's *Mother India* (1927) had blamed all of India's ills on the Indian male's 'manner of getting into the world and his sex-life thenceforth'. London's *New Statesman and Nation* said that the book demonstrated 'the filthy personal habits of even the most highly educated classes in India – which, like the denigration of Hindu women, are unequaled even among the most primitive African or Australian savages' (Joshi and Liddle 1986: 31). The supposed silence of Indian women enabled British feminists to claim a speaking part for themselves. In an editorial comment in *The Storm-bell* of June 1898, Josephine Butler commented that Indian women were

> indeed between the upper and nether millstone, helpless, voiceless, hopeless. Their helplessness appeals to the heart, in somewhat the same way in which the helplessness and suffering of a dumb animal does, under the knife of a vivisector. Somewhere, halfway between the Martyr Saints and the tortured 'friend of man', the noble dog, stand, it seems to me, these pitiful Indian women, girls, children, as many of them are. They have not even the small power of resistance which the western woman may have . . . .
>
> (Burton 1992: 144)

Butler and others could thus claim the necessity of representing their mute sisters, and hence legitimise themselves as 'the imperial authorities on "Indian womanhood" '. This is not to deny the important roles played by white women in the abolition of slavery, or in initiating colonial reform, but simply to remember that even these progressive roles were often premised on the idea of a racial hierarchy. Within colonial spaces, white women participated with varying degrees of alienation (and enthusiasm) in imperial projects; as teachers, missionaries, nurses, and the help-mates of colonial men, their roles varied both structurally and ideologically. According to Kumari Jayawardena the response of South Asian men was to divide foreign women into 'female devils' and 'white goddesses': the former were those who, like Mayo, critiqued South Asian societies; the latter were those who, like Sister Nivedita, participated in the national liberation struggle (1995: 2). As we might expect, colonised women also occupied contradictory positions vis-à-vis both indigenous and colonial social structures.

As my analysis has suggested, race, gender and sexuality are not just additive to one another in the colonial arena; they do not just provide metaphors and images for each other, but work together and develop in each other's crucible. It is important to remember that colonised women were not simply objectified in colonial discourses, but their labour (sexual as well as economic) fed into the colonial machine. If female slaves were the backbone of plantation economies, 'third world women remain the poorest of the poor in the 'post'-colonial world. Scholars such as Swasti Mitter have shown how colour and sex are 'the main principles behind the most recent international division of labour' (1986: 6). The majority of workers in transnational corporations are women. Third world women and women of colour provide the cheapest labour for sweatshops, the sex-trade, large multinationals as well as smaller industries, they are the guinea pigs for exploitative and dangerous experiments in health and fertility. Such exploitation is both a colonial legacy and the outcome of specific 'postcolonial' developments.

HYBRIDITY

Postcolonial studies have been preoccupied with issues of hybridity, creolisation, *mestizaje*, in-betweenness, diasporas and liminality, with the mobility and cross-overs of ideas and identities generated by colonialism. However, as some recent debates will serve to illustrate, there are widely divergent ways of thinking about these issues. Robert Young reminds us that a hybrid is technically a cross between two different species and that therefore the term 'hybridisation' evokes both the botanical notion of inter-species grafting and the 'vocabulary of the Victorian extreme right' which regarded different races as different species (1995: 10). However, in postcolonial theory, hybridity is meant to evoke all those ways in which this vocabulary was challenged and undermined. Even as imperial and racist ideologies insist on racial difference, they catalyse cross-overs, partly because not all that takes place in the 'contact zones' can be monitored and controlled, but sometimes also as a result of deliberate colonial policy. One of the most striking contradictions about colonialism is that it both needs to 'civilise' its 'others', and to fix them into perpetual 'otherness'. We have already discussed how colonial empires both fear and engender biological as well as intellectual hybridities. An early nineteenth-century Colombian, Pedro Fermín de Vargas, actually advocated a policy of interbreeding between whites and Indians in order to 'hispanicise' and finally 'extinguish' Indians. Benedict Anderson, who cites this example, rightly characterises as 'mental miscegenation' those colonial educational policies which aimed to create Europeanised natives, or to use Macaulay's famous words, 'a class of persons, Indian in blood and colour, but English in taste, in opinion, in morals and in intellect' (1991: 13, 91). The underlying premise was, of course, that Indians can mimic but never exactly reproduce English values, and that their recognition of the perpetual gap between themselves and the 'real thing' will ensure their subjection.

Colonial 'hybridity' in this particular sense, is a strategy premised on cultural purity, and aimed at stabilising the *status quo*. In practice, it did not necessarily work in that way: anti-colonial movements and individuals often drew upon Western ideas and vocabularies to challenge colonial rule. Indeed they often hybridised what they borrowed by juxtaposing it with indigenous ideas, reading it through their own interpretative lens, and even using it to assert cultural alterity or insist on an unbridgeable difference between coloniser and colonised. Thus Gandhi's notion of non-violence was forged by reading Emerson, Thoreau and Tolstoy, even though his vision of an ideal society evoked a specifically Hindu vision of 'Ram Rajya' or the legendary reign of Lord Rama. Thus too the theory of Negritude was articulated in a very French idiom, and drew upon French intellectual traditions. Hybridity or *mestizaje* is more self-consciously invoked as an anti-colonial strategy by some Caribbean and Latin American activists, most notably the Cuban writer Roberto Fernández Retamar. In a landmark 1971 essay, Retamar writes that 'our *mestizo* America' is unique in the colonial world because the majority of its population is racially mixed, it continues to use 'the languages of our colonisers', and 'so many of their conceptual tools . . . are also now *our* conceptual tools' (1974: 9–11). Retamar suggests that Caliban is the most appropriate symbol for this hybridity, although:

> I am aware that it is not entirely ours, that it is also an alien elaboration, although in our case based on our concrete realities. But how can this alien quality be entirely avoided? The most venerated word in Cuba – *mambí* – was disparagingly imposed on us by our enemies at the time of the war for independence, and we still have not totally deciphered its meaning. It seems to have an African root, and in the mouth of the Spanish colonists implied the idea that all *independentistas* were so many black slaves – emancipated by the very war for independence – who of course constituted the bulk of the

liberation army. The *independentistas*, white and black, adopted with honor something that colonialism meant as an insult. This is the dialectic of Caliban.

(1974: 27)

Although Retamar's vision of a radical hybridity sweeps under the carpet both gender difference and African culture in his region, it distinguishes between the hybridity of the 'creole exploiting classes' and the *mestizo* culture created by the oppressed classes, peasants and workers. Retamar connects the past history of colonialism and revolutions in Latin America to the United States's attempt to stifle the Cuban revolution at the time he was writing the essay. He explicitly urges the connection between colonised peoples and those fighting against capitalist domination. Although Retamar's invocation of 'a planetary vanguard' of 'socialist countries emerging on every continent' may feel out of date in today's world, his resolute connection between the colonial past and the neo-colonial present is salutary and necessary in the context of current discussions of postcoloniality where such linkages are rarely made.

Paul Gilroy's important book *The Black Atlantic* discusses another related but distinct dimension of colonial hybridities, i.e. the intellectual and political cross-fertilisations that resulted from the black diasporas or 'the movements of black people [from Africa to Europe and the Americas] not only as commodities but engaged in various struggles towards emancipation, autonomy and citizenship'. These movements created what Gilroy calls 'a black Atlantic', which he defines as an 'intercultural and transnational formation' which 'provides a means to re-examine the problems of nationality, location, identity, and historical memory' (1993: ix, 16). Gilroy shows the extent to which African-American, British and Caribbean diasporic cultures mould each other *as well as the metropolitan cultures with which they interacted*. Such diasporas have generated new and complex identities whose analysis demands new conceptual tools. If, on the one hand, there is no such thing as an uncontaminated white or European culture, then, on the other, as Stuart Hall points out, 'the black subject and black experience are . . . [also] constructed historically, culturally, politically'. The term 'ethnicity' has dominantly been used to indicate biologically and culturally stable identities, but Hall asks us to decouple it from its imperial, racist or nationalist deployment and to appropriate it to designate identity as a constructed process rather than a given essence. For Hall, the new black ethnicities visible in contemporary Britain are results of the 'cut-and-mix' processes of 'cultural *diaspora-ization*' (1996c: 446–447).

It is Homi Bhabha's usage of the concept of hybridity that has been the most influential and controversial within recent postcolonial studies. Bhabha goes back to Fanon to suggest that liminality and hybridity are necessary attributes of 'the' colonial condition. For Fanon, you will recall, psychic trauma results when the colonised subject realises that he can never attain the whiteness he has been taught to desire, or shed the blackness he has learnt to devalue. Bhabha amplifies this to suggest that colonial identities are always a matter of flux and agony. 'It is always', writes Bhabha in an essay about Fanon's importance for our time, 'in relation to the place of the Other that colonial desire is articulated'. Fanon's image of black skin/white masks is not, Bhabha explains 'a neat division' but

> a doubling, dissembling image of being in at least two places at once which makes it impossible for the devalued, insatiable evolué (an abandonment neurotic, Fanon claims) to accept the coloniser's invitation to identity: 'You're a doctor, a writer, a student, you're *different*, you're one of *us*'. It is precisely in that ambivalent use of 'different' – to be different from those that are different makes you the same – that the Unconscious speaks of the form of Otherness, the tethered shadow of deferral and displacement. It is not the Colonialist Self or the

Colonised Other, but the disturbing distance in between that constitutes the figure of colonial otherness – the White man's artifice inscribed on the Black man's body. It is in relation to this impossible object that emerges the liminal problem of colonial identity and its vicissitudes.

(1994: 117)

Terry Collits asks whether the image of 'black skin/white masks' indeed suggests hybridity or 'a violated authenticity'? Collits points out that Fanon reminds us that 'Skin is not just assumed like a mask: it is god-given even if its meanings are social, discursive. What skin and masks have in common is that they mark the interface between the self and the world: they are the border' (1994: 65–66). For Bhabha, however, this image evokes an ambivalence that can be read not just as marking the trauma of the colonial subject but also characterising the workings of colonial authority as well as the dynamics of resistance. Colonial authority, he suggests, undermines itself by not being able to replicate its own self perfectly. In one of his best-known essays, 'Signs Taken for Wonders', he discusses the transmission of the Bible in colonial India, and the way in which the Book is hybridised in the process of being communicated to the natives. He concludes that 'the colonial presence is always ambivalent, split between its appearance as original and authoritative and its articulation as repetition and difference' (1985: 150). For Bhabha, this gap marks a failure of colonial discourse and is a site for resistance:

resistance is not necessarily an oppositional act of political intention, nor is it the simple negation or the exclusion of the 'content' of another culture, as difference once perceived . . . [but] the effect of an ambivalence produced within the rules of recognition of dominating discourses as they articulate the signs of cultural difference.

(1985: 153)

If in Fanon's writings colonial authority works by inviting black subjects to mimic white culture, in Bhabha's work such an invitation itself undercuts colonial hegemony. Whereas Fanon's black mimics are dislocated subjects, here, as also in a wide range of writings on postcolonialism, mimicry has the effect of undermining authority.

We have already considered mimicry as an anti-colonial tool, but in Bhabha's work radical mimicry is not, as it is with Retamar, a weapon in the hands of a self-conscious Caliban. Rather it is an *effect* of the cracks within colonial discourse (with discourse being understood in entirely linguistic terms). Resistance is a condition produced by the dominant discourse itself, a rather problematic assumption that several critics have criticised. You will recall that Bhabha had critiqued Said's *Orientalism* for suggesting that colonial discourse was all powerful, and for not considering how it was forged *relationally*. Bhabha's writings are indeed useful in insisting that neither coloniser nor colonised is independent of the other. Colonial identities – on both sides of the divide – are unstable, agonised, and in constant flux. This undercuts both colonialist and nationalist claims to a unified self, and also warns us against interpreting cultural difference in absolute or reductive terms. However, despite the accent on hybridity and liminality, Bhabha generalises and universalises the colonial encounter. Thus, ironically, the split, ambivalent, hybrid colonial subject projected in his work is in fact curiously universal and homogeneous – that is to say he could exist anywhere in the colonial world. Hybridity seems to be a characteristic of his inner life (and I use the male pronoun purposely) but not of his positioning. He is internally split and agonistic, but undifferentiated by gender, class or location. As Ella Shohat suggests, we need to 'discriminate between the diverse modalities of hybridity, for example forced assimilation, internalized self-rejection, political co-optation, social conformism, cultural mimicry, and creative transcendence' (1993: 110).

The colonialist presence was felt differently by various subjects of the Empire – some never even saw Europeans in all their lives, and for them authority still wore a native face. For others, the foreign presence was daily visible but space was still divided into 'their' sphere and 'ours'. For others still, colonialism had penetrated still deeper into their everyday existence. Thus the resonances of both 'hybridity' and mimicry are enormously variable. As Rob Nixon writes in the context of the complex interchanges between South African and African-American cultures,

> the insights of the by now considerable literature around the issues of masking and mimicry ought always ... to be measured against conditions that are unavoidably local and immensely variable in the possibilities they allow. Otherwise the risk arises of sentimentalizing masquerade by abstracting it into a unitary phenomenon that is inherently, if ambiguously empowering.
>
> (1994: 24–25)

This universalising tendency in Bhabha's work (and other writings inspired by it) derives partly from the fact that in it colonial identities and colonial power relations are theorised entirely in semiotic or psychoanalytic terms. While theories of language and the psyche have given us sophisticated vocabularies of subjectivity, we also need to think about how subjectivities are shaped by questions of class, gender and context. We need to peg the psychic splits engendered by colonial rule to specific histories and locations. In making the point that 'there is no knowledge – political or otherwise – outside representation' Bhabha reduces colonial dynamics to a linguistic interchange. Or, as Benita Parry puts it in a detailed critique of Bhabha's work, 'what he offers us is The World according to The Word' (1994b: 9). And this 'Word' seems to lie largely with the coloniser: despite his critique of Said, in Bhabha's writings, everything outside colonial culture is treated with remarkable fuzziness. Indeed it seems as if the 'hybridity' of both coloniser and colonised can be understood only by tracing the vicissitudes of colonial discourse, or the mutations in European culture. We cannot appreciate the specific nature of diverse hybridities if we do not attend to the nuances of each of the cultures that come together or clash during the colonial encounter. Arif Dirlik also makes the point that currently, hybridity seems to be understood as 'uniformly between the post*colonial* and the First World, never, to my knowledge, between one post*colonial* intellectual and another', and he suggests that conditions of in-betweenness and hybridity cannot be understood without reference to the ideological and institutional structures in which they are housed (1994: 342).

One reason for the current imbalance may be that the experience of migration or of exile has become, in the Western academy, emblematic of the fissured identities and hybridities generated by colonial dislocations. Indeed, the critical fascination with Fanon may in part derive from the way in which his own complicated life (as a French educated Martiniquan who became an Algerian nationalist) mirrors themes of alienation, national longing and transnationalism that mark the experience of diaspora. It is true that the migration of peoples is perhaps the definitive characteristic of the twentieth century, and in crucial ways diasporic identities have come to represent much of the experience of 'postcoloniality'. And because in some senses the 'exile is a universal figure', as George Lamming put it (1960: 12) it is always tempting to present this experience in universalised terms. But while of course there are themes in common across different kinds of diasporic experiences and exiles, there are also enormous differences between them. The experiences and traumas generated by the single largest population shift in history – the division of India and Pakistan – are quite different from another enormous movement, that of immigrants from once-colonised nations to Europe or America. The experience of diaspora is also marked by class, and by the histories that shape each group that moves. Finally, it is important to recall that large numbers of people in the third world have not physically moved, and have to speak from 'where they are', which is also often an equally ideologically or politically or emotionally fractured space. These different kinds of dislocations cannot result in similarly split subjectivities: each demands dense contextualisation of the kind provided by Paul Gilroy and Stuart Hall.

There are other criticisms of current invocations of 'hybridity' within postcolonial theory: some critics (such as Parry 1994a) suggest that they work to downplay the bitter tension and the clash between the colonisers and the colonised and therefore misrepresent the dynamics of anti-colonial struggle. Nationalist struggles as well as pan-nationalist movements such as Negritude were fuelled by the alienation and the anger of the colonised, and cannot be understood, according to this view, within the parameters of current theories of hybridity. As mentioned earlier, many nationalists and anti-colonialists passionately, and often poetically appropriated the notion of a binary opposition between Europe and its others. Liberation, for them, hinged upon the discovery or rehabilitation of their cultural identity which European colonialism had disparaged and wrecked. Stuart Hall identifies this as a search for 'a sort of collective "one true self" . . . which people with a shared history and ancestry hold in common', or in Fanon's words, a search for 'some very beautiful splendid era whose existence rehabilitates us both in regard to ourselves, and in regard to others'. Such a search has been essential for anti-colonial struggles and postcolonial identities as well. But, as Hall goes on to suggest, it is possible to think about cultural identity in a related but different way, one which is 'much less familiar and more unsettling'. This second position recognises that identity is a matter of 'becoming' as well as of 'being'. Thus, colonised peoples cannot simply turn back to the idea of a collective pre-colonial culture, and a past 'which is waiting to be found, and which when found, will secure our sense of ourselves into eternity' (1994: 394). Hall is careful not to dismiss such a turning back as a romantic nativism, as some other postcolonial critics are apt to do. Although there are no pure and fixed origins to which cultures and peoples can return,

> it is no mere phantasm either. It is something – not a mere trick of the imagination. It has its histories – and histories have their real, material and symbolic effects. The past continues to speak to us. But it no longer addresses us as a simple, factual 'past', since our relation to it, like the child's relation to the mother, is always-already 'after the break'.
>
> (1994: 395)

This break is effected by colonial histories of domination. Colonialist categories of knowledge 'had the power to make us see and experience ourselves as "Other" . . . this kind of knowledge is internal, not external' and it is crucial to the process of colonial subject formation. It therefore cannot simply be erased or shrugged off as a kind of false consciousness. *That*, Hall reminds us, is the burden of Fanon's *Black Skin, White Masks*.

Hall thus refuses to choose between 'difference' and 'hybridity' and tries to keep alive a 'sense of difference which is not pure "otherness" '. He asks us to consider what Fanon's call for return to the past might entail. Is such a search an 'archaeology', a looking for something that always existed? Is it not really a 're-telling of the past', a process that requires an imaginative recognition of both what existed and what we continually create? Alterity, or a binary opposition between coloniser and colonised is an idea that has enormous force and power in the construction of anti-colonial narratives, by subjects who are themselves complex, mixed-up products of diverse colonial histories. As we sift through the often confusing positions on the subject, it will be useful to recall Neil ten Kortenaar's sensible reminder that '*neither* authenticity nor creolization has ontological validity, but both are valid as metaphors that permit collective self-fashioning'. Neither, he insists, is an inherently progressive or regressive position. Authenticity can be an enabling metaphor, as in the case of Ngũgĩ, or be 'mere obfuscation in the service of tyranny' as in the case of Mobuto in Zaire:

> One may not be able to return to the world of one's ancestors, but one can claim to be doing so, with political effect . . . . Like authenticity, hybridization is a metaphor that does not define a particular political program. Hybridization is most often invoked by advocates of pluralism and tolerance, but it can also underwrite imperialism (as in the case of French nationalist Jules Michelet). . . . Authenticity and creolization are best regarded as valuable rhetorical tools that can be made to serve liberation. It may also be liberating to remember that these constructions are effectively rhetorical.
>
> (Kortenaar 1995: 40–41)

The point, then, is not to simply pit the themes of migrancy, exile and hybridity against rootedness, nation and authenticity, but to locate and evaluate their ideological, political and emotional valencies, as well as their intersections in the multiple histories of colonialism and postcoloniality.

3

CHALLENGING COLONIALISM

NATIONALISMS AND PAN-NATIONALISMS

A civilization that proves incapable of solving the problems it creates is a decadent civilization.
A civilization that chooses to close its eyes to its most crucial problems is a stricken civilization.
A civilization that uses its principles for trickery and deceit is a dying civilization . . . .
Europe is indefensible.

Aimé Césaire's *Discourse on Colonialism* opens with this poetic and passionate indictment of European colonialism, and with an announcement that its days are numbered:

The colonialists may kill in Indochina, torture in Madagascar, imprison in Black Africa, crack down in the West Indies. Henceforth the colonised know that they have an advantage over them. They know that their temporary 'masters' are lying. And therefore that their masters are weak.

(1972: 9–10)

However, rebellion does not simply follow upon this knowledge of colonial duplicity. Caliban curses Prospero, and yet cannot revolt outright. He tells himself that 'he must obey' because Prospero's 'art is of such power' that it would control his mother's god Setebos. Prospero's continuing power lies not in his ability to fool Caliban or Ariel, but in the threat of violence:

> If thou more murmur'st, I will rend an oak
> And peg thee in his knotty entrails till
> Thou hast howled away twelve winters.
>   (*The Tempest*, I, ii, 294–296)

What does it take for colonial subjects to move from alienation to revolution, from a recognition of injustice to resistance? What are the dynamics of anti-colonial consciousness and revolt? Since no pre-colonial cultures, processes of colonisation or colonised subjects are identical, can we even begin to speak about resistance in general or global terms? Historically speaking, anti-colonial resistances have taken many forms, and they have drawn upon a wide variety of resources. They have inspired one another, but also debated with each other about the nature of colonial authority and how best it should be challenged. In each context, there have been sharp differences between the diverse groups within a 'colonised' population; even where they have managed to come together under the sweep of a particular movement, they have clashed at different points both before and after colonial rule has been formally dismantled.

Colonialism, we have seen, reshapes, often violently, physical territories, social terrains as well as human identities. As the Caribbean novelist George Lamming put it, 'the colonial experience is a *live* experience in the *consciousness* of these people . . . . The experience is a continuing *psychic* experience that has to be dealt with and will have to be dealt with long after the actual colonial situation formally "ends" ' (cited Hulme 1993: 120). Anti-colonial struggles therefore had to create new and powerful identities for colonised peoples and to challenge colonialism not only at a political or intellectual level, but also on an emotional plane. In widely divergent contexts, the idea of the nation was a powerful vehicle for harnessing anti-colonial energies at all these levels.

Although nationalism has been so crucial an aspect of modern history, and in some disciplines its study has been 'a minor industry', until recently it remained a curiously *undertheorised* phenomenon, especially in relation to non-European societies.[1] It is difficult to generalise about nationalism because none of the factors we might think of as responsible for forging national consciousness – language, territory, a shared past, religion, race, customs – are applicable in every instance. However, even as we know that each case of nationalism is unique, we do need to make linkages between different histories of the nation, and look for general patterns, if any. What, after all, makes a nation different from other sorts of communities? What is special about nations forged by struggles against colonialism?

Probably the most influential recent study of nationalism is Benedict Anderson's *Imagined Communities: Reflections on the Origin and Spread of Nationalism* (1991). Anderson, as the title makes clear, defines the nation as an 'imagined community', born with the demise of feudalism and the rise of capitalism. Feudal hierarchies, he suggests, allowed bonds to exist across national or linguistic boundaries (all European Catholics might feel part of a community, for example). The bourgeoisie, however, forged shared interests across class lines within a more bounded geography, and thus created a community among people who had never met and did not necessarily have interests or outlooks in common. Newspapers, novels and other new forms of communication were the channels for creating such a shared culture, interests and vocabularies. Such forms of communication were themselves made possible by 'print-capitalism' (or trade in books and printed materials) which had created certain 'mechanically reproduced print languages' by pruning out some vernaculars and modifying others, thereby creating certain standardised languages that could be used to reach diverse groups of people. Thus, 'the convergence of capitalism and print technology on the fatal diversity of human language created the possibility of a new form of imagined community, which in its basic morphology set the stage for the modern nation' (1991: 46).

However, Anderson tells us, in practice language was not even an issue in the formation of those states which were the first to define themselves as nations, i.e. 'the new American states of the late eighteenth and early nineteenth centuries'. Spanish-speaking creole communities in South and Central America developed the notion of 'nation-ness' well before most of Europe did, and they co-opted the indigenous oppressed non-Spanish speaking peoples into this idea of an 'imagined community' with them. Why did this happen, and why were otherwise comfortable landowning families so willing so risk ruin for this idea of the nation? For Anderson the answer lies in the fact that the creoles were marginalised in the imperial administration and sought advancement that the existing system denied them. Anderson further suggests that while the indigenous peoples were 'conquerable by arms and disease, and controllable by the mysteries of Christianity and a completely alien culture', the creoles 'had virtually the same relationship to arms, disease, Christianity and European culture as the metropolitans'. Thus they were privileged in all ways except in their independence from the colonial power: they were 'simultaneously a colonial community and an upper class' (Anderson 1991: 58). Their nationalism was born out of *both dispossession and privilege*: a dichotomy which also informs various anti-colonial nationalisms at a later time in history.

Anderson then traces the forms that this model of nationalism took in Europe, where language was much more fundamental to developing national consciousness. Here, initially, owing to the pivotal role played by the literate middle classes and the intelligentsia, nationalism appeared as all-inclusive, popular and based on language identifications. Such nationalism employed a democratic rhetoric, speaking out against serfdom or legal slavery. But then it was appropriated by the ruling European dynasties: in response to popular national movements and tendencies, these dynasties and aristocrats appeared 'in national drag' (1991: 86–87), which is to say they tried to forge new identifications with the people they ruled: 'Romanovs discovered they were Great Russians, Hanoverians that they were English' and so on. While these new identifications were often tenuous, they were the means of 'stretching the short, tight skin of the nation over the gigantic body of the empire'. Anderson reminds us that such 'official nationalism' (i.e. a nationalism forged by rulers) was 'an anticipatory strategy' adopted by dominant groups who feel they might be excluded from newer communities struggling to be born (1991: 101). Anderson contends that such a reactionary conservative nationalism was not confined to Europe, but extended to the colonies in Asia or Africa. There was a 'world-wide contradiction' whereby the ruled and the colonised were invited to become one of the rulers:

> Slovaks were to be Magyarized, Indians Anglicized, and Koreans Japanified, but they would not be permitted to join pilgrimages which would allow them to administer Magyars, Englishmen or Japanese. The banquet to which they were invited always turned out to be a Barmecide feast.
>
> (1991: 110)

The final form of the nation that Anderson considers is that of the 'nation-state' ushered in after the First World War and cemented after the Second World War. This includes, of course, nations born of anti-imperialist struggles. The nation-state, he argues, was conceptualised everywhere along the lines of the earlier models discussed by him. Anderson explains this dependency on the European models by the fact that the American and

European experiences 'were now everywhere modularly imagined' partly because the 'European languages-of-state they employed were the legacy of imperialist official nationalism' (1991: 113). In the colonies, the native intelligentsia played such a crucial role in forging nationalist consciousness because they were bilingual and had access 'to modern Western culture in the broadest sense, and in particular, to the models of nationalism, nation-ness, and nation-state produced elsewhere in the course of the nineteenth century' (1991: 116). In other words, anti-colonial nationalism is itself made possible and shaped by European political and intellectual history. It is a 'derivative discourse', a Calibanistic model of revolt which is dependent upon the coloniser's gift of language/ideas.

Anderson's argument here converges with the standard older understanding of nationalism in the colonised world. English historians had even suggested that Indians learnt their ideas of freedom and self-determination from English books, including the plays of Shakespeare! The phrase 'derivative discourse' is the subtitle of Partha Chatterjee's book *Nationalist Thought and the Colonial World* (1986) which challenges Anderson's model, suggesting that the relationship between anti-colonial and metropolitan nationalisms is structured by an intricate relationship of both borrowing and difference. In a later book, *The Nation and Its Fragments*, Chatterjee sums up his 'central objection' to Anderson's argument thus:

> If nationalisms in the rest of the world have to choose their imagined community from certain 'modular' forms already made available to them by Europe and the Americas, what do they have left to imagine? History, it would seem, has decreed that we in the postcolonial world shall only be perpetual consumers of modernity. Europe and the Americas, the only true subjects of history, have thought out on our behalf not only the script of colonial enlightenment and exploitation, but also

that of our anticolonial resistance and postcolonial misery. Even our imaginations must remain forever colonised.

(1993: 5)

Chatterjee attempts to break away from such a debilitating paradigm by locating the processes of ideological and political exchange in the creation of Indian nationalism – of identifying what he calls 'the ideological sieve' through which nationalists filtered European ideas.

He does this by drawing a distinction between nationalism as a political movement which challenges the colonial state, and nationalism as a cultural construct which enables the colonised to posit their difference and autonomy. The former is derivative but the latter draws its energies from other sources. Chatterjee points out that the official histories of Indian nationalism would in fact correspond to Anderson's thesis. They tell us that 'nationalism proper' began in 1885 with the formation of the Indian National Congress after a period of 'social reforms' when 'colonial enlightenment was beginning to "modernize" the customs and institutions of a traditional society . . . '. But such histories mistakenly believe that nationalism is only a political movement. Instead, he claims that well before it launches itself against the colonial state, anti-colonial nationalism attempts to create 'its own domain of sovereignty within colonial society'. It does so by dividing the world into a material, outside sphere constituted of the economy, statecraft, science and technology, and a spiritual, inner domain of culture (which includes religion, customs and the family). The supremacy of the West is conceded in the material world, whereas the spiritual world is claimed as the essence of national culture, one which must be protected and defended. The more colonised peoples imitate Western skills in the former sphere, the greater the need to protect the latter. Chatterjee clarifies that it is not as though this latter world is left unchanged:

In fact, here nationalism launches its most powerful, creative, and historically significant project: to fashion a 'modern' national culture that is nevertheless not Western. If the nation is an imagined community, then this is where it is brought into being. In this, its true and essential domain, the nation is already sovereign, even when the state is in the hands of the colonial power. The dynamics of this historical project is completely missed in conventional histories in which the story of nationalism begins with the contest for political power.

(1993: 6–7)

Thus, anti-colonial nationalism is not modelled upon simple imitation but also by defining its difference from Western notions of liberty, freedom and human dignity. All over Asia and Africa, Chatterjee claims, anti-colonial nationalisms worked in and through such a formula of a divided world.

In the colonial situation the development of 'print capitalism' and the construction of national languages also took a different form. In India, for example, colonised intellectuals were schooled in the coloniser's language but also asserted their claim over their mother tongues, set up the instruments for their dissemination and modernised them. Thus

the bilingual intelligentsia came to think of its own language as belonging to that inner domain of cultural identity, from which the colonial intruder had to be kept out; language therefore became a zone over which the nation first had to declare its sovereignty and then had to transform in order to make it adequate for the modern world.

(Chatterjee 1993: 7)

Therefore, despite their schooling in the Western fashion, and despite their Anglicisation, Bengali intellectuals also fervently tried to create, through theatre, novels and art, an aesthetic sphere that would be distinctively Indian. And they also took the lead in setting up educational institutions that would be distinct from those run by the missionaries and the colonial state. It was to such schools that women were allowed to go, because the family and women were firmly placed within the inner domain that was to remain outside the control of colonial authority.

Although Chatterjee's thesis is based on the study of Bengal, it helps us in thinking about the centrality of 'culture', and of gender, to nationalist discourses. In South Africa, for example, the family was central to the making of Afrikaner nationalism (Hofmeyr 1987). Here too 'white men were seen to embody the political and economic agency of the *volk*, while women were the (unpaid) keepers of tradition and the *volk*'s moral and spiritual mission' (McClintock 1995: 277). It also helps explain why anti-colonial nationalisms so persistently emphasised their *difference* from the imperial masters. As discussed earlier, in the colonial situation women were used as crucial markers of this cultural difference. Colonisers regarded their position within the family and within religious practices, in India, in Algeria, in South Africa and in countless other colonised countries, as indicative of a degenerate culture. 'Reform' of women's position thus became central to colonial rule. Nationalists regarded this as colonialist intrusion, and responded by initiating reforms of their own, claiming that only they had the right to intervene in these matters. Such tactics resulted in partial reform but also recast, and sometimes strengthened, indigenous patriarchal practices. In India, a 'new woman' and a new family structure, different both from the traditional and the Western versions were projected as nationalist ideals, a pattern that is also visible in other colonial situations.

Frantz Fanon's 'Algeria Unveiled' contains a fascinating discussion of the moulding of a nationalist woman. French colonialist doctrines, writes Fanon, identified Algerian women and family relations as the crucial site for their onslaught against native culture:

If we want to destroy the structure of Algerian society, its capacity for resistance, we must first of all conquer the women; we must go and find them behind the veil where they hide themselves and in the houses where the men keep them out of sight. It is the situation of woman that was accordingly taken as the theme of action. The dominant administration solemnly undertook to defend this woman, pictured as humiliated, sequestered, cloistered . . . transformed by the Algerian man into an inert, demonetized, indeed dehumanized object . . . . After it had been posited that the woman constituted the pivot of Algerian society, all efforts were made to obtain control over her.

(1965: 37–38)

For the colonisers unveiling the Arab woman becomes an obsession. The veil becomes a symbol of colonial frustration for it lets the woman gaze upon the world while shielding her from prying eyes: 'Thus the rape of the Algerian woman in the dream of the European is always preceded by a rending of the veil' (1965: 44). The colonial struggle becomes a sort of war of the veils because 'to the colonialist offensive against the veil, the colonised opposes the cult of the veil'. The colonialist identification of woman with Algeria thus 'had the effect of strengthening the traditional patterns of behaviour'.

Fanon goes on to describe how the resistance movement demanded that the nationalist Algerian woman both veil and unveil herself in its cause. She was asked at first to Europeanise herself to penetrate the European quarters of the city, since the colonial regime assumed that Westernised women would not be part of the resistance. The unveiled Algerian woman had to fashion her body to being 'naked' and scrutinised, she had to move 'like a fish in the Western waters' while 'carrying revolvers, grenades, hundreds of false identity cards or bombs'. But such a woman is not unveiled at Europe's bidding, hence she does not signify loss of cultural identity but the forging of a new nationalist self. Fanon describes how this woman would be seen by a relative and friend, and various reports would reach her father: 'Zohra or Fatima unveiled, walking like a . . . My Lord, protect us!' But his protests would melt in the face of the young woman's 'firmness' and 'commitment' and soon 'the whole family – even the Algerian father, the authority for all things, the founder of every value – following in her footsteps, becomes committed to the new Algeria' (1965: 60). Some years later, when the colonial state understood that not all unveiled women were alienated from the nationalists, the Algerian woman was ordered to veil herself again:

> The Algerian woman's body, which in an initial phase was pared down, now swelled. Whereas in the previous period the body had to be made slim and disciplined to make it attractive and seductive, it now had to be squashed, made shapeless and even ridiculous. This . . . is the phase during which she undertook to carry bombs, grenades, machine-gun clips . . . . Spontaneously and without being told, the Algerian women who had long since dropped the veil once again donned the *haïk*, thus affirming that it was not true that woman liberated herself at the invitation of France and of General de Gaulle.
>
> (1965: 62)

But if a certain sphere or domain, such as gender, is regarded as intrinsic to national culture, such a domain cannot be addressed as other than national. Thus, as Vilashini Cooppan points out, Fanon is interested in Algerian and other women of colour only to the extent that they are useful for discussing the nation:

> Gender and nation do more than intersect in Fanon's analysis: nation subsumes gender. Within Fanon's scheme, gender seems to represent a particularity that should be translated,

> with all possible speed, into the universality and strategic unity
> of revolutionary culture and the new nation.
>
> (1996: 193–194)

Thus too, Indian nationalism takes up and discards the woman question, depending upon the exigencies of the moment, as we'll discuss at some length in a later section.

The assertion of a gendered spiritual or inner core thus becomes the site for the construction of national identities across a wide political and ideological anti-colonial spectrum. The communities that are imagined by anti-colonial nationalism often invoke a shared past or a cultural essence that is regarded as synonymous with a religious or racial identity. Gandhi declared not just the British but all of modern industrial society to be the enemy. Although such an idea was not shaped by a simple nativism and drew upon the Romantic critique of industrialism, it nevertheless also invoked the idea of an Eastern anti-materialism, spiritualism and asceticism. Jawaharlal Nehru, so different from Gandhi in his Anglicisation, his belief in socialism, modernity and Western science, was passionately eloquent about the 'Idea of India' which had been shaped at the dawn of civilisation and had survived for thousands of years. Such an idea, he suggested had changed through the ages but still clung to some of its originary foundations. We can find similar resurrections of the past in many African, Arab, and other nationalisms. Such a going back is actually quite modern in itself – it is a product of a *present* need, which reshapes, rather than simply invokes the past.

A national 'memory', or rather a memory which creates a national identity is the subject of Ernest Renan's 1882 essay 'What is a Nation?', which remains a foundational text on the subject. 'A nation is a soul, a spiritual principle', Renan says, and of all its cults 'that of the ancestors is the most legitimate, for the ancestors have made us what we are. A heroic past, great men, glory . . . this is the social capital upon which one bases a national idea' (1990: 19). Renan is emphatic, too, that *'forgetting* . . . is a crucial factor in the creation of a nation' (1990: 11; emphasis added). Thus, forging the idea of a unifying past collectivity involves careful *selection* from multiple histories. And although Renan is resolutely Euro-centric in his focus, his perception that where 'national memories are concerned, griefs are of more value than triumphs, for they impose duties and require a common effort' is true of the colonial situation where nationalists repeatedly invoke a glorious pre-colonial past or traditions (symbolised by 'culture', the family, language, religion and women) that has been trampled upon by the invader.

Nationalism engages in a complex process of contesting as well as appropriating colonialist versions of the past. Anthony Appiah has accused nationalists in Africa of making 'real the imaginary identities to which Europe has subjected us' (1991: 150). Nativists, he says, are of the West's party without knowing it, and in fact 'few things . . . are less native than nativism in its current forms' (1991: 145–146). Eric Hobsbawm and Terence Ranger's well-known book, *The Invention of Tradition*, had earlier documented how many 'traditions' are not traditional at all, but are continually invented and re-invented both by colonialists as well as nationalists who continually engage with one another's creations in order to reinforce or challenge authority. Of course not just tradition, but nations themselves in many parts of the colonised world were invented by colonialists. These newly created nations altered previous conceptions of the community, or of the past. For example, in Rwanda, at the onset of colonial rule,

> only in the central core of the Rwandan kingdom had 'Tutsi' and 'Hutu' acquired comprehensive social meaning as labels associated with dominance and subordination, respectively. In the outer perimeter of this expanding state, where looser tributary relations applied, the evidence of oral tradition shows that 'Tutsihood' and 'Hutuhood' were much more diffuse concepts.

The colonial state absorbed the ideology of domination of the central Rwandan state, codified and rationalized it, and extended it throughout the domain. The consequences of this are illustrated in the intriguing difference today between 'kiga' in southwest Uganda and those labelled 'Hutu' across the border in Rwanda; a century ago there was no meaningful linguistic, cultural, or identity difference.

(Young 1994: 227–228)

These new identities were often appropriated for anti-colonial purposes: thus Arab nationalisms in the Middle East and North Africa invested colonially created territorial units with their own meaning of community or nation by drawing upon myths of Arab origin or the Islamic golden age of the Caliphates, even though some early Arab nationalists were Christian. As Dipesh Chakrabarty puts it, European imperialism and third world nationalisms have *together* achieved the 'universalization of the nation-state as the most desirable form of political community' (1992: 19).

Benita Parry and Neil Lazarus, among other postcolonial critics, have insisted that it is important to remember and acknowledge the enormous power and appeal of anti-colonial nationalism. It would be foolish to deny this. But the anti-colonial, radical thrust of nationalism ought not to be celebrated by forgetting its exclusions. Nationalism itself invites us to disregard these. Both as an oppositional and as a state ideology, it claims to include 'all' the people, the ordinary folk, to celebrate diversity and speak for the 'entire' imagined community. Thus, Benedict Anderson argues that 'Regardless of the actual inequality and exploitation that may prevail in each, the nation is always conceived as a deep, horizontal comradeship' (1991: 6–7). But several critics have suggested that *Imagined Communities* pays so much attention to who is included in the communities that it fails to consider those who are excluded and marginalised, such as women, or lower classes, races, or castes. The 'fraternity' which represents the nation does not explicitly include them as equals, however, it always implicitly claims to represent them. Creole nationalism, for example, which Anderson regards as foundational, was forged by working through and incorporating existing hierarchies of gender and class (Skurski 1994). The forms of marginalisation differ during the forging of various national communities: women for example, may either be openly excluded from citizenship as in Napoleonic France, or even be invited to embody the nation but in terms that enforce their subordination, as during the *swadeshi* movement in India. These exclusions are sometimes enforced, but often won by the 'consent' of the people. The power of nationalism, its continuing appeal, lies precisely in its ability to successfully speak on behalf of all the people. In this context, it is significant that many nationalist leaders offer their autobiographies as emblematic of and representative of their nation's birth: Jawaharlal Nehru's *An Autobiography*, Kwame Nkrumah's *Autobiography*, Kenneth Kaunda's *Zambia Shall be Free* (see Boehmer 1995: 192).

When nationalist thought becomes enshrined as the official dogma of the postcolonial State, its exclusions are enacted through the legal and educational systems, and often they simply duplicate the exclusions of colonialism. Women's movements, peasant struggles or caste- and class-based dissent, both during and after colonial rule sometimes (but not always) allow us to explore the distance between the rhetoric and the reality of the nation-state. In recent years, the effort to uncover the histories and standpoint of people excluded by nationalist projects has multiplied across the disciplines. 'Histories from below' have attempted to tell other stories of rebellion and struggle, as well as to interrelate them to the narratives of nationalism and decolonisation. In this context, an important document was Ranajit Guha's 'On Some Aspects of the Historiography of Colonial India' which announced a revisionist agenda for the (by now extremely influential) Subaltern Studies volumes on Indian history.

It accused the dominant historiography of Indian nationalism of leaving out 'the subaltern classes and groups constituting the mass of the labouring population and the intermediate strata in town and country – that is, the people'. Guha's essay inaugurated the widespread use of the term 'subaltern' in postcolonial studies, which he defined as 'the demographic difference between the total Indian population and all those we have defined as elite'. The elite was composed of 'dominant groups, foreign as well as indigenous' – the foreign including British officials of the colonial state and foreign industrialists, merchants, financiers, planters, landlords and missionaries, and the indigenous divided into those who operated at the 'all-India level' , i.e. 'the biggest feudal magnates, the most important representatives of the industrial and mercantile bourgeoisie and the native recruits to the uppermost levels of the bureaucracy' and those who operated at 'the regional and local levels', either as 'members of the dominant all-India groups', or 'if socially inferior', those who 'still acted in the interests of the latter and not in conformity to interests corresponding truly to their own being' (1982: 8).

Such a definition asks us to re-view colonial dichotomies; it shifts the crucial social divide from that between colonial and anti-colonial to that between 'elite' and 'subaltern'. Recently, the same point is made by a slim and passionate volume called *Why I am not a Hindu*, a book that has been compared to Fanon's *Wretched of the Earth*. Its author, Kancha Ilaiah, writes as one of the 'dalitbahujans', whom he defines as 'people and castes who form the exploited and suppressed majority' in India (1996: ix). He describes the alienation of the castes excluded as 'backward' or 'untouchable' by Hinduism, not merely from the colonial or neo-colonial Western culture, but also from the dominant postcolonial 'Indian' one (that reflects the upper-caste Hindu culture and interests):

What difference did it make to us whether we had an English textbook that talked about Milton's *Paradise Lost* or *Paradise*

Regained, or Shakespeare's *Othello* or *Macbeth* or Wordsworth's poetry about nature in England, or a Telegu text-book which talked about Kalidasa's *Meghasandesham,* Bommera Potanna's *Bhagvatam,* or Nannaya and Tikkana's *Mahabharatham* except the fact that one textbook is written with 26 letters and the other in 56 letters? We do not share the contents of either, we do not find our lives reflected in their narratives. We cannot locate our family settings in them. In none of these books do we find words that are familiar to us. Without the help of a dictionary neither makes any sense to us. How does it make any difference to us whether it is Greek and Latin that are written in Roman letters or Sanskrit that is written in Telegu?

(1996: 15)

In a situation where the Hindu right has begun to aggressively define what is Indian (and it does so by invoking both the West and Islam as foreign elements that threaten to pollute the nation), Ilaiah challenges its right to represent or speak for the enormous numbers of oppressed castes that 'had been excluded from history'. Now, there *is* an obvious nativism at work here: Ilaiah defends Dalit cultures as intrinsically more creative, democratic and humanitarian (and even feminist) than Hindu society, close to the manner in which Césaire had argued that all non-Western societies were superior to European ones. The line between oppressor and oppressed is, however, drawn by caste and not colonial oppression. Thus, if we are to give 'two cheers for nativism' or nationalism and celebrate 'reverse-discourse', as Benita Parry suggests we should, it should be with the knowledge that 'nativism' itself is not a unitary phenomenon.

The wretched of the earth have been rarely been represented by competing visions of the nation. But nationalism, Ranajit Guha contends, simply cannot be understood without locating how subaltern groups contributed to it, not at the behest of nationalist leaders but '*on their own,* that is, *independently of the elite*'. Subaltern and elite politics were not simply demarcated, but they were not identical either, and their difference can be grasped by what Guha calls 'the failure of the Indian bourgeoisie to speak for the nation. There were vast areas in the life and consciousness of the people which were never integrated into their hegemony' (1982: 5–6). Thus the millions who contributed to the nationalist project were also both excluded by it and resistant to it. What, then were their agendas, their struggles, and their relationship to colonialism and postcolonial societies? How can we recover them? We will return to such questions in the section on subaltern speech. However, we should note that recovering the viewpoint of 'the people' does not necessarily indicate a historian's radical sympathies. Belinda Bozzoli and Peter Delius trace pioneering oral history work in South Africa to liberal historians W.M. MacMillan and C.W. de Kiewiet, who, during the 1920s and 1930s argued that history should speak of the everyday lives of ordinary folk in order to support their argument that 'contemporary forms of racism were rooted in a preindustrial world and imperialism was a benign force'. Today, histories 'from below' are committed not simply to unravelling colonialism but tracing 'how colonised peoples have been drawn into capitalist society and have resisted their incorporation, leaving their mark on the form taken by the "big" categories of class, race and state' (Bozzoli and Delius 1990: 34).

In such relational histories, nationalism emerges as a wider and yet more limited force than in its own narration. Wider because, as it turns out in Shahid Amin's gripping account of a single, pivotal event in the Indian struggle for independence, nationalism is also created by people, narratives and perspectives beyond its own imaginings, and more limited because, when placed within this larger context, its scope, ambitions and reach are revealed as severely constricted. Amin's book *Event, Metaphor, Memory* re-tells the story of Chauri Chaura, the place where twenty-three policemen were burnt to death by an angry 'mob' in February 1922, leading Mahatma Gandhi to suspend the struggle against the British, and the event itself to become the 'great unremembered episode of modern Indian history', read only as 'a figure of speech, a trope for all manner of untrammelled peasant violence, specifically in opposition to disciplined non-violent mass satyagrahas' (Amin 1995: 3). Perceived as criminals by both nationalists and imperialists, the rioting peasants have been entirely obscured by subsequent histories as crucial actors both in this local drama and in the larger nationalist struggle. By re-reading the archives, and reconstructing local memories of the event as well as local cultural history Amin tries to interconnect 'peasant nationalism' to the Gandhian movement. Although it has the structure of an exciting 'who-dunnit', the book in fact leads one away from the judicial/nationalist perspectives of the 'crime', and asks us to re-examine the ideologies and cultures of the peasants who made Gandhi into a Mahatma and yet were far from being represented by him.

Thus, nations are communities created not simply by forging certain bonds but by fracturing or disallowing others; not merely by invoking and remembering certain versions of the past, but making sure that others are forgotten or repressed. Only select aspects of Chauri Chaura can be remembered. What is forgotten, however, is as necessary to the nationalist imagining, to the fabrication of a modern India and its stories of the anti-colonial struggle as what is remembered. Such selections ensure that the partition of India in 1947 is virtually erased both from official, but also from a larger collective memory, or at least its memory is rarely articulated in any of the nation-states (Bangladesh, Pakistan or India) that were spawned by the colonial carving up of the subcontinent. Partly because some key writings on these issues (such as the *Subaltern Studies* volumes) have dealt with India, this section has favoured materials from that part of the world: however, similar patterns of recall and repression are at the heart of nearly every national 'community'.

As we ponder the distance between the nation and the people, as well as the enormous force of nationalism, Amilcar Cabral's writings take on an especial validity. Cabral, who was Secretary-General of the African party for the Independence of Guinea and the Cape-Verde Islands (PAIGC), was committed to the idea of forging a national culture, and yet committed also to the idea that 'the movement must be able to preserve the positive cultural values of every well-defined social group, of every category, and to achieve the confluence of these values in the service of the struggle, giving it a new dimension – *the national dimension*' (1994: 59). In 'metropolitan' nations as well as 'third world' ones, the difficulty of creating national cultures that might preserve, indeed nourish internal differences has emerged as a major issue in our time. Cabral's insistence that 'no culture is a perfect, finished whole. Culture, like history, is an expanding and developing phenomenon' (1994: 61) reminds us that nations, like other communities, are not transhistorical in their contours or appeal, but are continually being re-imagined.

Literature and 'the nation'

European nationalism was discredited over the course of the twentieth century by its association with fascism and colonialism. At the same time, its third world variant was legitimised by being read as synonymous with anti-colonialism. In contemporary mainstream European or American discourse, however, nationalism is often regarded as an exclusively 'Third World problem' (and for that reason almost always implies atavistic religious fundamentalism and bigotry). Even in the writings of radical Western academics, there is often a reductive equation of nationalism with the third world. Thus Aijaz Ahmad criticises Frederic Jameson's well-known essay 'Third World Literature in the Era of Multinational Capital' for suggesting that 'a certain nationalism is fundamental in the third world' where 'the telling of the individual story, the individual experience cannot but ultimately involve the whole laborious telling of the experience of the collectivity itself' (Jameson 1986: 85–86). How can widely divergent cultures, histories and narratives be squeezed into a single formal pattern? Ahmad points out that such a generalisation relies on the Three Worlds Theory according to which the 'First' and 'Second Worlds' are defined in terms of their systems of production (i.e. capitalism and socialism) and the 'Third World' is defined in terms of its experience of an 'externally inserted phenomena' (colonialism):

> If this 'Third World' is *constituted* by the singular 'experience of colonialism and imperialism', and if the only possible response is a nationalist one, what else is there that is more urgent to narrate than this 'experience'? . . . For if societies here are defined not by relations of production but by relations of international domination; if they are forever suspended outside the sphere of conflict between capitalism (First World) and socialism (Second World); if the motivating force for history here is neither class formation and class struggle nor the multiplicities of intersecting conflicts based upon class, gender, nation, race, region, and so on, but the unitary 'experience' of national oppression, . . . then what else *can* one narrate but that national oppression? Politically we are Calibans all . . . .
>
> (Ahmad 1987: 20)

Ahmad's questioning of the theoretical and political underpinnings of the term 'Third World' and his plea against the homogenisation of the literatures of vast areas of Asia, Africa and Latin America are compelling. But whereas he implies that to speak of the 'national oppression' is necessarily to highlight the colonial experience at the expense of issues such as 'class formation' or 'the multiplicities of intersecting conflicts', in fact these are not issues that need to be counterposed to one another. We have seen how the nation emerged as a site where these conflicts – of class, or gender, caste, region and language – were played out. As Ranajit Guha's statement on the Subaltern Studies project (cited above) notes, the *failure* of the postcolonial nation-state can only be understood by looking at class, region, gender and other social formations and tensions in once colonised countries. Thus to pose the question as a choice between an account of colonial domination and nation-formation on the one hand, and an analysis of modes of production or internal dynamics on the other is itself reductive.

Finally, despite the flaws in his conceptualisation, is Jameson entirely wrong in suggesting that 'a certain nationalism' is crucial to understanding postcolonial societies? Timothy Brennan's essay, 'The National Longing for Form' suggests that the burden of one strain of writing from the so-called third world has been to *critique* 'the all inclusive gestures of the nation-state and to expose the excesses which the a priori state, chasing a national identity after the fact, has created at home' (1990: 58, 56). Brennan suggests that such writing appropriates and inverts the form of the European novel; writers like Rushdie and Vargas Llosa are 'well poised to thematize the centrality of nation-forming while at the same time demythifying it from a European perch', and that such challenges are 'easier to embrace in our metropolitan circles than the explicit challenges of, say, the Salvadoran protest-author Manlio Argueta, or the sparse and caustic satires of the Nigerian author, Obi Egbuna'. While such a thesis locates the reception of the 'third world novel' in the West within the political and thematic differences between writers, Brennan nevertheless conceptualises the novel in once-colonised countries as 'the form through which a thin, foreign-educated stratum (however sensitive or committed to domestic political interests) has communicated to metropolitan reading publics, often in translation' (1990: 56). Such a definition of course leaves out the enormous production of literature within once-colonised countries which is written by those who were not 'foreign-educated', often not even educated within the colonial educational apparatus – literature which is not translated or circulated abroad, and which cannot be understood as 'Third World thematics as seen through the elaborate fictional architecture of European high art' (Brennan's wonderfully suggestive phrase for the novels he discusses). It is a matter of some alarm that not just in Western academic circles but also beyond, writing in non-European languages is excluded or marginalised – the latest instance being Salman Rushdie's wild assertion in the pages of the *New Yorker* that in India, writing in English is 'a stronger and more important body of work than most of what has been produced in the eighteen "recognized" languages' of the country (1997: 50)!

Neil Lazarus validates Jameson's connection between the nation and 'third world' societies on the grounds that:

> it is only on the terrain of the nation that an articulation between cosmopolitan intellectualism and popular consciousness can be forged; and *this* is important, in turn, because in the era of multinational capitalism it is only on the basis of such a universalistic articulation – that imperialism can be destabilised.
>
> (1994: 216)

In his view, the 'specific role' of postcolonial intellectuals is 'to construct a standpoint – nationalitarian, liberationist, internationalist – from which it is possible to assume the burden of speaking for all humanity' (1994: 220). Given the history of exclusions that accompanied the earlier constructions of an all-inclusive nation, postcolonial intellectuals may in fact be sceptical about such a prescription. Postcolonial women's struggles for example are less concerned with speaking on behalf of all the people than claiming their own place within the national polity. It is even more doubtful whether the construction of a national identity can be adequate grounds for forging an anti-imperialist struggle. The postcolonial state often uses an anti-imperialist rhetoric of nationalism to consolidate its own power while making enormous concessions to multinational interests. And then, it is not just merely the state but other social and political configurations that lay claim to the rhetoric of 'the nation'. Hindu fundamentalists in India, or Muslim fundamentalists in Iran have most aggressively tried to reconstruct a national identity along exclusionary religious lines, and this has always included a diatribe not only against other religions and communities but also against the West, and often against 'imperialism'. Finally, racist organisations also lay claim to nationalism, and as Etienne Balibar reminds us: 'the discourses of race and nation are never very far apart' (1991: 37).

Perhaps the connection between postcolonial writing and the nation can be better comprehended by understanding that the 'nation' itself is a ground of dispute and debate, a site for the competing imaginings of different ideological and political interests. If so many so-called 'third world' writings return to this site, it is not at the expense of, but as an expression of, 'other' concerns – those of gender, ethnicity, race, religion, caste, language, tribe, class, region, imperialism and so on. While it is patently excessive to claim that 'all third world texts' are allegories of nationalism, we can certainly see why the construction of, and contestation of, 'the nation' becomes such a charged issue for so many writers.

Salman Rushdie's latest novel, *The Moor's Last Sigh*, for example, fluctuates between a celebration and a critique of competing versions of the Indian nation. Written in the aftermath of the communal riots that tore Bombay apart in January 1993 following the destruction of the Babri Mosque by Hindu fundamentalists, *The Moor's Last Sigh* nostalgically evokes the Nehruvian vision of a free, hybrid India:

above religion because secular, above class because socialist, above caste because enlightened, above hatred because loving, above vengeance because forgiving, above tribe because unifying, above language because many-tongued, above colour because multi-coloured, above poverty because victorious over it, above ignorance because literate, above stupidity because brilliant . . . .

(1995: 51)

The lineage of Rushdie's Moor invokes the intricate histories of such a hybridity. His mother is from the Catholic da Gama family of Cochin, pepper traders by profession. His father is Abraham Zogoiby whose ancestry invokes the intermingling histories of Moors and Jews, both of whom had arrived on the Kerala coast in the wake of their expulsion from Spain:

Thus Abraham learned that, in January 1492, while Christopher Columbus watched in wonderment and contempt, the Sultan Boabdil of Granada had surrendered the keys to the fortress-palace of the Allahambra, last and greatest of all the Moors' fortifications, to the all-conquering Catholic Kings Fernando and Isabella . . . . He departed into exile with his mother and retainers, bringing to a close centuries of Moorish Spain, and reigning in his horse upon the Hill of Tears, he turned to look for one last time upon his loss, upon the palace and the fertile plains and all the concluded glory of al-Andalus . . . at which the Sultan sighed, and hotly wept . . . .

(1995: 79–80)

In Rushdie's novel, both Jews and Moors fled South, and Boabdil takes on a Jewish lover who steals his crown and moves to India. Aurora and Abraham's fourth child unites their double Moorishness and is born dark, and monstrously quick-growing. Rushdie's central figure, the Moor, born of a hybrid lineage is like Bombay:

Like the city itself, Bombay of my joys and sorrows, I mush-
roomed into a huge urbane sprawl of a fellow, expanded without time for proper planning, without any pauses to learn from
my experiences or my mistakes or my contemporaries, without
time for reflection. How then could I have turned out to be
anything but a mess?

(1995: 161–162)

At the end of the novel, this hybrid figure moves back to
Spain, driven by the increasingly communal atmosphere of contemporary Bombay. He dies in Spain, looking at the 'Allahambra,
Europe's red fort, sister to Delhi's and Agra's' and hoping to
awake in better times (1995: 433). Rushdie thus juxtaposes the
recent escalation of anti-Muslim fundamentalism in India, the
drive towards ethnic cleansing and purity alongside its layered
and multicultural histories. Arrivals from the outside mirror ex-
pulsions from the inside:

Christians, Portuguese and Jews; Chinese tiles promoting god-
less views; pushy ladies, skirts not saris, Spanish shenanigans,
Moorish crowns . . . can this really be India? *Bharat-mata,
Hindustan-hamara*, is this the place? War has just been declared. Nehru and the All-India Congress are demanding that
the British must accept their demand for independence as a
precondition for Indian support in the war effort; Jinnah and
the Muslim League are refusing to support that demand; Mr.
Jinnah is busily articulating the history-changing notion that
there are two nations in the sub-continent, one Hindu, the
other Mussulman . . . .

(1995: 87)

Shakespeare's Othello, who haunts Rushdie's novel, had died
testifying to an impossible split between his black, African self
and his Christianised, Europeanised 'mask'. He had described his

suicide as the killing of a 'malignant and turban'd Turk' who acts against the Venetian State: thus, in his own words, Othello is both the defender of the state and the rebel, the insider and the outsider. Rushdie's Moor invokes a different sort of hybridity – a history of minglings that has created hybrid, complex nations which are now being whittled away and 'traduc'd' (to use Othello's word for the Turk's act against Venice) in the name of the nation.

Rushdie's novel thus both retains the vision of an all-inclusive nation, and sees its historic degeneration into communal hatred and violence. Is the latter a necessary outcome of the former, or its travesty? Can the former be used to resist the new narrow uses of the nation, or is it time to discard such a nationalist conception altogether? Answers to such questions will surely depend on specific contexts: perhaps in the building of a 'new South Africa' today, the language of the 'rainbow nation', an all inclusive community, carries a radical charge even though similar rhetoric may have exhausted its emancipatory potential elsewhere. In a very useful essay, Ruth Frankenberg and Lata Mani point out that whereas real and imagined diasporic identities take on a political edge within British South Asian, Black and Caribbean communities or among African-Americans, in other postcolonial locations, such as India, 'the nation-state' and its exclusions are far more important (1996: 357). Finally, the political meaning or centrality of the nation is also dependent on the relation of individual nation-states to the processes of globalisation. For, as Anthony Giddens reminds us, we live in a world where rapid 'globalisation' has been accompanied by a proliferation of 'local' nationalisms, which have reshaped the contours of the modern globe: 'In circumstances of accelerating globalisation, the nation-state has become "too small for the big problems of life and too big for the small problems of life" ' (1994: 182).[2]

Pan-nationalisms

Anti-colonial thought has not always equated the notion of a 'shared' racial/cultural memory or experience with the nation understood as a distinct geographical or political entity. In the writings of the Negritude movement, or of Pan-Africanism, 'nation' itself takes on another meaning, a sense of shared culture and subjectivity and spiritual essence that stretches across the divisions of nations as political entities. Negritude (the word itself was coined by Aimé Césaire) refers to the writings of French-speaking black intellectuals, such as Léopold Sédar Senghor (who became the President of independent Senegal) the Martiniquan poet Aimé Césaire, or Bernard Binlin Dadié from the Ivory Coast. Pan-Africanism generally refers to a similar movement in the English-speaking world, by and large the work of black people living in Britain. Both these movements articulated pan-national racial solidarity, demanded an end to white supremacy and imperialist domination and positively celebrated blackness, and especially African blackness, as a distinct racial-cultural way of being.

It was Jean-Paul Sartre who, in his collection of black poetry, *Black Orpheus* (1963), first identified the shared sentiment of a collective black consciousness in the poetry of several black writers whom he was introducing. For Sartre, Negritude was a particular historical phase of black consciousness, 'a weak stage of a dialectical progression' which will be transcended in 'the realization of the human society without racism'. However, for Léopold Senghor, considered by many to be the most important philosopher of Negritude, racial difference and consciousness were part of human reality, moulded historically, and yet reflecting an inner state that is not just a passing phase of history. For Senghor, the experience of colonialism, for black people, is a racial experience, and it creates what Irele describes as a 'community of blood', and what Senghor calls a 'collective personality of the black people'. Thus Negritude does not contest the colonial assertion that race signifies both outer and inner traits, or the connections between race and culture: it is, in fact, 'a sum of the cultural value of the black world' (Senghor 1994: 28). However, it does challenge the meaning and values attached to these associations.

In Senghor's work, the black race is associated exclusively with Africa. Africa provides a common cultural root for black peoples all over the world, and a common African culture is seen to survive in black subcultures everywhere, notably in the Americas: 'What strikes me about the Negroes in America is the permanence not of the physical but of the psychic characteristics of the Negro-African, despite race-mixing, despite the new environment' (cited Irele 1971: 167). African civilisation is described in terms of precisely those supposed markers of African life that had been for so long reviled in colonialist thought – sensuality, rhythm, earthiness and a primeval past. For Senghor, Africans 'belong to the mystical civilizations of the senses', and for Aimé Césaire, these civilisations are communal and non-individualistic in nature. But sensuality and community are separated from the negative implications of barbarism attached to them within colonialist thought. Césaire thus claims that these communal societies were fundamentally democratic, anti-capitalist, 'courteous' and therefore civilised (1972: 23). It is Europe which is barbaric. Negritude is thus a reactive position, and yet it tries to create a black identity free of colonialism's taint. Like Césaire, Senghor charts a dichotomy between Africa and Europe in terms that celebrate the former: whereas the 'traditional philosophy of Europe . . . is essentially static, objective, dichotomic' and 'founded on separation and opposition: on analysis and conflict', '[t]he African, on the other hand, conceives the world, beyond the diversity of its forms, as a fundamentally mobile, yet unique, reality that seeks synthesis' (1994: 30). Césaire pointed out that they adopted the word 'nègre' as a term of defiance, out of 'a violent affirmation' (1972: 74). Fanon also understood the relationship between Negritude and colonial categories: 'It is the white man who creates the Negro. But it is the Negro who creates Negritude' (1965: 47). Except that for the Negritude writers, the Negro is not created only by Europe, but also by a shared pre-colonial past, in Césaire's words, a 'sort of black civilization spread throughout the world' (1972: 77). Of course, as Ran Greenstein points out:

> No pre-colonial discourses of Africa are known and it is highly doubtful that indigenous conceptualizations of Africa as a whole (as opposed to specific groups and regions within it) ever existed. Pan-Africanism, Negritude and Black Conscious-ness have all emerged in the aftermath of the colonial en-counter, and not just in their written forms, although they have drawn on and sought to mobilize pre-colonial dis-courses.
>
> (1995: 227)

Fanon was highly critical of the Negritude movement, and he described its literature as 'a violent, resounding, florid writing which on the whole serves to reassure the occupying power', writ-ten as it is from within the terms, in the language of, and for the benefit of that power by an assimilated, albeit protesting, native intelligentsia (1963: 192). Against this Fanon proposes a 'na-tional literature', a 'literature of combat' directed towards the people, engaged in the formation of 'national consciousness' and committed to the struggle for national liberation. For Fanon, na-tive intellectuals who take to 'the unconditional affirmation of African culture' are mistaken since such a category simply inverts colonial stereotyping. For Césaire, on the other hand, it is the na-tion that is 'a bourgeois phenomenon' (1972: 57), and true radi-calism demands forging solidarities across its boundaries.

Thus, both 'the nation' and a pan-national racial essence are contentious conceptions which have nevertheless helped mobilise anti-colonial consciousness. Both nationalism and pan-nationalisms create communities which then have to be endowed with a historical, racial and cultural unity which in practice both simplifies complex cultural formations and performs its own exclusions. However, there may be an alternative way of thinking about transnational solidarities and connections. Paul Gilroy's book *The Black Atlantic* charts a pan-national black culture along very different lines. Gilroy is critical both of 'ethnic absolutism' and 'cultural nationalism'. He points out that the nation is too often considered, even by radical analysts, as the privileged site of material production, political domination and rebellion. It is rarely acknowledged how syncretic the nation itself is. Gilroy traces a shared culture of blackness – a 'transcultural, international formation I call the black Atlantic' – which is rooted not in any racial essence but the shared historical experiences and geographic movements of black peoples through the colonial period. He suggests that Western nations are themselves deeply permeated and shaped by this African diaspora, whose historical experiences form the basis of a shared black culture which can thus never be thought of in racially essentialist terms, or by simply referring back to pre-colonial African roots. Thus his idea of 'the black Atlantic' shows us the inadequacy of both 'nation' or 'race' as privileged markers of cultural identity.

The intellectual and political connections between peoples of Asian, Caribbean and African descent within Britain are traced by Peter Fryer's *Staying Power: The History of Black People in Britain*. The histories charted by Gilroy and Fryer's books and the issues they highlight are important for contemporary attempts to negotiate the legacies of colonialism and deal with the challenges and problems thrown up by both a global resurgence of nationalisms and the 'globalisation' of different nations. They remind us that there were important political and intellectual exchanges between different anti-colonial movements and individuals and that even the most rooted and traditional of these was shaped by a syncretic history so that, despite the rhetoric used by many of the participants, 'nationalism' is not the simple opposite of 'pan-nationalism' or 'hybridity' the neat inverse of 'authenticity'. Finally, we need also to recall Frederick Cooper's caution that, 'Politics in a colony should not be reduced to anticolonial politics or to nationalism: the "imagined communities" Africans saw were both smaller and larger than the nation, sometimes in creative tension with each other, sometimes in repressive antagonism' (1994: 1519).

FEMINISM, NATIONALISM AND POSTCOLONIALISM

If the nation is an imagined community, that imagining is profoundly gendered. We have already discussed how gender and sexuality are central to the conceptualisation, expression and enactment of colonial relations. National fantasies, be they colonial, anti-colonial or postcolonial, also play upon and with the connections between women, land or nations. To begin with, across the colonial spectrum, the nation-state or its guiding principles are often imagined literally *as* a woman. The figures of Britannia and Mother India, for example, have been continually circulated as symbols of different versions of the national temper.[3] Such figures can be imagined as abstractions, allegories, goddesses or real-life women (such as Britomart or Queen Elizabeth in the first case, and Kali or the Rani of Jhansi in the latter). Resistance itself is feminised – Delacroix commemorated the spirit of the French Revolution as the bare breasted Liberty (who was later transformed into Marianne, the figure symbolising the French Republic and the Statue of Liberty in New York). Sometimes the nation-state is represented as a woman as in the former Stalingrad where stands a colossal statue of the Motherland. Sometimes the spirit or dilemma of an entire culture is sought to be expressed via a female figure – the story of Malintzin (or La Malinche) occupies such a place in Chicano culture.

As national emblems, women are usually cast as mothers or

wives, and are called upon to literally and figuratively reproduce the nation. As Nira Yuval-Davis and Floya Anthias point out, feminist literature on reproduction considers the biological and economic aspects of the term but 'has generally failed to consider the reproduction of national, ethical and racial categories' (1989: 7). Anti-colonial or nationalist movements have used the image of the Nation-as-Mother to create their own lineage, and also to limit and control the activity of women within the imagined community. They have also literally exhorted women to produce sons who may live and die for the nation. Hamas or the Palestinian Islamic resistance movement makes this point rather blatantly: 'In the resistance, the role of the Muslim woman is equal to the man's. She is a factory to produce men, and she has a great role in raising and educating the generations' (Jad 1995: 241).

The identification of women as national mothers stems from a wider association of nation with the family. The nation is cast as a home, its leaders and icons assume parental roles (Mahatma Gandhi is the 'Father of the Nation', and until recently, Winnie Mandela was 'Mother of the Nation') and fellow-citizens are brothers and sisters. This association is not just metaphoric, nor is it new. Under feudalism, the King was a Father to his people, and patriarchy provided the vocabulary for explaining political hierarchies too. Thus King James I proclaimed that 'by the Law of Nature the King becomes a naturall Father to all his Lieges at his Coronation'. The family and the State shaped each other's development. A seventeenth-century French ordinance recognised that 'Marriages are the seminaries of States'. Natalie Zemon Davis tells us that 'Kings and political theorists saw the increasing legal subjection of wives to their husbands (and of children to their parents) as a guarantee of the obedience of both men and women to the slowly centralizing state . . . ' (1965: 128).

This vocabulary translated easily to the colonial situation. The colonial state cast itself as the *parens patriae*, controlling but also supposedly providing for its children. In the colonial situation, the familial vocabulary was not limited to the relations between state and subject but became the means of expressing racial or cultural relations as well. The white man's burden was constructed as a parental one: that of 'looking after' those who were civilisationally underdeveloped (and hence figured as children), and of disciplining them into obedience. In his autobiography, Nelson Mandela describes how the South African prison system enforced racial discrimination by not allowing African prisoners (unlike their white or coloured counterparts) to wear long trousers in prison. They had to wear shorts 'for only African men are deemed "boys" by the authorities' (1994: 396). We have already discussed how this homology between the child and the non-European was advanced by psychoanalytic ethnography. Isabel Hofmeyr (1987) shows how the ideology of the family played a crucial role in consolidating the Afrikaner nationalist ideology as well as its racism in early twentieth-century South Africa. The image of the *volksmoeder* (mother of the nation) was central to such consolidation. Afrikaner women were denied any agency outside of the family, but the authority and power of motherhood was marshalled in the service of white racism.

The family is both used as metaphor for the nation, and as an institution, cast as the antithesis of the nation. It is itself dehistoricised, seen as timeless and unchanging (McClintock 1995: 357). Further, it is increasingly spoken of as a 'private' realm, as opposed to the public space of the nation, although, as I have discussed earlier, in the colonial situation, this division breaks down as the family becomes both the domain and the symbol of public anti-colonial activity. In many situations, especially that of slavery, colonialism violently intruded upon, broke up and appropriated families of colonised subjects. In such cases and where intrusions were only imagined or feared, the family becomes a symbol of resistance. Anti-colonial nationalism is a struggle to represent, create or recover a culture and a selfhood that has been systematically repressed and eroded during colonial rule. As we have already discussed, for both colonisers and the colonised, women, gender relations as well as patterns of sexuality come to symbolise both such a cultural *essence* and cultural *differences*. Veiling, clitoral excision, polygamy, widow immolation, matriliny or same-sex relations (to take just a few examples) are interpreted as symptoms of the untranslatable cultural essence of particular cultures. Maintaining or undermining these practices or the social relations they signify thus becomes central to colonial struggles, often tinting them with an extremely patriarchal hue.

Under colonial rule, the image of nation or culture as a woman (often conjured up via images of goddesses as primary life-givers or manifestations of female energy) worked to evoke both female power and female helplessness. The nation as mother protected her son from colonial ravages, but was also herself ravaged by colonialism and in need of her son's protection. 'I know', writes the Indian nationalist Sri Aurobindo, 'my country as Mother. I offer her my devotions, my worship. If a monster sits upon her breast and prepares to suck her blood, what does her child do? Does he quietly sit down to his meal... or rush to her rescue?' (quoted Nandy 1983: 92). Thus the image of nation as mother both marshals and undercuts female power.

As mothers to the nation, women are granted limited agency. Arguments for women's education in metropolitan as well as colonial contexts rely on the logic that educated women will make better wives and mothers. At the same time, educated women have to be taught not to overstep their bounds and usurp authority from men. Thus, for example, in Renaissance Europe, humanist arguments in favour of women's education were also careful to distinguish between a learned woman and a virago who would usurp male authority. Humanist writings visualised women as companions and help-mates to their men, and yet as completely subservient to the male head of the household. Sir Thomas More, for example, championed the cause of female education, and yet passionately proscribed the role of leaders or teachers for educated women. In the colonial context, the debates on women's education echo these earlier histories but of course they are further complicated by racial and colonial hierarchies. The question of female education itself became a colonial battlefield. If colonialists claimed to reform women's status by offering them education, nationalists countered by charting a parallel process of education and reform, one which would simultaneously improve the women's lot and protect them from becoming decultured. In nineteenth-century Bengali discourses, for instance, the over-educated woman is represented as becoming a *memsahib* or Englishwoman who neglects her home and husband. Too much education, like too little, results in bad domestic practices:

> If you have acquired real knowledge, then give no place in your heart to *memsahib* like behaviour. That is not becoming in a Bengali housewife. See how an educated woman can do housework thoughtfully and systematically in a way unknown to an ignorant, uneducated woman. And see if God had not appointed us to this place in the home, how unhappy a place this world would be.
>
> (quoted Chatterjee 1989: 247)

This appeal, incidentally, is issued by a woman.

Although the ideal woman here is constructed in opposition to the spectre of the *memsahib*, it fuses together older brahminical notions of female self-sacrifice and devotion with the Victorian ideal of the enlightened mother, devoted exclusively to the domestic sphere. Women may have become the grounds for colonial battle, but according to Rosalind O'Hanlon, colonial history also reveals a reverse pattern whereby colonial officials and native men 'came to share very similar language and preconceptions about the significance of women and their proper sphere and duties'. The construction of an ideal *bhadramahila* (or gentlewoman), educated yet ladylike, also entailed the isolation of upper- and middle-class women from their lower-class sisters, who were not only servants but also repositories of folk or popular music and tales, dramas and wit. As a result, many 'indigenous forms of women's popular culture were suppressed' and marginalised. These forms often voiced the plight of women in a male-dominated society or expressed sexual desire using robust humour, sharp wit and frankness which was deemed vulgar or too explicit for a gentlewoman's ears (Banerjee 1989). Thus iconic motherhood or wifehood is also constructed by purging the ghosts of racial or class 'others' and in the effort to harness women to the nation, certain traditions are repressed and others invented anew.

If the strengthening of patriarchy within the family became one way for colonised men to assert their otherwise eroded power, women's writings often testify to the confusion and pain that accompanied these enormous changes. From the autobiography of Ramabai Ranade, married at the age of eleven to the well-known scholar and jurist Mahadev Govind Ranade, we can glimpse what a tortuous process it was to be fashioned from a traditional child bride into the nationalist ideal of the wife as help-mate and companion. Ramabai describes how she was torn between her husband's desire that she be literate and schooled, and the taunts of her mother-in-law and other women in the family who disapproved. One day, she was faced with the choice of sitting with either orthodox or reformist women at the temple, and thought herself very clever for refusing to chose by pretending to be ill and going home. Her husband punished her by refusing to discuss the issue or even to speak to her. The ultimate rejection came when:

> I started rubbing his feet with the ghee myself. I wanted him at least to say, 'Now that's enough!' But no, he went off to sleep as soon as I started rubbing his feet. *Usually, after an hour's massage, he would extend his other foot and ask us to start working on that.* But today, I don't know how, he did not forget

his resolve of silence even in his sleep. He didn't speak a single word. And turning on the other side, he pretended to be fast asleep.

(Tharu and Lalita 1991: 288; emphasis added)

While she does not even know the nature of her fault, the situation is only resolved when she goes up and apologises to her husband. His response is to scold her:

Who would like it if his own one didn't behave according to his will? Once you know the direction of my thoughts, you should always try to follow the same path so that neither of us suffers. Don't ever do such things again.

(1991: 289)

The self-fashioning of the nationalist male thus required his fashioning of his wife into a fresh subservience, even though this new role included her education and freedom from some older orthodoxies.

Critics have pointed out that even though the reform of women's position seems to be a major concern within nationalist (and colonialist) discourses, and even though female power, energy and sexuality haunt these discourses, women themselves, in any real sense, seem to 'disappear' from these discussions about them. From colonial as well as nationalist records, we learn little about how they felt or responded, and until recently, there was little attempt to locate them as subjects within the colonial struggle. For example, Lata Mani suggests that the entire colonial debate on sati was concerned with re-defining tradition and modernity, that 'what was at stake was not women but tradition' (1989: 118) and that women 'become sites on which various versions of scripture/tradition/law are elaborated and contested' (1989: 118, 115). Hence, she argues, nowhere is the sati herself a subject of the debate, and nowhere is her subjectivity represented.

Thus, we learn little or nothing about the widows themselves, or their interiority, or even of the fact of their pain. The debates around widow immolation have come to occupy a prominent place within postcolonial theory, and especially within debates on the agency of the colonised. This is in part due to Gayatri Spivak's work, especially her oft-cited essay, 'Can the Subaltern Speak', in which the complete absence of women's voices in the immolation debates is read as a particularly apt emblem of the intermixed violence of colonialism and of patriarchy. We will return to this essay in the next section; for the moment let us pursue the formulation that women are the 'site' rather than the subjects of certain historical debates, a formulation which has become rather fashionable in postcolonial studies.

While it captures how gender functions as a currency in all political exchanges, and how women are marginalised by discourses 'about' them, such a formulation also implies that gender politics is only a metaphor for the articulation of other issues. This somewhat confuses women's relationship to any social structure. Women are not just a symbolic space but real *targets* of colonialist and nationalist discourses. Their subjection and the appropriation of their work is crucial to the workings of the colony or the nation. Thus, despite their other differences, and despite their contests over native women, colonial and indigenous patriarchies often collaborated to keep women 'in their place'. The spectre of their real independence haunted both colonialists and their opponents. Such collaborations, or overlaps in ways of thinking about women, do not indicate that patriarchy is more fundamental than class or race or colonialism. They do remind us that women are not just a vocabulary in which colonial and colonised men work out their relations with each other but at least half the population of any nation. This is not to pit 'symbolic' and 'real' against each other, but to remember that symbolism shapes the real-life roles women are called upon to play.

But if women are and have always been at stake, we must look for them – both within discourses which seek to erase their self-representation and elsewhere. The writings of women who worked alongside, within or in opposition to the nationalist and anti-colonial movements are increasingly becoming available for feminist scholars. These writings help us understand that the debate over tradition and modernity specifically targeted those who challenged or critiqued the patriarchal underpinnings of nationalist discourses. In 1883, for example, Pandita Ramabai's attack against the domestic roles enshrined by both orthodox and nationalist Hindus led her to convert to Christianity. Her 'betrayal' aroused widespread anger precisely because it contested the nationalist attempt to identify the Hindu home as the domain of Indian culture. Thus while women and gender are seen as emblematic of culture and nation, they also signify breaks or faultlines within these categories. Rosalind O'Hanlon (1994) describes how women who broke the codes of silence and subservience became the objects of extreme hostility, which, in some cases, succeeded in silencing outspoken women. The more feminist research uncovers either the hidden and erased voices of women's colonial history, or reinterprets events from a new perspective, the clearer it becomes that the precursors of today's feminists, as individuals and as a potential collectivity, constituted a threat and were thus at least partially the target of earlier patriarchal re-writings of 'tradition'.

Like any other political mass movements, anti-colonial struggles have also varied greatly in their attitudes to female agency and women's rights. Throughout Latin America, *machismo* has posed a real problem for women in political struggle (Fisher 1993). The Black Consciousness movement has also often been aggressively macho. According to some critics, others, such as Gandhi's non-co-operation movement were feminist in nature, not only because they mobilised enormous numbers of women, but also because they adopted attributes (such as passivity) and activities (such as spinning) that are traditionally considered female. But one may question whether such attributes are really 'female', and recall that Gandhi's movement censored women's militancy, and adhered to entirely patriarchal conceptions of the family and society. In a variety of places, including India, women's increasing militancy met with an intense backlash. Even where women were called upon to be militant, as in Algeria, it was resolutely on behalf of the emergent nation. In some contexts the exclusion and inclusion are intimately connected. To continue with the example of colonial India, the ideal of the *bhadramahila* constructed during the nineteenth century (when women seem to be absent from any public anti-colonial protests) shaped the terms on which they were finally allowed participation in the nationalist movement from the 1920s onwards (O'Hanlon 1994: 61). They were then recruited in enormous numbers as followers as well as leaders, but their roles were seen as extensions of their domestic selves – caring, subservient, non-militant.

Women themselves responded in a variety of ways to these attempts to harness and limit their agency. Often the iconography of motherhood was appropriated by women. Millions of women actively fought in anti-colonial struggles as followers, but also as leaders in their own right. Most of them were not feminist, nor did they usually perceive a tension between their own struggles and those of their community at large. By and large perhaps they could not challenge the terms of their participation in these movements, because they themselves often subscribed to the nationalist logic that the colonial masters must first be gotten rid of. Nevertheless, because these women were politically active, worked and lived outside of purely domestic spaces, sometimes in positions of leadership, they opened up new conceptual spaces for women. Even when they moved into public spaces in the name of motherhood and family, they challenged certain notions of motherhood as well as about female roles. (A good relatively recent example of this is the Madres of Plaza de Mayo in

Argentina.) Often, women did depart from the nationalist script and were militant or transgressive. In some rare cases, as in contemporary South Africa, women's voices and increasing grass-roots activism can be seen to alter the shape and ideology of nationalism itself.

How can we make sense of these different patterns? They seem to suggest that women and gender work both as markers of colonial collaboration as well of colonial difference. They suggest also that anti-colonial movements have a complex, ambiguous and shifting relationship with the question of women's rights (see Jayawardena 1986). They have to work through a basic contradiction: on the one hand, the principle of universal equality from which they are launched demands certain concessions to women's rights. This explains why many newly liberated nations conceded certain rights to women (such as the right to vote) even before their European counterparts had it. On the other hand, as we earlier discussed, national culture is built upon a series of exclusions. Thus, even in the case of the African National Congress, which may be reckoned to be more progressive than many nationalist organisations,

> While the language of the ANC was the *inclusive* language of national unity, the Congress was in fact *exclusive* and hierarchical, ranked by an upper house of chiefs (which protected traditional patriarchal authority through descent and filiation), a lower house of elected representatives (all male) and an executive (always male). Indians and so-called coloureds were excluded from full membership.
>
> (McClintock 1995: 380)

While this hierarchy is not equivalent to the brahminical upper-class hierarchy of the Indian National Congress, in both cases the pattern ensures that women's struggles for equality will continue after formal independence and define the nature of postcoloniality. On the whole, however, anti-colonial nation-alisms did open up spaces for women, largely by legitimising their public activity. Women's participation in politics is often more easily accepted in certain postcolonial countries than in 'metropolitan' ones precisely because of this nationalist legacy.

But we must guard against a simple celebration of female mil-itancy or political participation, because the key question is for what purpose it is used. This question becomes especially urgent in postcolonial societies. Not only does women's active participa-tion in politics not necessarily indicate a feminist consciousness or agenda but in recent years there has been an effort to harness women's political activity and even militancy to right-wing movements and especially to religious fundamentalism. In vari-ous parts of the world, women have been active campaigners for the Hindu, Islamic or Christian right-wing movements. This question of religion is an especially tricky one for postcolonial feminists, as it has surfaced as a major factor in women's relation-ship to 'the nation' and to postcolonial politics. Many postcolo-nial regimes have been outrightly repressive of women's rights, using religion as the basis on which to enforce their subordina-tion. National identity in Pakistan, Bangladesh, Iran and re-cently Afghanistan is being moulded on the basis of the Islamicisation of civil society, and severe curtailment of freedoms for women. There is a rich literature about women and Islam, and I do not wish to explore their relationship here, but only to indi-cate that postcolonial identities are not static but shifting, and that religion plays a key role in defining these shifts.[4] The al-liance between fundamentalism and the State has resulted in a se-ries of anti-women legislations in Pakistan which are blatantly discriminatory. It is a measure of the persistence of Orientalist discourses that Islam is often read as especially prone to funda-mentalist appropriation (and to misogyny) than any other reli-gion. However other religious groupings (such as certain Hindu groups in India or the Christian right-wing in the United States) have been equally guilty on both counts. The crucial point here is that often women themselves are key players in the fundamentalist game: in India women like Sadhvi Rithambara and Uma Bharati have stridently mobilised for Hindu nationalism by invoking fears of Muslim violence. In other words, women are objects as well as subjects of fundamentalist discourses, targets as well as speakers of its most virulent rhetoric.

The relationship between women, nation and community is thus highly variable and complicated both in the colonial period and afterwards. The important point is that if on the one hand, questions of women's rights and autonomy complicate any simple celebration of anti-colonialism, nation and liberation, then on the other, these issues also shape approaches to feminism and to the understanding of women's place in society. In 1984, Robin Morgan's anthology *Sisterhood is Global* claimed that women seem, cross-culturally, to be deeply opposed to nationalism. Today, this once-influential view stands challenged by the nature of women's movements in large parts of the once-colonised world which have often emerged and been shaped by the struggles for self-determination, democracy and anti-imperialism, as in the Occupied Territories of the West Bank, Namibia or South Africa. Women had to overcome male opposition to their equal participation in these struggles. Amrita Basu points out that such an association has benefited women more in the case of contemporary nationalist movements than it did in the earlier anti-colonial period. Thus in Namibia (which gained independence in 1990), the constitution forbids sex discrimination, and authorises affirmative action for women, whereas in India (which became free in 1947) the constitution explicitly excludes women from the affirmative action programmes designed for the so-called backward castes and upholds customary law in relation to the family. In the United States, it should be remembered, the Equal Rights Amendment has yet to be ratified (Basu 1995: 14). Women's movements have often been closely aligned with working-class struggles, as in Mexico, Chile and Peru. In Brazil feminism was transformed and expanded by working-class women. At a national feminist conference in 1987, for example, 79 per cent of the participants were also active in black, labour, working-class, church and other political movements, and feminists from autonomous groups were dubbed 'fossils' (Soares *et al*. 1995: 309). It is easy to understand why women in several colonial or neo-colonial situations would identify more readily with anti-imperialist or working-class struggles than with the dominant images or concerns of white First World feminism. As a South African feminist puts it:

> burning one's bra to declare one's liberation as a woman did not connect psychically as did the act of a Buddhist monk who made a human pyre of himself to protest the American occupation of Vietnam. And perhaps that was the point – we were a people under siege. As women we identified with this – the national liberation struggle was our struggle.
>
> (Kemp *et al*. 1995: 138)

Of course, in the process of drawing these distinctions between women's movements, we should be careful not to homogenise either 'First World' or 'Third World' women. In each case, considerations of class, colour, religion, location, sexuality and politics have divided the women's movements and their dominant concerns. If black women within the United States have questioned the politics of white feminism in that country, then independent feminists in India have also made valuable contributions in raising certain issues that neither nationalist nor left-wing women's groups had articulated earlier. If, on the one hand, middle-class white women's movements have not sufficiently addressed questions of class and race, then, on the other hand, nationalist or class-based struggles have historically subordinated questions of women's autonomy or sexuality to supposedly 'larger' concerns.

So it has not been easy for postcolonial women to raise questions of sexuality and sexual orientation. In several countries, including Bangladesh, China, Eastern Europe, Kenya and Nigeria, lesbianism has been rendered invisible (Basu 1995: 13). But in many other places, such as the Philippines, it has become a major issue. In other countries, such as India, there has been an attempt by a wide spectrum of women's organisations to articulate questions of sexual and domestic violence alongside those of secularism, or of equal pay for equal work. Thus the fight against state repression and rape, against racism and patriarchy or for better working conditions and for choice of sexual orientation, cannot be pitted against each other but need to be simultaneously addressed.

However the fact remains that the word 'feminism' and the agendas popularly associated with Western feminism are often viewed with deep scepticism within several postcolonial women's movements. But, both those who are sceptical and those who are not have tried to establish indigenous roots for the women's movement and thus challenge the assumption that women's activism in the postcolonial world is only inspired by its Western counterparts. Such a move has involved re-writing indigenous histories, appropriating pre-colonial symbols and mythologies, and amplifying, where possible, the voices of women themselves. Since, as we have already discussed, colonialism often eroded certain women-friendly traditions, images and institutions, such moves to recover aspects of the pre-colonial past can certainly be extremely useful for feminists. However, there is the obvious danger of glossing over the patriarchal aspects of indigenous cultures, especially as these are constantly being amplified and strengthened, in some cases by postcolonial states and in others by fundamentalist groupings within the state.

While it is impossible to sum up or homogenise the range of concerns that affect women in various post and neo-colonial situations, we may identify certain variable patterns. Today, postcolonial women's movements have to negotiate the dynamics of globalisation on the one hand, and of the postcolonial nation-state on the other. The first often reproduces the general effects of colonialism. Colonialism and imperialism, we have seen, generally entrenched women's subordination. Women's labour was universally expropriated, either directly or indirectly, to feed the colonial machine, and this legacy dovetails with patterns of globalisation to ensure that third world women and women of colour remain the most exploited of the world's workers today. Moreover, such women are the guinea-pigs for fertility and other medical experiments, and the recipients of drugs and contraceptives banned in the West. Thus, if there is a 'Sisyphus stratum' (the phrase is Gloria Joseph's (1995: 147)) which consists of people 'endlessly toiling at the bottom of the socio-economic stratification', then women from once-colonised countries or peoples form a major part of that stratum.

On the other hand, postcolonial women's lives are equally structured by economic and political developments at the more local level. Often there is a declared animosity between the local and the global: thus revivalists and fundamentalists may declare that it is Western or imperialist forces that are responsible for all manner of evil, including women's oppressions. But globalisation has also spawned an international 'women's development' network, linked to non-governmental organisations, international aid-giving bodies and development agencies which tour the world with programmes for women's 'empowerment'. While some of them have certainly helped women from the 'Sisyphus stratum' and have worked alongside governmental or feminist organisations to better women's health, or working conditions, others have worked very much within the colonialist legacy of carrying enlightenment from the West to the rest of the world. In this way, global imbalances profoundly structure feminist agendas in the postcolonial world.

However, the image of the Sisyphus stratum should not lead us to suppose an eternal victim-status for those within it. We will discuss the question of agency at greater length in the next section, but here it is important to note that women have increasingly participated in the full range of postcolonial politics, ranging from the more established forms of political action to the new social movements (such as those for the preservation of the environment). In 1987, one South African feminist predicted: 'I think there will be a different kind of feminism coming out of Africa'. To the extent that postcolonial women's movements have increasingly begun to articulate both the specificity of women's issues and their profound inter-linkage with the community at large, that prediction is certainly coming true.

CAN THE SUBALTERN SPEAK?

To what extent did colonial power succeed in silencing the colonised? When we emphasise the destructive power of colonialism, do we necessarily position colonised people as victims, incapable of answering back? On the other hand, if we suggest that the colonial subjects can 'speak' and question colonial authority, are we romanticising such resistant subjects and underplaying colonial violence? In what voices do the colonised speak – their own, or in accents borrowed from their masters? Is the project of recovering the 'subaltern' best served by locating her separateness from dominant culture, or by highlighting the extent to which she moulded even those processes and cultures which subjugated her? And finally, can the voice of the subaltern be represented by the intellectual? It will be clear by now that such questions are not unique to the study of colonialism but are also crucial for any scholarship concerned with recovering the histories and perspectives of marginalised people – be they women, non-whites, non-Europeans, the lower classes and oppressed castes – and for any consideration of how ideologies work and are transformed. To what extent are we the products of dominant ideologies, and to what extent can we act against them? From where does rebellion arise?

These issues have been centre-stage in postcolonial studies since Said's *Orientalism*. From diverse theoretical perspectives it has been argued that *Orientalism* concentrated too much on imperialist discourses and their positioning of colonial peoples, neglecting the way in which these peoples received, contributed to, modified, or challenged such discourses. Some scholars nevertheless acknowledged that, despite this shortcoming, Said's project inspired or coincided with widespread attempts to write 'histories from below' or 'recover' the experiences of those who have been hitherto 'hidden from history'. The desire to articulate the standpoint of the downtrodden is of course not new – Marxists, feminists, and even liberal historians have all attempted to amplify the voices of sections of the oppressed. Jean Baudrillard remarks that 'the masses' are 'the leitmotif of every discourse, they are the obsession of every social project' which claims to make the oppressed speak (1983: 48–49). Baudrillard himself believes that such projects are doomed, for the masses 'cannot be represented'. Others, who believe they can, differ about how their voices can be articulated. In this section, we will trace some of the debates on this question as it pertains to the colonial subject.

In Homi Bhabha's view, highlighting the formation of colonial subjectivities as a process that is never fully or perfectly achieved helps us in correcting Said's emphasis on domination, and in focusing on the agency of the colonised. Drawing upon both psychoanalytical and post-structuralist notions of subjectivity and language, Homi Bhabha suggests that colonial discourses cannot smoothly 'work', as *Orientalism* might seem to suggest. In the very processes of their delivery, they are diluted and hybridised, so that the fixed identities that colonialism seeks to impose upon both the masters and the slaves are in fact rendered unstable. In discursive terms, there is no neat binary opposition between the coloniser and the colonised, both are caught up in a complex reciprocity and colonial subjects can negotiate the cracks of dominant discourses in a variety of ways. Other critics, however, suggest that it is the post-structuralist, psychoanalytic and deconstructive perspectives within Said's work and that of subsequent postcolonial critics which are to blame for their inability to account for oppositional voices. Where Bhabha posits the process of subject-formation as central to the delineation of agency, for example, Arif Dirlik complains that 'postcolonial criticism has focused on the postcolonial subject to the exclusion of an account of the world outside of the subject' (1994: 336). This is a somewhat unhelpful formulation, because most Marxists and post-structuralists would in fact agree that 'the subject' and the 'world outside the subject' cannot be easily separated. The real differences between them have to do with varying conceptions of the acting colonial or postcolonial subject, and of *the manner* in which the world determines this subject.

As we have discussed earlier, for post-structuralist thinkers, human subjects are not fixed essences, but are discursively constituted. Human identities and subjectivities are shifting and fragmentary. While some critics and historians find that such accounts of subject-formation facilitate our understanding of the possible give-and-take, negotiations and the dynamics of power and resistance of colonial relations, for others such theories of fragmented, unstable identity do not allow us to conceptualise agency, or to define subjects who are the makers of their own history. One widespread critique of postcolonial theory is that it is too pessimistic because it the child of post-modernism, a subject that we will return to shortly. For the moment, let us turn to an influential essay by Gayatri Chakravorty Spivak, from whose title this section derives its heading.

In 'Can the Subaltern Speak?' (1985b), Spivak suggests that it is impossible for us to recover the voice of the 'subaltern' or oppressed subject.[5] Even a radical critic like Foucault, she says, who so thoroughly decentres the human subject, is prone to believing that oppressed subjects can speak for themselves, because he has no conception of the repressive power of colonialism, and especially of the way in which it historically intersected with patriarchy. Spivak turns to colonial debates on widow immolation in India to illustrate her point that the combined workings of colonialism and patriarchy in fact make it extremely difficult for the subaltern (in this case the Indian widow burnt on her husband's pyre) to articulate her point of view. Scholars such as Lata Mani, as mentioned earlier, have shown that in the lengthy debates and discussions that surrounded the British government's legislations against the practice of sati, the women who were burnt on their husband's pyres as satis are absent as subjects. Spivak reads this absence as emblematic of the difficulty of recovering the voice of the oppressed subject and proof that 'there is no space from where the subaltern [sexed] subject can speak'. She thus challenges a simple division between colonisers and colonised by inserting the 'brown woman' as a category oppressed by both. Elite native men may have found a way to 'speak', but, she suggests, for those further down the hierarchy, self-representation was not a possibility.

Spivak's point here is also to challenge the easy assumption that the postcolonial historian can recover the standpoint of the subaltern. At the same time, she takes seriously the desire, on the part of postcolonial intellectuals, to highlight oppression and to provide the perspective of oppressed people. She therefore suggests that such intellectuals adapt the Gramscian maxim – 'pessimism of the intellect, optimism of the will' – by combining a philosophical scepticism about recovering any subaltern agency with a political commitment to making visible the position of the marginalised. Thus it is the intellectual who must 'represent' the subaltern:

> The subaltern cannot speak. There is no virtue in global laundry lists with 'woman' as a pious item. Representation has not withered away. The female intellectual as intellectual has a circumscribed task which she must not disown with a flourish.
>
> (1988: 308)

Spivak effectively warns the postcolonial critic against romanticising and homogenising the subaltern subject. However, her insistence on subaltern 'silence' is problematic if adopted as the definitive statement about colonial relations. Benita Parry finds that Spivak's reading of Jean Rhys's novel *Wide Sargasso Sea*, for example, does not pick up on traces of female agency within that text and in Caribbean cultures generally, and is insensitive to the ways in which 'women inscribed themselves as healers, ascetics, singers of sacred songs, artisans and artists' in colonised societies. Therefore, she accuses Spivak of 'deliberate deafness to the native voice where it *can* be heard' (1987: 39; emphasis added). Parry suggests that such a deafness arises out of Spivak's theory of subaltern silence which attributes 'an absolute power to the hegemonic discourse'. Spivak responds by renewing her earlier warning against what she calls 'a nostalgia for lost origins', or the assumption that native cultures were left intact through colonial rule, and are now easily recoverable: 'the techniques of knowledge and the strategies of power . . . have a history rather longer and broader than our individual benevolence and avowals' (1996: 204).

It is difficult (and in my view unnecessary) to chose *between* these two positions. Parry takes anti-colonial nationalism as emblematic of the native ability to question and counter colonial discourses. But 'natives' are divided by differences of gender, as Spivak so effectively points out, and by those of class, caste and other hierarchies. As we have discussed earlier, anti-colonial nationalism can only be taken as representative of the subaltern voice if we homogenise the category 'subaltern' and simplify enormously our notion of 'speaking'. At the same time, too inflexible a theory of subaltern silence, even if offered in a cautionary spirit, can be detrimental to research on colonial cultures by closing off options even before they have been explored. Spivak's choice of the immolated widow as emblematic of the 'subaltern' is thus significant. Such a figure is in fact the most perfect instance of subaltern silence, since she is a conceptual and social category that comes into being only when the subject dies. The to-be-sati is merely a widow, the sati is by definition a silenced subject. Her silencing points to the oppression of all women in colonial India, but at the same time not all women in colonial India can be collapsed into such a figure. Elsewhere I have suggested that we need to reposition the sati by concentrating not just on the widow who died but also on some of those widows who survived to tell the tale (Loomba 1993). Of course, not all of those who survived told any tales, and colonial as well as indigenous archives are not particularly hospitable to the preservation of the tales that were told. Further, the stories they tell are not straightforward testimonials to female 'agency,' if by agency we mean an oppositional consciousness. For example, in an article called 'The Plight of Hindu Widows as Described by a Widow Herself', written in 1889, the writer describes the misery of a wife following the death of her husband:

> None of her relatives will touch her to take her ornaments off her body. That task is assigned to three women from the barber caste . . . those female fiends literally jump all over her and violently tear all the ornaments from her nose, ears etc. In that rush, the delicate bones of the nose and ear are sometimes broken. Sometimes . . . tufts of hair are also plucked off. . . . At such times grief crashes down on the poor woman from all sides . . . there is nothing in our fate but suffering from birth to death. When our husbands are alive, we are their slaves; when they die, our fate is even worse . . . . Thousands of widows die after a husband's death. But far more have to suffer worse fates throughout their lives if they stay alive. Once, a widow who was a relative of mine died in front of me. She had fallen ill before her husband died. When he died, she was so weak that she could not even be dragged to her husband's cremation. She had a burning fever. Then her mother-in-law dragged her down from the cot onto the ground and ordered

the servant to pour bucketfuls of cold water over her. After some eight hours, she died. But nobody came to see how she was when she was dying of the cold. After she died, however, they started praising her, saying she had died for the love of her husband . . . . If all [such] tales are put together they would make a large book. The British government put a ban on the custom of sati, but as a result of that several women who could have died a cruel but quick death when their husbands died now have to face an agonizingly slow death.

(Tharu and Lalita 1991: 359–363)

Despite the fact that this narrative is written by a woman, a widow and a potential sati, its picture of widows comes closest to the one constructed by colonial records and accounts. The speaker herself does not offer a critique of the practice of sati, but a functionalist explanation of the widow's desire to die. And yet, she herself did *not* die. While her voice is no straightforward testimony to rebellion, it also militates against too absolute a theory of subaltern silence.

Many upper-class women, from whose ranks a majority of satis were drawn, learnt to write and expressed themselves, participated in anti-colonial activities, and, in rare cases, spoke out against British and indigenous patriarchal oppression. Now of course we can argue that such women were usually privileged in terms of class, no matter how oppressed they might have been in other ways. So can they even be thought of as 'subalterns'? And then again, many upper-class women, as we have discussed earlier, offered elaborate justifications for restrictions on female education and freedom. Others adopted Christianity as a platform from which to attack Hindu patriarchy. Their writings, like the fragment quoted above, will only underline the fact that subaltern agency, either at the individual level or at the collective, cannot be idealised as pure opposition to the order it opposes; it works both within that order and displays its own contradictions.

We can usefully turn to debates in feminist theory and historiography where the question of recovering women's consciousness has been fraught with similar problems. Judith Walkowitz rightly points out that:

> Foucault's insight that no one is outside of power has important implications for expressions from the margins. Just because women are excluded from centres of cultural production, they are not left free to invent their texts, as some feminist critics have suggested. They are not 'innocent' just because they are often on the cultural sidelines. They draw on the cultural resources available to them – they make some amendments, they refocus or rewrite them in a different direction – yet they are basically bounded by certain cultural parameters . . . . That individuals do not fully author their texts does not falsify Marx's insight that men (and in parenthesis women) make their own history, albeit under circumstances that they do not fully control or produce. *They are makers as well as users of culture, subjected to the same social and ideological constraints, yet forcefully resisting those same constraints.*
>
> (Walkowitz 1989: 30; emphasis added)

This applies to the 'subaltern' subject under colonialism as well. Scholars of colonial Africa have emphasised the various ways in which Africans 'have always been active in making their histories (not waiting for them to be conjured up by white men)' (Vaughan 1994: 1). 'Active', if we keep Walkowitz's qualifications in mind, does not mean free, and it does not imply either a simple collaboration or a straightforward opposition. Rather, as Ran Greenstein says of some recent studies of the Shaka, 'History is seen as a process that allows alliances across a colonial divide, not a dichotomy between the powerful and the powerless' (1995: 225).

But 'the powerful' and 'the powerless' are not unitary categories.

When black and white people belonging to poor farming communities bonded across racial lines in the first half of this century in South Africa, they simultaneously consolidated class divisions even as they may have strained some racial boundaries. More importantly, when the colonial authorities 'negotiated' with the colonisers, they did so selectively, and in the process often consolidated existing hierarchies. For example, when, in nineteenth-century Punjab, British colonialists consulted the natives as they recorded (and thus codified) local customs, it is possible to conclude that 'the native voice was inscribed within imperial discourse'. However, to the extent that only upper-class men were consulted, we can also see how 'this was a patriarchal voice, the voice of the dominant proprietary body speaking against the rights of non-proprietors, females and lower castes' (Bhattacharya 1996: 47).

It is not the case that only the very lowliest of the low can be understood as 'true' subalterns, worthy of being 'recovered'. At the same time, we should keep in mind that those who, following Gramsci, revived the term in historical studies, did so to draw distinctions *within* colonised peoples, between the elite and the non-elite. But whoever our subalterns are, they are positioned simultaneously within several different discourses of power and of resistance. The relations between coloniser and colonised were, after all, constantly intersected, spliced by many other forms of power relations. This also means that any instance of agency, or act of rebellion, can be truthfully assessed in many different ways. For example, Frederick Cooper (1994) asks us to consider whether African working-class actions in French and British Africa are to be thought of an instance of African militancy, or an example of the universal struggle of the working class, or of the successful co-optation of Africans into Western practices? He reminds us that 'all three readings have some truth, but the important point is their dynamic relationship': labour movements were in creative tension with anti-colonial struggles, as were rural and peasant movements with urban and more Westernised forms of rebellion. Thus individual and collective subjects can be thought of in multiple ways at any given time, and we must keep open the very meanings of subalternity and domination.

This is an important point. Situating the subaltern within a multiplicity of hierarchies is not enough: we must also think about the crucial relations *between* these hierarchies, between different forces and discourses. Because post-modern thinkers (including Foucault) do not consider this interrelation, their work does not help us in the task of recovering the subaltern subject in colonial history. Rosalind O'Hanlon and David Washbrook, for example, contend that 'Derridean and post-modern perspectives' display a 'depthlessness' and make it impossible for us to understand how societies function (1992: 148–153). These historians write in response to Gyan Prakash's essay 'Writing Post-Orientalist Histories of the Third World: Perspectives from Indian Historiography', which has sparked off a wide-ranging discussion about the politics of postcolonial theory by suggesting that histories of marginalised, subaltern subjects can only be written by moving away from a 'post-foundational perspective', i.e. by moving away from the grand narratives which occluded such subjects and their stories. While many critics believe that post-modern ideas of multiplicity and fragmentation make the standpoint of marginalised historical subjects visible, others argue that post-modernism carries these ideas to the extreme so that we cannot understand historical dynamics at all.

It is possible to make the case for a productive synthesis here: we can abandon the grand narratives which once dominated the writing of history without also abandoning all analysis of the *relationships* between different forces in society. To insert gender into our understanding of history, for example, is to move away from class as a 'grand narrative', according to which historical development can be understood as the product of class struggle alone. But gender and class should not be thought of as different elements, a multiplicity of narratives that we can choose between. Their full force is uncovered only by locating their articulation with each other and with other social forces. In fact if we really believe that human subjects are constituted by several different discourses then we are obliged to consider these articulations. Thus, in order to listen for subaltern voices we need to uncover the multiplicity of narratives that were hidden by the grand narratives, but we still need to think about how the former are woven together.

In practice, it has not been easy for critics to maintain a balance between 'positioning' the subject and amplifying her/his voice. Several attempts to write 'histories from below' have come close to essentialising the figure or the community of the resistant subaltern. It is indeed a difficult task to demarcate some sort of autonomy for oppressed people without projecting a timeless culture of subjectivity for such people, to suggest that the subaltern was a 'conscious subject-agent' without reverting to humanist notions of subjectivity. In trying to show how peasant struggles in India were distinct from the elite anti-colonial movements, the subaltern historians, Rosalind O'Hanlon suggests, repeatedly construct an essential peasant identity in India, not fractured by differences of gender, class or location. As a corrective, she cites the work of Fanon, Said and Bhabha on how colonial identities are *constructed* rather than given (1988: 204–205). But at the same time, she is also deeply sceptical about adopting in full measure post-structuralist or post-modern views about identity:

> *Some conception of experience and agency are absolutely required by the dispossessed's call for a politics of contest*, for it is not clear how a dispersed effect of power relations can at the same time be an agent whose experience and reflection form the basis of a striving for change. To argue that we need these categories in some form does not at all imply a return to

undifferentiated and static conceptions of nineteenth-century liberal humanism. Our present challenge lies precisely in understanding how the underclasses we wish to study are at once constructed in conflictual ways as subjects yet also find the means through struggle to realize themselves in coherent and subjectively centred ways as agents.

(O'Hanlon and Washbrook 1992: 153; emphasis added)

This view – that to regard human beings as fragmented discursive constructs is incompatible with understanding them as experiencing agents – is widespread within critics of post-modernism. On this question, Joan Scott's essay on 'Experience' is extremely useful because it argues that experience itself is constructed rather than simply given:

experience works as a foundation providing both a starting point and a conclusive kind of explanation, beyond which few questions need to or can be asked. And yet it is precisely the questions precluded – questions about discourse, difference and subjectivity, as well as about what counts as experience and who gets to make that determination – that would enable us to historicize experience, to reflect critically on the history we write about it, rather than to premise our history upon it.

(1992: 33)

If we are not to take either identity or experience for granted, she writes, we should look at how they are 'ascribed, resisted or embraced'.

Therefore, 'experience' and 'constructedness' need not be thought of as polar opposites. The process of 'acting' is not outside the process by which identities are formed, but equally 'action' and 'consciousness' are not attributes of some static inner force but of our changing selves. Today, there are heated debates between historians of colonialism on how to achieve such a balance. For many,

'colonial discourse theory' has become synonymous with emphasising colonial power, and they sometimes suggest that older historical methodologies were more helpful in uncovering subaltern
agency. For example, Megan Vaughan, whose work on colonial
medicine we have discussed in earlier sections, counterposes oral
histories of Africa against 'colonial discourse theory'. The former
have documented a more interactive version of colonialism: the
way in which Africans participated in the creation of 'custom'
and 'tradition' in colonial Africa, and how colonial discourses and
practices 'were created out of the face-to face encounters of
coloniser and colonised' (Vaughan 1994: 13) whereas the latter is
more concerned with colonial power and hegemony. Thus she pits
a post-modern, Western, pessimistic 'colonial discourse theory'
against older traditions of historical writing, rooted in Africa and
drawing upon oral sources. Oral histories have in fact been an especially important method of assessing Africans' participation in
the formation of both oppressive and oppositional discourses, and
of filling the gaps in written documents and archives. But they
cannot simply reflect the point of view of 'the people', they too
are mediated by the scholar, the historian or the critic. As David
Bunn (1994) rightly points out, one 'cannot attack the excesses of
post-structuralist analysis by smothering it with oral historical
narrative'; oral evidence too 'functions within the domain of narrative' (1994: 31).

Is objectivity possible, or are we merely ventriloquising our
own concerns when we make the subaltern speak? Of course, to
some extent, our investments in the past are inescapably coloured
by our present-day commitments. We are interested in recovering
subaltern voices because we are invested in changing contemporary power relations. Thus, when Baudrillard speaks of the masses
as an implosive force that 'can no longer be spoken for, articulated and represented', Stuart Hall is justified in reading this statement as exemplifying the pessimistic politics of post-modernism.
However, it should not be the case that we begin to measure our

own radicalism mechanically in terms of our ability to find 'resistance' in any given text or historical situation. If I cannot locate the voices of nineteenth-century widows it surely does not mean that I am party to the process of silencing them. Conversely, critics often lay claim to a radical politics by suggesting a radical consciousness on the part of those they study. This often leads to a reductive understanding of 'resistance', which seems to mushroom too easily everywhere. Thus, *our desire* to make the subaltern speak may or may not be gratified by our historical researches.

Finally, what exactly do we mean by 'resistance' or 'speaking'? Often these terms are invoked without any clear understanding of what exactly is being resisted, or what the process of resistance involves. Moreover, the concept of resistance is vaguely and endlessly expanded until, as Frederick Cooper puts it, 'it denies any other kind of life to the people doing the resisting. Significant as resistance might be, Resistance is a concept that may narrow our understanding of African history rather than expand it' (Cooper 1994: 1532). Gayatri Spivak suggests that precisely because the subaltern cannot speak, it is the duty of postcolonial intellectuals to represent her/him. Stuart Hall offers another way of interpreting the supposed passivity of the subalterns: 'in spite of the fact that the popular masses have never been able to become in any complete sense the subject-authors of the cultural practices in the twentieth century', he writes, 'their continuing presence, as a kind of passive historical-cultural force, has constantly interrupted, limited and disrupted everything else' (1996d: 140). Therefore, we can make visible the importance of subalterns to history without necessarily suggesting that they are *agents* of their own histories.

The connections between us and the 'subalterns' we seek to recover exist also in the fact that past histories continue to inform the world we live in. To continue with the example of widow immolation: although cases of sati in modern India are relatively few, the issue has resurfaced in recent years. The politics of this renewal help us in some ways in understanding, and reconfiguring, the dynamics of sati debates in the past, just as colonial politics to some extent are revisited by contemporary ones. To isolate colonialism from its later evolution is to deflect attention from the narratives of nationalism, communalism and religious fundamentalism which are the crucibles within which gender, class, caste, or even neo-colonialism function today. Lata Mani points out that our investments in finding subaltern voices may shift over different locations. Thus she draws a distinction between the way in which her work on the silenced sati resonates within the United States academy, in Britain and in India. Attending to these differences leads her to offer a useful rephrasing of the query with which we began:

> The question 'Can the subaltern speak?' then, is perhaps better posed as a series of questions: Which group constitute the subalterns in any text? What is their relationship to each other? How can they be heard to be speaking or not speaking in any given set of materials? With what effects? Rephrasing the questions in this way enables us to retain Spivak's insight regarding the positioning of women in colonial discourse without conceding to colonial discourse what it, in fact did not achieve – the erasure of women.
>
> (Mani 1992: 403)

POST-MODERNISM AND POSTCOLONIAL STUDIES

At many points in this book we have touched upon the view that postcolonial theory and criticism are inadequate to the task of either understanding or changing our world because they are the children of post-modernism. In this section, we shall consider this problem in the light of recent debates on the politics of postcolonial studies. In an oft-cited essay, Kwame Anthony Appiah pronounced that:

Postcoloniality is the condition of what we might ungenerously call a comprador intellegentsia: a relatively small, Western-style, Western trained group of writers and thinkers, who mediate the trade in cultural commodities of world capitalism at the periphery. In the West they are known through the Africa they offer; their compatriots know them both through the West they present to Africa and through an Africa they have invented for the world, for each other, and for Africa.

(1996: 62–63)

Appiah makes his point by contrasting such Westernised intellectuals with others who live in Africa: whereas postcolonial intellectuals are always at the risk of becoming 'otherness machines, with the manufacture of alterity as our principal role', in Africa itself 'there are those who will not see themselves as other'. Whereas 'postcoloniality' as it pertains to these 'Western-style' intellectuals 'has become . . . a condition of pessimism,' in Africa,

Despite the overwhelming reality of economic decline; despite unimaginable poverty; despite wars, malnutrition, disease, and political instability . . . popular literatures, oral narrative and poetry, dance, drama, music and visual art all thrive. The contemporary cultural production of many African societies, and the many traditions whose evidences so vigorously remain, is an antidote to the dark vision of the postcolonial novelist.

(1996: 69)

Certainly, art and culture may 'thrive' amidst poverty and disease, but does such art and culture necessarily share a common, optimistic 'vision'? Even though they may not agree with this easy generalisation about indigenous cultural production, however, several recent critiques of postcolonial studies reiterate the crux of Appiah's argument about 'postcoloniality'. Arif Dirlik calls 'postcolonialism' a 'child of postmodernism' which is born not out of new perspectives on history and culture but because of 'the increased visibility of academic intellectuals of Third World origin as pacesetters in cultural criticism' (1994: 330). He too argues for the 'First world origins (and situation)' of the term postcoloniality. Similarly, Aijaz Ahmad's work, even though it challenges the ideologies behind the break-up of the globe into First, Second and Third Worlds ('Three-Worlds Theory'), also attributes a post-modern outlook and sensibility to what he calls 'literary postcoloniality', and contrasts this unfavourably with a Marxist radicalism.

Of the various critics who have written in this vein, Dirlik formulates the case against 'postcolonialism' most vehemently: he argues that David Harvey and Frederic Jameson have established an interrelation between post-modernism and late capitalism that can now be extended to postcolonialism. In other words, if postmodernism is, in Jameson's words, the 'cultural logic' of late capitalism, then postcolonialism is also complicit with the latter. Both post-modernists and postcolonialists celebrate and mystify the workings of global capitalism. Even the 'language of postcolonialism . . . is the language of First World post-structuralism'. Therefore, postcolonialism, which appears to critique the universalist pretensions of Western knowledge systems, and 'starts off with a repudiation of the universalistic pretensions of Marxist language ends up not with its dispersal into local vernaculars but with a return to another First World language with universalist epistemological pretensions' (1994: 342). So Dirlik modifies Appiah's critique to suggest that 'Postcoloniality is the condition of the intelligentsia of global capitalism' (1994: 356).

This is a scathing indictment indeed, and at many points it touches several earlier critiques, articulated by intellectuals within as well outside the Western academy, of post-structuralism and post-modernism as Euro-centric philosophies. Ten years ago, for example, Nancy Hartsock pointed out that post-structuralist theories of split and agonistic subjectivity came into vogue just at the moment when marginalised subjects were finding a more powerful collective voice (1987: 160). Is the notion of the decentred subject the latest strategy of Western colonialism? As Denis Epko puts it:

> nothing stops the African from viewing the celebrated post-modern condition . . . as nothing but the hypocritical self-flattering cry of overfed and spoilt children of hypercapitalism. So what has hungry Africa got to do with the post-material disgust . . . of the bored and the overfed?
>
> (1995: 122)

But does hungry Africa or naked India need to resurrect older ideas of the unified humanist subject, or go back to older accounts of human history?

Recently, the debates on these questions have focused upon whether we need a 'world system analysis' or a 'postfoundational understanding' (Dirlik 1994: 306). Is the modern world to be understood as fundamentally capitalist in nature, or should we understand modernity as basically a fragmentary affair? Some critics ask us to place colonialism and postcolonialism within the structuring rubric of capitalism, whereas others point out that such a structure telescoped marginal histories *into* the story of capitalism. But this debate often reproduces reductive versions of both Marxism and post-structuralism or post-modernism, and, as such, retards the possibility of a more nuanced dialogue. For example, critics who persuasively suggest that the post-structuralist critique of a foundational history is useful for uncovering marginalised histories, sometimes go on to make the more dubious claim that to view capitalism as foundational is to become complicit with capitalist development itself. Others, who correctly point out that to regard capitalism as foundational is not necessarily to endorse its ideologies, then sometimes go on to suggest the reverse, an equally simplistic connection between arguing for multiplicities of histories and a celebration of fragmentation as our new reality.

Surely there should be another way of rethinking the relationship between the local and marginalised, on the one hand, and the larger structures in which they are housed, on the other. The narratives of women, colonised peoples, non-Europeans *revise* our understanding of colonialism, capitalism and modernity: these global narratives do not disappear but can now be read differently. We need to move away from global narratives not because they necessarily *always* swallow up complexity, but because they historically have done so, and once we have focused on these submerged stories and perspectives, the entire structure appears transformed. For example, capitalism as it was theorised by classical Marxism was not enough for understanding colonialism. Histories written from anti-colonialist perspectives have re-written the 'story' of capitalist development itself so that the 'grand narrative' of capitalism now appears in a very different light – no longer can it be told as a story scripted entirely in European centres, or as one of peaceful evolution. Instead, we see it a violent narrative in which far flung 'peripheries' played a crucial role. Hence:

> the transition from feudalism to capitalism (which played such a talismanic role in, for example, Western Marxism) [becomes a tale of] . . . the formation of the world market . . . . In this way, the 'postcolonial' marks a critical interruption into that whole grand historiographical narrative which, in liberal historiography and Weberian historical sociology, as much as in the dominant traditions of Western Marxism, gave this global dimension a subordinate presence in a story which could essentially be told from within its European parameters.
>
> (Hall 1996a: 250)

Having said that, we cannot *abandon* thinking about capitalism altogether. How can one work out the articulations between the various local narratives of our world without also paying serious attention to the operations of global capitalism today? Dirlik correctly points out that postcolonial criticism has not seriously considered the way in which postcoloniality today is necessarily shaped by the operations of capitalism – both the way in which capitalism globalises, drawing various local cultures and economies into its vortex, and how it weakens older boundaries and decentres production and consumption. Actually, this problem is not unique at all – feminist critiques of Marxist economism were also in some danger of privileging cultural analysis. To ignore the economic dimension of the global order is to construct what Dirlik calls a 'shapeless' world which is all more or less postcolonial:

> Postcolonial critics have . . . had little to say about . . . contemporary figurations. . . . They have rendered into problems of subjectivity and epistemology concrete and material problems of the everyday world. While capital in its motions continues to structure the world, refusing it foundational status renders impossible the cognitive mapping that must be the point of departure for any practice of resistance . . . .
>
> (1994: 356)

The ways in which global capitalism might be re-configuring postcolonial relations are thus obscured, says Dirlik, by postcolonial critics. Whether, this neglect is due to the disciplinary training and affiliations of postcolonial critics or their political/philosophical orientation, there is no doubt that neither local nor global cultures, neither nation nor hybridity can be thought about seriously without considering how they are shaped by economic systems. However, it is more debatable whether such a neglect makes postcolonial critics agents of global capital!

Finally, it may be helpful to rethink the term post-modernism itself. Stuart Hall helpfully points out that 'post-modernism' does not signify a completely new epoch or absolute rupture with the modern era. It is 'the current name we give to how several old certainties began to run into trouble from about 1900s onwards' . But certain post-modernist thinkers suggest that it is 'a kind of final rupture or break with the modern era'. This gesture, this attempt to *fix* a dynamic history into something called the postmodern condition is what causes a problem:

> What this says is: this is the end of the world. History stops with us and there is no place to go after this. But whenever it is said that *this* is the last thing that will ever happen in history, that is the sign of the functioning, in the narrow sense, of the ideological – what Marx called 'the eternalizing effect'. Since most of the world has not yet properly entered the modern era, who is it who 'has no future left'?
>
> (1996d: 134)

Elsewhere Hall pleads for more discrimination between different kinds of post-modern critics: some of them '*may* believe that the global has fragmented into the local but most of the serious ones argue that what is happening is a mutual reorganization of the local and the global, a very different proposition' (1996a: 257). In other words, we need to distinguish between thinkers who adopt postmodernism as a philosophical creed, and others who signal the need for new tools to understand the contemporary world.

So also, the local and the global need not be thought of as mutually exclusive perspectives, but as aspects of the same reality which help reposition each other in more nuanced ways. Peter Hulme sensibly points out another reason for moving away from grand narratives,

> not because the age of grand narratives has been left behind

on epistemological grounds, but rather that the grand narrative of decolonisation has, for the moment, been adequately told and widely accepted. Smaller narratives are now needed, with attention paid to local topography, so that maps can become fuller.

(1994: 71–72)

We need to consider the utility of both Marxist as well as post-structuralist perspectives for thinking about colonialism and its aftermath. As Annamaria Carusi cautions,

while the usefulness of Marxist strategies for opposition movements should not be minimized, their terms need to be looked at more closely ... [the] critique of humanism (and economism, one might add) cannot simply be brushed away; one cannot continue as though it had never been.

(1989: 88)

I will suggest that above all, we should not homogenise either position. While minority intellectuals and feminists have felt affinities with post-structuralists, there have also been sharp debates *between* them. Feminists of different persuasions have been sceptical about post-modernism, which is not to say that there have not been overlaps and dialogue between feminist and post-structuralist questioning of dominant narratives. But at least some feminists have suggested that they did not simply follow in post-structuralism's wake, but pioneered certain alternative ways in thinking about history, language and subjectivity which were subsequently made fashionable in a different way by academic post-structuralism (Newton 1989). In fact, considerations of gender are either entirely left out or minimised as the battlelines are drawn today between post-modernism and Marxism, or between postcolonial intellectuals inside and outside the Western academy. For feminists, but also for others, the sweeping divide between a 'Third World Marxism' and a 'First World' post-modernism, as suggested by writers like Ahmad, is extremely problematic. Feminist politics in the third world ranges across a large spectrum, but it has always had to negotiate a complex relationship with Marxist struggles at home, as well as with women's movements and writing in the West. Their affinities and disagreements thus do not follow either the neat division between good Marxists and bad post-structuralists that has been suggested by recent critiques of postcolonial theory, or the reverse binary of bad Marxists and good post-structuralists that has also circulated for a while within postcolonial studies.

However, is it possible to simply pick and choose between theoretical perspectives? Gyan Prakash suggests that the Subaltern Studies project 'derives its force as postcolonial criticism from a catachrestic combination of Marxism, post-structuralism, Gramsci and Foucault, the modern West and India, archival research and textual criticism' (1994: 1490). Prakash's use of the term 'catachresis' derives from Gayatri Spivak, who uses it to suggest transformation. Thus, he implies, when the subaltern historians combine these different perspectives, they also transform each of them. There is a long-standing debate, outside of postcolonial criticism as such, whether Marxism and deconstruction are philosophically compatible. Said's *Orientalism* has also been subject to a similar charge of trying to combine Foucaultian and Derridean methods and Gramscian dedication to social change. Some critics liken trying to combine Marxist and post-structuralist insights to trying to ride two horses at the same time (O'Hanlon and Washbrook 1992). Others reply that methodological purity can only be achieved by sweeping marginalised narratives and perspectives once again under the carpet of class and capitalism: instead, as Prakash suggests, 'let us hang on to two horses, inconstantly' (1992: 184). Other writers have also persuasively asserted the value of negotiating the 'fertile tensions' between different theoretical approaches and the necessity of postcolonial critics and historians becoming what one historian calls 'stunt riders' (Mallon 1994: 1515).

Within the literary academy, we often see a too-easy pluralism, where all theories are regarded as equally and unproblematically available for the scholar. However, Mallon's term, 'fertile tensions', does not simply ignore the possible contradictions between a Gramscian project committed to uncovering the agency of colonised people and a more Foucaultian assessment of the way in which individuals are positioned in oppressive structures, but also recognises that postcolonial studies demand theoretical flexibility and innovation. This is a tall order, but if postcolonial studies demands both a revision of the past, and an analysis of our fast-changing present, then we cannot work with closed paradigms.

CONCLUSION

In an influential article, Dipesh Chakrabarty suggests that

> insofar as the academic discourse of history – that is 'history'
> as a discourse produced at the institutional site of the univer-
> sity is concerned, 'Europe' remains the sovereign, theoretical
> subject of all histories, including the ones we call 'Indian',
> 'Chinese', 'Kenyan' and so on . . . . Third-world historians feel a
> need to refer to works in European history, historians of
> Europe do not feel any need to reciprocate . . . . The everyday
> paradox of third-world social science is that we find these theo-
> ries, in spite of their inherent ignorance of 'us' eminently use-
> ful in understanding our societies. What allowed the modern
> European sages to develop such clairvoyance with regard to
> societies of which they were empirically ignorant? Why cannot
> we, once again, return the gaze?
>
> (1992: 1–3)

Chakrabarty's declared project is to return the gaze by 'provin-
cializing Europe' although he is doubtful that the problem of 'asym-
metric ignorance' can be made to vanish simply by analysing it.
He points out that the very categories employed in the writing of
most third world histories are borrowed from Europe, and that the

institutions within which 'history' as a discipline is produced and taught are deeply Euro-centric. Many critics, located both within the Western academy and in diverse 'postcolonial' locations, have suggested that postcolonial studies are caught in the horns of a similar dilemma: they remain curiously Euro-centric, dependent upon Western philosophies and modes of seeing, taught largely in the Western academy, unable to reject convincingly European frames of reference, and guilty of telescoping the complexity of diverse parts of the world into 'the colonial question'. This is partly why the question of the postcolonial critic's location and political affiliations has become a contentious, often bitterly fraught issue in recent years. Are academics located in the West, or working with Western conceptual and narrative paradigms, incapable of opening up the perspectives within which we can view the non-Western world? Or have they adopted reactive perspectives which lock them into a reductive position whereby they can return the colonial gaze only by mimicking its ideological imperatives and intellectual procedures?

For Chakrabarty, within the discipline of 'history', 'the project of provincialising Europe must realise within itself its own impossibility' since the subject is, both philosophically and in institutional terms, inextricably bound to its European cradle. Postcolonial studies is not a discipline in the same way as history is, but it too inherits the burden of a Euro-centric past, even as so much of its energy and revisionist power is derived from its provenance within anti-colonial and progressive political movements. This energy is enhanced when postcolonial studies keeps in mind or addresses directly neo-colonial imbalances in the contemporary world order. These imbalances, as Dirlik and others allege, have in fact not been engaged with enough by postcolonial critics who grapple with the shades of the colonial past much more than with the difficulties of the postcolonial present. If postcolonial studies is to survive in any meaningful way, it needs to absorb itself far more deeply with the contemporary world, and with the local circumstances within which colonial institutions and ideas are being moulded into the disparate cultural and socio-economic practices which define our contemporary 'globality'. This globality is often reduced to discussions of literatures written or translated into English, reminding us that in many ways postcolonial studies is simply a reworking of the older concepts of 'Commonwealth literatures' or 'Third World literatures'. But even these literatures cannot be adequately discussed outside of the difficult interplay between their local and global contexts, an awareness that is all too often erased as we celebrate the hybridity or polyphony or magic realism of these texts!

Even if postcolonial critics sometimes forget the links between the recasting of third world cultures and the spread of consumer capitalism, the *New York Times* does not: in recent essays on the 'liberalised' India this newspaper suggests that the increasing flood of Western commodities in the 'third world' markets and the desires of local middle-class consumers for these goods should be seen as a giant step towards a more democratic globe. And often globalisation is celebrated as the producer of a new and 'liberating' hybridity or multiculturalism, terms that now circulate to ratify the mish-mash of cultures generated by the near unipolar domination of the Western, particularly United States, media machine. In this situation, it is even more important for us to think about the relation of culture to economic and political structures, as also to remind ourselves that the 'provincialising' of Europe cannot be the work of intellectuals alone. This does not mean that we should simply undermine the importance of academic and intellectual work, or, as is often the case, all too easily counterpose it to something that is vaguely but powerfully invoked as 'the political'. Ran Greenstein points out that often 'histories from below' are usually 'written from above' – a reminder of the enormous distance between subalterns and intellectuals. But he also reminds us that in recent years the 'insurrection of subjugated voices in the fields of feminism, black, gay, and postcolonial studies has been led by members of marginalized groups . . . and the creation of new scholarly fields was implicated in fierce struggles over control of academic boundaries' (1995: 231). These have been large and valuable gains, and they serve to remind us that, as students and academics, we should at the very least place our discussions of postcoloniality in the context of our own educational institutions and practices. Such institutional critiques will inevitably demand an awareness of the relationships between First and Third World academies, and will re-emphasise the fact that these relationships are not separate from the inequities which contour our newly 'globalised' world. Out of such empirical specificity might emerge the hindsight that returns the colonial gaze by diagnosing its occlusions and mystifications, as also the look away, the clairvoyance, the vision more focused on, more true to, our own developing histories and possibilities.

Notes

INTRODUCTION

1   Robbins is quoted by Barker, Hulme and Iverson (1994: 11) and their discussion of these issues is useful.

CHAPTER 1

1   For a fascinating account of how Afrikaner nationalism constructed its difference with Western capitalism as well as communism see Nixon 1994.
2   Eagleton (1991) and Hawkes (1996) provide useful general introductions to ideology.
3   All references to Shakespeare's plays are from *The Riverside Shakespeare*. Marx and Engels (1976: 230–231).
4   Stuart Hall rightly points out that Althusser's cryptic and condensed formulation 'Disappear; the term ideas' leads to such a conflation (Hall 1985: 100).
5   For an excellent introduction to these see Belsey (1980).
6   He was delivering the V. Krishna Memorial Lecture on 'Literature and Politics' at Miranda House College on 19 February 1996.
7   Jenny Sharpe (1993) uses the term 'colonial text' as a subtitle of her book. For a perceptive analysis of rumour see Shahid Amin's discussion of the construction of Gandhi as 'Mahatma' or a 'great soul' among the peasantry (1988).

CHAPTER 2

1   In this section, I am indebted to Stuart Hall (1980), John Rex (1980) and Robert Miles(1989).
2   Melanie Klein and Karen Horney initiated the debate on Freud's phallocentricism. The feminist debate on psychoanlysis is extensive. Useful starting points are Mitchell (1974), Feldstein and Roof (1989) and Rose (1986).

CHAPTER 3

1   The phrase is Timothy Brennan's (1990: 47). Hutchinson and Smith (1994), and Bhabha (1990) are useful collections of current writings on the nation.
2   Giddens (1994: 182). Giddens is quoting Daniel Bell, 'The World and the United States in 2013', *Deadalus*, (1987: 116).
3   Warner (1987) discusses the iconography of the female form, although she never ventures outside Europe in her study.
4   See Leila Ahmed (1992); Mernissi (1987); el Saadawi (1986); Azar Tabari and Nahid Yahgeneh (1983).
5   There are several versions of this essay: Spivak (1988) and (1985a). See also Spivak (1987) for further discussion of colonial archives and the recovery of the colonial subject.

BIBLIOGRAPHY

Achebe, C. (1975) *Morning Yet on Creation Day*, New York: Anchor Press/Doubleday.

—— (1989) 'An Image of Africa, Racism in Conrad's *Heart of Darkness*', in *Hopes and Impediments, Selected Essays*, New York: Doubleday/Anchor Press, pp. 269–274.

Adas, M. (1989) *Machines as the Measure of Men*, Ithaca, NY: Cornell University Press.

Africanus, L. (1905) 'Navigations, Voyages, and Land-Discoveries, with other Historical Relations of Afrike . . . taken out of John Leo', in S. Purchas (ed.), *Hakluytus Posthumus*, vol. 5, Glasgow: James Maclehose and Sons, pp. 307–529.

Ahmad, A. (1992) *In Theory, Classes, Nations, Literatures*, London: Verso.

—— (1987) 'Jameson's Rhetoric of Otherness and the "National Allegory"', *Social Text* 17, Fall, pp. 3–25.

Ahmed, L. (1992) *Women and Gender in Islam, Historical Roots of a Modern Debate*, New Haven, CT: Yale University Press.

Althusser, L. (1971) *Lenin and Philosophy and Other Essays*, trans. B. Brewster, New York: Monthly Review Press.

Alva, J.J.K. de (1995) 'The Postcolonization of the (Latin) American Experience, A Reconsideration of "Colonialism", "Postcolonialism" and "Mestizaje"', in G. Prakash (ed.), *After Colonialism, Imperial Histories and Postcolonial Displacements*, Princeton, NJ: Princeton University Press, pp. 241–275.

Amin, S. (1988) 'Gandhi as Mahatma, Gorakhpur District, Eastern UP, 1921–2', in *Selected Subaltern Studies*, Delhi: Oxford University Press, pp. 288–346.

—— (1995) *Event, Metaphor, Memory, Chauri Chaura 1922–1992*, Delhi: Oxford University Press.

Anderson, B. (1991) *Imagined Communities: Reflections on the Origin and Spread of Nationalism*, London and New York: Verso.

Appiah, K.A. (1991) 'Out of Africa, Topologies of Nativism', in D. LaCapra (ed.), *The Bounds of Race, Perspectives on Hegemony and Resistance*, Ithaca, NY and London: Cornell University Press, pp. 134–163.

—— (1996) 'Is the Post in Postmodernism the Post in Postcolonialism?', in P. Mongia (ed.), *Contemporary Postcolonial Theory: A Reader*, London: Arnold.

Arnold, D. (1993) *Colonizing the Body: State Medicine and Epidemic*

Disease in Nineteenth-century India, Berkeley, CA: University of California Press.

—— (1994) 'Public Health and Public Power: Medicine and Hegemony in Colonial India', in D. Engels and S. Marks (eds), *Contesting Colonial Hegemony*, London and New York: British Academic Press, pp. 131–151.

Arunima, G. (1996) 'Multiple Meanings: Changing Conceptions of Matrilineal Kinship, in Nineteenth- and Twentieth-century Malabar', *The Indian Economic and Social History Review* 33 (3): pp. 283–307.

Ashcroft, B., Griffiths, G. and Tiffin, H. (eds) (1995) *The Post-colonial Studies Reader*, London and New York: Routledge.

Baldick, C. (1983) *The Social Mission of English Criticism*, Oxford: Clarendon Press.

Balibar, E. (1991) 'Racism and Nationalism', in E. Balibar and I. Wallerstein, *Race, Nation, Class*, London and New York: Verso.

Banerjee, S. (1989) 'Marginalization of Women's Popular Culture in Nineteenth Century Bengal', in K. Sangari and S. Vaid (eds), *Recasting Women: Essays in Colonial History*, New Delhi: Kali for Women, pp. 127–179.

Barker, F., Hulme, P. and Iversen, M. (eds) (1994) *Colonial Discourse/Postcolonial Theory*, Manchester and New York: Manchester University Press.

Barrell, J. (1991) *The Infection of Thomas De Quincey: A Psychopathology of Imperialism*, New Haven, CT and London: Yale University Press.

Basu, A. (ed.) (1995) *Women's Movements in Global Perspective*, Boulder, CO: Westview Press.

Baudrillard, J. (1983) *In the Shadow of the Silent Majorities . . . or the End of the Social and Other Essays*, trans. P. Foss, P. Patton and J. Johnston, New York: Semiotext(e).

Behn, A. (1986) *Oroonoko and other Stories*, M. Duffy (ed.), London: Methuen.

Belsey, C. (1980) *Critical Practice*, London: Methuen.

Berger, J. (1972) *Ways of Seeing*, London: BBC and Penguin Books.

Bergner, G. (1995) 'Who is that Masked Woman? or The Role of Gender in Fanon's *Black Skin, White Masks*', *PMLA* 110 (1), January: pp. 75–88.

Bernal, M. (1987) *Black Athena: The Afroasiatic Roots of Classical Civilization*, New Brunswick, NJ: Rutgers University Press.

Bhabha, H.K. (1983) 'Difference, Discrimination, and the Discourse of Colonialism', in F. Barker, P. Hulme, M. Iversen and D. Loxley (eds),

The Politics of Theory, Colchester: University of Essex Press, pp. 194–211.

—— (1984) 'Of Mimicry and Man: The Ambivalence of Colonial Discourse', *October* 28 Spring: pp. 125–133.

—— (1985) 'Signs Taken for Wonders: Questions of Ambivalence and Authority under a Tree Outside Delhi, May 1817', *Critical Inquiry* 12 (1), Autumn: pp. 144–165.

—— (ed.) (1990) *Nation and Narration*, London and New York: Routledge.

—— (1994) 'Remembering Fanon: Self, Psyche and the Colonial Condition', in P. Williams and L. Chrisman (eds), *Colonial Discourse and Postcolonial Theory*, New York: Columbia University Press, pp. 112–123.

Bhattacharya, N. (1996) 'Remaking Custom, the Discourse and Practice of Colonial Codification', in R. Champakalakshmi and S. Gopal (eds), *Tradition, Dissent and Ideology*, New Delhi: Oxford University Press.

Bishop, A.J. (1990) 'Western Mathematics: The Secret Weapon of Cultural Imperialism', *Race and Class* 32 (2): 51–65.

Bottomore, T. (ed.) (1983) *A Dictionary of Marxist Thought*, Oxford: Basil Blackwell.

Boehmer, E. (1995) *Colonial and Postcolonial Literature*, Oxford and New York: Oxford University Press.

Boone, J.A. (1995) 'Vacation Cruises; or, The Homoerotics of Orientalism', *PMLA* 110 (1), pp. January: pp. 89–107.

Bozzoli, B. and Delius, P. (1990) 'Radical History and South African Society', *Radical History Review* 46/47: pp. 13–45.

Brennan, T. (1990) 'The National Longing for Form', in H.K. Bhabha (ed.), *Nation and Narration*, London and New York: Routledge, pp. 44–70.

Brontë, C. (1981) *Jane Eyre*, London: Zodiac Press.

Brotherstone, G. (1986) 'A Controversial Guide to the Language of America, 1643', in F. Barker, P. Hulme, D. Loxley and M. Iverson (eds), *Literature, Politics and Theory*, London and New York: Routledge, pp. 84–100.

Bunn, D. (1994) 'The Insistence of Theory', *Social Dynamics* 20 (2): pp. 24–34.

Burton, A.M. (1992) 'The White Woman's Burden, British Feminists and "The Indian Woman", 1865–1915', in N. Chaudhuri and M. Strobel (eds), *Western Women and Imperialism*, Bloomington, IN: Indiana University Press, pp. 137–157.

Cabral, A. (1994) 'National Liberation and Culture', in P. Williams and
L. Chrisman (eds), *Colonial Discourse and Postcolonial Theory: A Reader*, New York: Columbia University Press, pp. 53–65.

Carby, H. (1982) 'White Woman Listen! Black Feminism and the Boundaries of Sisterhood, in, *The Empire Strikes Back: Race and Racism in 70s Britain* (Centre for Contemporary Cultural Studies), London: Hutchinson.

Carr, H. (1985) 'Woman/Indian, the "American" and his Others', in F. Barker, P. Hulme, M. Iversen and D. Loxley (eds), *Europe and Its Others*, vol. 2, Colchester: University of Essex Press.

Carusi, A. (1989) 'Post, Post and Post. Or, Where is South African Literature in All This?', *Ariel* 2014, October.

Césaire, A. (1950) *Discourse on Colonialism*, New York and London: Monthly Review Press, 1972.

Chakrabarty, D. (1992) 'Postcoloniality and the Artifice of History, Who Speaks for "Indian" Pasts?', *Representations* 37 Winter: pp. 1–24.

Chatterjee, P. (1986) *Nationalist Thought and the Colonial World: A Derivative Discourse?*, London: Zed Books.

—— (1989) 'The Nationalist Resolution of the Women's Question', in K. Sangari and S. Vaid (eds), *Recasting Women: Essays in Colonial History*, New Delhi: Kali for Women, pp. 233–253.

—— (1993) *The Nations and Its Fragments: Colonial and Postcolonial Histories*, Princeton, NJ: Princeton University Press.

Chew, S. (1937) *The Crescent and the Rose: Islam and England During the Renaissance*, New York: Oxford University Press.

Chrisman, L. (1994) 'The Imperial Unconscious? Representations of Imperial Discourse', in P. Williams and L. Chrisman (eds), *Colonial Discourse and Postcolonial Theory: A Reader*, New York: Columbia University Press, pp. 498–516.

Christian, B. (1990) 'The Race for Theory', in A. JanMohamed and D. Lloyd (eds), *The Nature and Context of Minority Discourse*, New York and Oxford: Oxford University Press, pp. 37–49.

Collits, T. (1994) 'Theorizing Racism', in C. Tiffin and A. Lawson (eds), *Describing Empire, Postcolonialism and Textuality*, London and New York: Routledge, pp. 61–69.

Conrad, J. (1975) *Heart of Darkness*, Harmondsworth: Penguin.

Cooper, F. (1994) 'Conflict and Connection: Rethinking Colonial African History', *American Historical Review* 99 (5), December: pp. 1516–1545.

Cooppan, V. (1996) 'Inner Territories: Postcoloniality and the Legacies of Psychoanalysis', Ph.D. Dissertation, Stanford University.

Cowhig, R. (1985) 'Blacks in English Renaissance Drama and the Role of Shakespeare's *Othello*', in D. Dabydeen (ed.), *The Black Presence in English Literature*, Manchester: Manchester University Press, pp. 1–25.

Crawford, R. (1992) 'The Scottish Invention of English Literature', in *Devolving English Literature*, Oxford: Clarendon Press.

Davis, A.Y. (1982) *Women, Race and Class*, London: Women's Press.

Davis, N.Z. (1965) *Society and Culture in Early Modern France*, Stanford, CA: Stanford University Press.

Deleuze, G. and Guattari, F. (1977) *Anti-Oedipus, Capitalism and Schizophrenia*, trans. R. Hurley, H.R. Lane and M. Seem, New York: Viking Press.

Derrida, J. (1994) 'Structure, Sign and Play in the Discourse of the Human Sciences', in D. Keesey (ed.), *Contexts for Criticism*, Mountain View, CA: Mayfield, pp. 347–358.

Dirks, N. (1992) 'Introduction, Colonialism and Culture', in N. Dirks (ed.), *Colonialism and Culture*, Ann Arbor, MI: University of Michigan Press.

Dirlik, A. (1994) 'The Postcolonial Aura: Third World Criticism in the Age of Global Capitalism', *Critical Inquiry* 20 (2), Winter: pp. 328–356.

Donne, J. (1985) *The Complete English Poems of John Donne*, C.A. Patrides (ed.), London and Melbourne: Dent.

Dubow, S. (1993) 'Wulf Sachs's Black Hamlet: A Case of Psychic Vivisection?', *African Affairs* 92: pp. 519–556.

Eagleton, T. (1991) *Ideology: An Introduction*, London and New York: Verso.

—— (1994) 'Goodbye to the Enlightenment', *The Guardian*, 5 May.

Elliot, G. (1996) 'Ideology', in M. Payne (ed.), *A Dictionary of Cultural and Critical Theory*, Oxford and Cambridge, MA: Blackwell, pp. 252–257.

Engels, D. and Marks, S. (eds) (1994) *Contesting Colonial Hegemony: State and Society in Africa and India*, London and New York: British Academic Press.

Epko, D. (1995) 'Towards a Post-Africanism', *Textual Practice* 9 (1), Spring: pp. 121–135.

Fanon, F. (1963) *The Wretched of the Earth*, trans. C. Farrington, New York: Grove Press.

—— (1965) *A Dying Colonialism*, trans. H. Chevalier, New York: Grove Press.

—— (1967) *Black Skin, White Masks*, trans. C.L. Markmann, New York: Grove Press.

Feldstein, R. and Roof, J. (eds) (1989) *Feminism and Psychoanalysis*, Ithaca, NY: Cornell University Press.

Ferguson, M. (1991) 'Juggling the Categories of Race, Class and Gender, Aphra Behn's *Oroonoko*', *Women's Studies* 19: pp. 159–181.

Fieldhouse, D.K. (1989) *The Colonial Empires*, London: Macmillan.

Fields, B. (1982) 'Ideology and Race in American History', in J.M. Kousser and J.M. McPherson (eds), *Region, Race and Reconstruction*, New York: Oxford University Press.

Fisher, J. (1993) *Out of the Shadows: Women, Resistance and Politics in South America*, London: Latin America Bureau.

Foucault, M. (1970) *The Order of Things: An Archeology of the Human Sciences*, trans. A. Sheridan-Smith, New York: Pantheon Books.

—— (1990) *The History of Sexuality*, trans. R. Hurley, New York: Vintage Books.

Frank, A.G. (1969) *Capitalism and Underdevelopment in Latin America*, New York: Monthly Review Press.

Frankenburg, R. and Mani, L. (1996) 'Crosscurrents, Crosstalk, Race, "Postcoloniality" and the Politics of Location', in P. Mongia (ed.), *Contemporary Postcolonial Theory: A Reader*, London: Arnold, pp. 347–364.

Freud, S. (1947) *The Question of Lay Analysis*, trans. N. Proctor-Gregg, London: Imago Publishing Company.

—— (1953) 'Three Essays on the Theory of Sexuality', in James Strachey (ed.), *The Complete Psychological Works of Sigmund Freud*, vol. VII, London: The Hogarth Press.

Friel, B. (1984) *Translations*, in *Selected Plays*, London: Faber and Faber.

Fryer, P. (1984) *Staying Power: The History of Black People in Britain*, London: Pluto Press.

Gates, H.L. Jr (1991) 'Critical Fanonism', *Critical Inquiry* 17, Spring: 457–470.

—— (1994) *The New Republic*, 31 October.

Gibbons, L. (1991) 'Race Against Time, Racial Discourse and Irish History', *Oxford Literary Review* 13 (1–2): pp. 95–117.

Giddens, A. (1994) 'From *The Consequences of Modernity*', in P. Williams and L. Chrisman (eds), *Colonial Discourse and Postcolonial Theory: A Reader*, New York: Columbia University Press, pp. 181–189.

Gillies, J. (1994) *Shakespeare and the Geography of Difference*, Cambridge: Cambridge University Press.

Gilman, S. (1985a) 'Black Bodies, White Bodies, Towards an Iconography of Female Sexuality in Late Nineteenth-Century Art, Medicine and Literature', in H.L. Gates, Jr (ed.), *Race, Writing and Difference*, Chicago, IL: Chicago University Press, pp. 223–261.

—— (1985b) *Difference and Pathology: Stereotypes of Sexuality, Race and Madness*, Ithaca, NY and London: Cornell University Press.

—— (1993) *Freud, Race and Gender*, Princeton, NJ: Princeton University Press.

Gilroy, P. (1993) *The Black Atlantic: Modernity and Double Consciousness*, Cambridge, MA: Harvard University Press.

—— (1994) 'Urban Social Movements, "Race" and Community', in P. Williams and L. Chrisman (eds), *Colonial Discourse and Postcolonial Theory*, New York: Columbia University Press, pp. 404–420.

Gould, S.J. (1996) *The Mismeasure of Man*, New York: Norton.

Gramsci, A. (1971) *Selections from the Prison Notebooks*, Q. Hoare and G.N. Smith (eds), London: Lawrence and Wishart.

Greenblatt, S. (1991) *Marvelous Possessions: The Wonder of the New World*, Chicago, IL: University of Chicago Press.

Greenstein, R. (1995) 'History and the Production of Knowledge', *South African Historical Journal* 32, May: pp. 217–232.

Grove, R.H. (1995) *Green Imperialism: Colonial Expansion, Tropical Island Edens and the Origins of Environmentalism 1600–1860*, Cambridge: Cambridge University Press.

Guha, R. (1982) 'On Some Aspects of the Historiography of Colonial India', in R. Guha (ed.) *Subaltern Studies*, vol. I, New Delhi: Oxford University Press, pp. 1–8.

Habib, I. (1990) 'Merchant Communities in Pre-colonial India', in J.D. Tracy (ed.), *The Rise of Merchant Empires*, Cambridge: Cambridge University Press, pp. 371–399.

Hall, K. (1995) *Things of Darkness, Economies of Race and Gender in Early Modern England*, Ithaca, NY and London: Cornell University Press.

Hall, S. (1980) 'Race, Articulation and Societies Structured in Dominance', in *Sociological Theories, Race and Colonialism*, Paris: Unesco, pp. 305–345.

—— (1985) 'Signification, Representation, Ideology: Althusser and the Post-Structuralist Debates', *Critical Studies in Mass Communication* 2 (2), June: pp. 91–114.

—— (1994) 'Cultural Identity and Diaspora', in P. Williams and L.

Chrisman (eds), *Colonial Discourse and Postcolonial Theory*, New York: Columbia University Press, pp. 392–403.

—— (1996a) 'When Was "the Post-colonial"? Thinking at the Limit', in I. Chambers and L. Curti (eds), *The Post-colonial Question, Common Skies, Divided Horizons*, London and New York: Routledge, pp. 242–259.

—— (1996b) 'Gramsci's Relevance for the Study of Race and Ethnicity', in D. Morley and K.H. Chen (eds), *Stuart Hall, Critical Dialogues in Cultural Studies*, London and New York: Routledge, pp. 411–440.

—— (1996c) 'New Ethnicities', in D. Morley and K.H. Chen (eds), *Stuart Hall, Critical Dialogues in Cultural Studies*, London and New York: Routledge, pp. 441–449.

——(1996d) 'On Postmodernism and Articulation' (interview with Stuart Hall), in D. Morley and K.H. Chen (eds), *Stuart Hall, Critical Dialogues in Cultural Studies*, London and New York: Routledge, pp. 131–150.

Hall, S., Critcher, C., Jefferson, T., Clarke, J. and Roberts, B. (1978) *Policing the Crisis, Mugging, the State, Law and Order*, London: Macmillan.

Hardayal, L. (1934) *Hints for Self-Culture*, Dehradun: Current Events.

Harding, S. (1986) *The Science Question in Feminism*, Ithaca, NY: Cornell University Press.

Harley, B. (1988) 'Maps, Knowledge and Power', in D. Cosgrove and S. Daniels (eds), *The Iconography of Landscape*, Cambridge: Cambridge University Press, pp. 277–312.

Hartsock, N. (1987) 'Rethinking Modernism, Majority versus Minority Theories', *Cultural Critique* 7: pp. 187–206.

—— (1990) 'Foucault on Power: A Theory for Women?', in L.J. Nicholson (ed.), *Feminism/Postmodernism*, New York and London: Routledge.

Hawkes, D. (1996) *Ideology*, London and New York: Routledge.

Head, R. (1666) *The English Rogue*, part III, London.

Hitchcott, N. (1993) 'African Oedipus?', *Paragraph* 16 (1): pp. 59–66.

Hobsbawm, E. and Ranger, T. (1983) *The Invention of Tradition*, Cambridge and New York: Cambridge University Press.

Hofmeyr, I. (1987) 'Building a Nation from Words: Afrikaans Language, Literature and Ethnic Identity, 1902–1924', in S. Marks and S. Trapido (eds), *The Politics of Race, Class and Nationalism in the Twentieth-century South Africa*, London and New York: Longman, pp. 95–123.

Hulme, P. (1985) 'Polytropic Man: Tropes of Sexuality and Mobility in Early

Colonial Discourse', in F. Barker, P. Hulme, M. Iversen and D. Loxley (eds), *Europe and its Others*, vol. 2, Colchester: University of Essex Press, pp. 17–32.

—— (1986a) *Colonial Encounters, Europe and the Native Caribbean 1492–1797*, London: Methuen.

—— (1986b) 'Hurricane in the Caribbees, the Constitution of the Discourse of English Colonialism', in F. Barker, P. Hulme, M. Iversen and D. Loxley (eds), *Literature, Politics and Theory*, Papers from the Essex Conference 1976–1984, London: Methuen.

—— (1993) 'The Profit of Language', in J. White (ed.), *Recasting the World: Writing After Colonialism*, Baltimore, MD and London: Johns Hopkins University Press.

—— (1994) 'The Locked Heart: The Creole Family Romance of *Wide Sargasso Sea*', in F. Barker, P. Hulme and M. Iversen (eds), *Colonial Discourse/Postcolonial Theory*, Manchester: Manchester University Press, pp. 73–88.

—— (1995) 'Including America', *Ariel* 26 (1), January: pp. 117–123.

Hurtado, A. (1989) 'Relating to Privilege: Seduction and Rejection in the Subordination of White Women and Women of Color', *Signs* 14 (4), Summer: pp. 833–855.

Hutchinson, J. and A.D. Smith (eds) (1994) *Nationalism*, Oxford: Oxford University Press.

Hyam, R. (1990) *Empire and Sexuality: The British Experience*, Manchester: Manchester University Press.

Ilaiah, K. (1996) *Why I am not a Hindu: A Sudra Critique of Hindutva Philosophy, Culture and Political Economy*, Calcutta: Samya.

Irele, F.A. (1971) 'The Theory of Negritude', in *Political Theory and Ideology in African Society*, Edinburgh: Centre of African Studies Seminar Papers, University of Edinburgh.

Jacoby, R. (1995) 'Marginal Returns: The Trouble with Post-colonial Theory', *Lingua Franca*, September/October: pp. 30–37.

Jad, I. (1995) 'Claiming Feminism, Claiming Nationalism: Women's Activism in the Occupied Territories', in A. Basu (ed.), *Women's Movements in Global Perspective*, Boulder, CO: Westview Press.

Jameson, F. (1981) *The Political Unconscious: Narrative as a Socially Symbolic Act*, Ithaca, NY: Cornell University Press.

—— (1986) 'Third World Literature in the Era of Multinational Capitalism', *Social Text* 15, Fall: pp. 65–88.

JanMohamed, A.R. (1985) 'The Economy of Manichean Allegory: The

Function of Racial Difference in Colonialist Literature', *Critical Inquiry* 12: pp. 59–87.

Jayawardena, K. (1986) *Feminism and Nationalism in the Third World*, London: Zed Books.

—— (1995) *The White Woman's Other Burden: Western Women and South Asia During British Rule*, New York and London: Routledge.

Johnson, D. (1996) *Shakespeare and South Africa*, Oxford: Clarendon Press.

Jolly, R. (1995) 'Contemporary Postcolonial Discourse and the New South Africa', *PMLA* 110 (1), January: pp. 17–29.

Jones, A.R. (1981) 'Writing the Body: Towards an Understanding of *l'ecriture feminine*', *Feminist Studies* 7 (2), Summer: pp. 247–263.

Joshi, R. and Liddle, J. (1986) *Daughters of Independence: Gender, Caste and Class in India*, London: Zed Books.

Joseph, G.I. (1995) 'Caribbean Women: The Impact of Race, Sex and Class', in A. Basu (ed.), *Women's Movements in Global Perspective*, Boulder, CO: Westview Press.

Kabbani, R. (1986) *Europe's Myths of the Orient*, London: Pandora.

Kelman, J. (1992) *Some Recent Attacks: Essays Cultural and Political*, Stirling: AK Press.

Kemp, A., Madlala, N., Moodley, A. and Salo, E. (1995) 'The Dawn of a New Day: Redefining South African Feminism', in A. Basu (ed.), *Women's Movements in Global Perspective*, Boulder, CO Westview Press.

Kiberd, D. (1995) *Inventing Ireland*, London: Jonathan Cape.

Kortenaar, N. ten (1995) 'Beyond Authenticity and Creolization: Reading Achebe Writing Culture', *PMLA* 110 (1), January: pp. 30–42.

Laclau, E. (1977) *Politics and Ideology in Marxist Theory*, London: New Left Books.

LaCapra, D. (ed.) (1991) *The Bounds of Race: Perspectives on Hegemony and Resistance*, Ithaca, NY and London: Cornell University Press.

Lamming, G. (1960) 'The Occasion for Speaking', in *The Pleasures of Exile*, London: Michael Joseph.

Lawrence, E. (1982) 'Just Plain Common Sense: The "Roots" of Racism', in *The Empire Strikes Back, Race and Racism in 70s Britain*, Centre for Contemporary Cultural Studies, London: Hutchinson, pp. 47–94.

Lazarus, N. (1994) 'National consciousness and intellectualism', in Francis Barker *et al.* (eds), *Colonial Discourse/Postcolonial Theory*, Manchester: Manchester University Press, pp. 197–220.

Lenin, V.I . (1947) *Imperialism, the Highest Stage of Capitalism*, Moscow: Foreign Languages Publishing House (first published 1916).

Lithgow, W. (1928) 'Rare Adventures and Painefull Peregrinations', B.I. Lawrence (ed.), London: Jonathan Cape.

Lloyd, D. (1994) 'Ethnic Cultures, Minority Discourse and the State', in F. Barker, P. Hulme and M. Iversen (eds), *Colonial Discourse/ Postcolonial Theory*, Manchester: Manchester University Press, pp. 221–238.

Loomba, A. (1989) *Gender, Race, Renaissance Drama*, Manchester: Manchester University Press.

—— (1993) 'Dead Women Tell No Tales: Issues of Female Subjectivity, Subaltern Agency and Tradition in Colonial and Post-colonial Writings on Widow Immolation in India', *History Workshop Journal* 36: pp. 209–227.

Macaulay, T.B. (1972) 'Minute on Indian Education', J. Clive (ed.), *Selected Writings*, Chicago, IL: University of Chicago Press.

Macherey, P. (1978) *A Theory of Literary Production*, trans. G. Wall, London and Boston, MA: Routledge and Kegan Paul.

Mahasweta Devi (1993) 'Shishu', in S. Tharu and K. Lalita (eds), *Women Writing in India*, vol. II, New York: The Feminist Press, pp. 236–250.

Majumdar, B.P. (1973) *First Fruits of English Education*, Calcutta: Bookland Private Limited.

Mallon, F.E. (1994) 'The Promise and Dilemma of Subaltern Studies: Perspectives from Latin American History', *American Historical Review* 99 (5), December: pp. 1491–1515.

Mandela, N. (1994) *Long Walk to Freedom*, London: Abacus.

Mani, L. (1989) 'Contentious Traditions: The Debate on Sati in Colonial India', in K. Sangari and S. Vaid (eds), *Recasting Women*, New Delhi: Kali for Women, pp. 88–126

—— (1992) 'Cultural Theory, Colonial Texts: Reading Eyewitness Accounts of Widow Burning', in L. Grossberg, C. Nelson and P. Treichler (eds), *Cultural Studies*, New York and London: Routledge.

Mannoni, O. (1956) *Prospero and Caliban: The Psychology of Colonisation*, trans. P. Powesland, London: Methuen.

Marx, K. (1961) *Capital*, vol. 1, Moscow: Foreign Languages Publishing House.

—— (1973) *Surveys from Exile*, D. Fernbach (ed.), London: Pelican Books.

Marx, K. and Engels, F. (1976) *Collected Works*, London: Lawrence and Wishart.

Masters, J. (1952) *The Deceivers*, London: Michael Joseph.

Mayo, K. (1927) *Mother India*, New York: Blue Ribbon Books.

McClintock, A. (1992) 'The Angel of Progress: Pitfalls of the Term "Post-colonialism" ', *Social Text* 31/32: pp. 84–98.

—— (1995) *Imperial Leather: Race, Gender and Sexuality in the Colonial Contest*, New York and London: Routledge.

Memmi, A. (1967) *The Colonizer and the Colonized*, Boston, MA: Beacon Press.

—— (1973) 'The Impossible Life of Frantz Fanon', *The Massachusetts Review* XIV (1), Winter: pp. 9–39.

Mernissi, F. (1987) *Beyond the Veil: Male–Female Dynamics in Modern Muslim Society*, Bloomington, IN: Indiana University Press.

Mies, M. (1980) *Indian Women and Patriarchy*, New Delhi: Concept Books.

Miles, R. (1989) *Racism*, London: Routledge.

Mishra, V. and Hodge, B. (1991) 'What is Post(-)colonialism?', *Textual Practice* 5 (3): pp. 399–415.

Mitchell, J. (1974) *Psychoanalysis and Feminism*, New York: Vintage Press.

Mitter, S. (1986) *Common Fate, Common Bond: Women in the Global Economy*, London: Pluto.

Mohanty, C.T. (1988) 'Under Western Eyes: Feminist Scholarship and Colonial Discourses', *Feminist Review* 30 Autumn: pp. 61–102.

Morley, D. (1996) 'EurAm, Modernity, Reason and Alterity', in D. Morley and K.H. Chen (eds), *Stuart Hall, Critical Dialogues in Cultural Studies*, London and New York: Routledge.

Morgan, R. (1984) *Sisterhood is Global: The International Women's Movement Anthology*, Garden City, NY: Anchor Press/Doubleday.

Morris, J. (1982) *The Spectacle of Empire: Style, Effect and the Pax Britannia*, London and Boston, MA: Faber.

—— (1994) *Stones of Empire: The Buildings of British India*, London: Penguin.

Murray, C. and Herrnstein, R.J. (1994) *The Bell Curve*, New York: Free Press.

Nandy, A. (1980) *At the Edge of Psychology: Essays in Politics and Culture*, New Delhi: Oxford University Press.

—— (1983) *The Intimate Enemy: Loss and Recovery of Self under Colonialism*, New Delhi: Oxford University Press.

Neill, S. (1966) *Colonialism and the Christian Missions*, New York: McGraw Hill.

Newton, J. (1989) 'History as Usual? Feminism and the "New

Historicism" ', in H.A. Veeser (ed.), *The New Historicism*, New York and London: Routledge, pp. 152–167.

Nixon, R. (1994) *Homelands, Harlem and Hollywood*, New York and London: Routledge.

Obeyesekere, G. (1992) ' "British Cannibals", Contemplation of an Event in the Death and Resurrection of James Cook, Explorer', *Critical Inquiry* 18 (Summer): 630–654.

O'Hanlon, R., (1988) 'Recovering the Subject, *Subaltern Studies* and Histories of Resistance in Colonial South Asia', *Modern Asian Studies* 22 (1): pp. 189–224.

—— (1994) *A Comparison Between Men and Women: Tarabai Shinde and the Critique of Gender Relations in Colonial India*, Madras: Oxford University Press.

O'Hanlon, R. and Washbrook, D. (1992) 'After Orientalism: Culture, Criticism, and Politics in the Third World', *Comparative Studies in Society and History* 34 (1), January: pp. 141–167.

Orkin, M. (1987) *Shakespeare Against Apartheid*, Craighall: AD Donker.

Osborne, T. (ed.) (1745) *A Collection of Voyages and Travels*, London.

Pal, B.C. (1958) *The Soul of India: A Constructive Study of Indian Thoughts and Ideals*, Calcutta: Yugayatri Prakashak.

Palmer, T. (1988) *The Emblems of Thomas Palmer: Two Hundred Posies*, J. Manning (ed.), New York: AMS Press.

Pannikar, K.N. (1996) 'Creating a New Cultural Taste: Reading a Nineteenth-century Malayalam Novel', in R. Champakalakshmi and S. Gopal (eds), *Tradition, Dissent and Ideology*, New Delhi: Oxford University Press.

Parker, G. (1990) 'Europe and the Wider World, 1500–1750', in J.D. Tracy (ed.), *The Rise of Merchant Empires*, Cambridge: Cambridge University Press.

Parker, P. (1994) 'Fantasies of "Race" and "Gender", Africa, *Othello*, and Bringing to Light', in M. Hendricks and P. Parker (eds), *Women, 'Race' and Writing in the Early Modern Period*, London and New York: Routledge, pp. 84–100.

Parmar, P. and Amos, V. (1984) 'Challenging Imperial Feminism', *Feminist Review* 17 Autumn: 3–19.

Parry, B. (1987) 'Problems in Current Theories of Colonial Discourse', *Oxford Literary Review* 9 (1–2): 27–58.

—— (1994a) 'Resistance Theory/Theorising Resistance or Two Cheers for Nativism', in F. Barker, P. Hulme and M. Iversen (eds), *Colonial*

Discourse/Postcolonial Theory, Manchester: Manchester University Press, pp. 172–196.

—— (1994b) 'Signs of Our Times. Discussion of Homi Bhabha's *The Location of Culture*', *Third Text* 28/29, Autumn/Winter: pp. 5–24.

Porter, D. (1983) '*Orientalism* and its Problems', in F. Barker, P. Hulme, M. Iversen and D. Loxley (eds), *The Politics of Theory*, Proceedings of the Essex Sociology of Literature Conference, Colchester: University of Essex Press, pp. 179–193.

Pratt, M.L. (1992) *Imperial Eyes: Travel Writing and Transculturation*, London and New York: Routledge.

Prakash, G. (1990) 'Writing Post-Orientalist Histories of the Third World: Perspectives from Indian Historiography', *Comparative Studies in Society and History* 32 (2), April: pp. 383–408.

—— (1992) 'Can the "Subaltern" Ride? A Reply to O'Hanlon and Washbrook', *Comparative Studies in Society and History* 34 (1), January: pp. 168–184.

—— (1994) 'Subaltern Studies as Postcolonial Criticism', *American Historical Review* 99 (5), December: pp. 1475–1490

Purchas, S. (1614) *Purchas His Pilgrimage*, London, 2nd edn.

Rabasa, J. (1985) 'Allegories of the Atlas', in F. Barker, P. Hulme, M. Iversen and D. Loxley (eds), *Europe and its Others*, vol. 2, Colchester: University of Essex Press, pp. 1–16.

Ranade, R. (1991) *Amachya Ayushyatil Kahi*, in S. Tharu and K. Lalita (eds), *Women Writing in India*, vol. 1, New Delhi: Oxford University Press, pp. 281–290.

Ranger, T. (1982) 'Race and Tribe in Southern Africa: European Ideas and African Acceptance', in R. Ross (ed.), *Racism and Colonialism*, The Hague: Martinus Nijhoff Publishers.

—— (1983) 'The Invention of Tradition in Colonial Africa', in E. Hobsbawm and T. Ranger (eds), *The Invention of Tradition*, Cambridge: Cambridge University Press, pp. 211–262.

Renan, E. (1990) 'What is a Nation?', trans. by M. Thom, in H.K. Bhabha (ed.), *Nation and Narration*, London and New York: Routledge.

Retamar, R.F. (1974) 'Caliban, Notes Towards a Discussion of Culture in Our America', *Massachusetts Review* 15 Winter/Spring: pp. 7–72.

Rex, J. (1980) 'Theory of Race Relations: A Weberian Approach', in *Sociological Theories, Race and Colonialism*, Paris: Unesco, pp. 116–142.

Robbins, B. (1992) 'Comparative Cosmopolitanism', *Social Text* 31/32: pp. 169–186.

Robinson, C. (1983) *Black Marxism, The Making of a Black Radical Tradition*, London: Zed Books.

Roe, T. (1926) *The Embassy of Sir Thomas Roe To India 1615–19*, Sir W. Foster (ed.), Oxford: Oxford University Press.

Rosaldo, R. (1994) 'Social Justice and the Crisis of National Communities', in F. Barker, P. Hulme and M. Iversen (eds), *Colonial Discourse/Postcolonial Theory*, Manchester: Manchester University Press, pp. 238–252.

Rose, J. (1986) *Sexuality in the Field of Vision*, New York: Verso.

—— (1993) *Why War? Psychoanalysis, Politics, and the Return to Melanie Klein*, Oxford: Blackwell.

Rushdie, S. (1995) *The Moor's Last Sigh*, London: Jonathan Cape.

—— (1997) 'Damme, This is the Oriental Scene for You', *The New Yorker*, June 23–30: pp. 50–61.

Ryan, S. (1994) 'Inscribing the Emptiness, Cartography, Exploration and the Construction of Australia', in C. Tiffin and A. Lawson (eds), *De-Scribing Empire, Postcolonialism and Textuality*, London and New York: Routledge, pp. 115–130.

Saadawi, N. el (1986) *The Hidden Face of Eve*, London: Zed Press.

Sachs, W. (1947) *Black Hamlet*, Boston, MA: Little, Brown and Company.

Said, E.W. (1978) *Orientalism*, London and Henley: Routledge and Kegan Paul.

—— (1984) *The World, the Text and the Critic*, London: Faber and Faber.

—— (1989) 'Representing the Colonized, Anthropology's Interlocuters', *Critical Inquiry* 15, Winter: pp. 205–225.

—— (1994) *Culture and Imperialism*, New York: Vintage.

—— (1995) 'Secular Interpretation: The Geographical Element, and the Methodology of Imperialism', in G. Prakash (ed.), *After Colonialism*, Princeton, NY: Princeton University Press, pp. 21–39.

Sandys, G. (1627) *A Relation of a Journey begun An. Dom. 1610*, London, 3rd edn.

Sarkar, S. (1994) 'Orientalism Revisited, Saidian Frameworks in the Writing of Modern Indian History', *Oxford Literary Review* 16 (1–2): 205–224.

Sarkar, T. (1989) 'Politics and Women in Bengal, the Conditions and Meaning of Participation', in J. Krishnamurthy (ed.), *Women in Colonial India, Essays on Survival, Work and the State*, Delhi: Oxford University Press.

Sartre, J.-P. (ed.) (1963) *Black Orpheus*, trans. S.W. Allen, Paris: Presence Africaine.

Scott, J. (1992) 'Experience', in J. Butler and J.W. Scott (eds), *Feminists Theorize the Political*, New York and London: Routledge, pp. 22–40.

Senghor, L.S. (1994) 'Negritude: A Humanism of the Twentieth Century', in P. Williams and L. Chrisman (eds) *Colonial Discourse and Postcolonial Theory*, New York: Columbia University Press, pp. 27–35.

Seshadri-Crooks, K. (1994) 'The Primitive as Analyst: Postcolonial Feminism's Access to Psychoanalysis', *Cultural Critique* 28, Fall: pp. 175–218.

Shakespeare, W. (1974) *The Riverside Shakespeare*, Boston, MA: Houghton Mifflin.

Sharpe, J. (1993) *Allegories of Empire: The Figure of Woman in the Colonial Text*, London and Minneapolis, MN: University of Minnesota Press.

Shiva, V. (1988) *Staying Alive: Women, Ecology and Survival in India*, New Delhi: Kali; London: Zed Books.

Shohat, E. (1993) 'Notes on the "Post-colonial" ', *Social Text* 31/32: pp. 99–113.

Silverblatt, I. (1995) 'Becoming Indian in the Central Andes of Seventeenth-Century Peru', in G. Prakash (ed.), *After Colonialism*, Princeton, NJ: Princeton University Press, pp. 279–298.

Skurski, J. (1994) 'The Ambiguities of Authenticity in Latin America, *Dona Barbara* and the Construction of National Identity', *Poetics Today* 15 (4), Winter: pp. 605–642.

Soares, V. *et al.* (1995), 'Brazilian Feminisms and Women's Movements, A 2-way Street', in A. Basu (ed.), *Women's Movements in Global Perspective*, Boulder, CO: Westview Press.

Spillers, H. (1987) 'Mama's Baby, Papa's Maybe: An American Grammar Book', *Diacritics* 17: pp. 65–71.

Spivak, G.C. (1985a) 'Three Women's Texts and a Critique of Imperialism', *Critical Inquiry* 12 (1): pp. 243–261.

—— (1985b) 'Can the Subaltern Speak? Speculations on Widow-Sacrifice', *Wedge*, Winter/Spring: pp. 120–130.

—— (1987) 'The Rani of Sirmur: An Essay in Reading the Archives', *History and Theory* 24 (3): pp. 247–272.

—— (1988) 'Can the Subaltern Speak?', in C. Nelson and L. Grossberg (eds), *Marxism and the Interpretation of Culture*, Basingstoke: Macmillan Education, pp. 271–313.

—— (1990) 'The Political Economy of Women as Seen by a Literary Critic', in E. Weed (ed.), *Coming to Terms*, London and New York: Routledge.

—— (1996) 'Post-structuralism, Marginality, Postcoloniality and Value', in P. Mongia (ed.), *Contemporary Postcolonial Theory*, London: Arnold, pp. 198–222.

Spurr, D. (1993) *The Rhetoric of Empire: Colonial Discourse in Journalism, Travel Writing and Imperial Administration*, Durham, NC and London: Duke University Press.

Stepan, N.L. (1982) *The Idea of Race in Science, Great Britain 1800–1960*, London: Macmillan.

—— (1990) 'Race and Gender: The Role of Analogy in Science', in D.T. Goldberg (ed.), *The Anatomy of Racism*, Minneapolis, MN and London: University of Minnesota Press.

Stepan, N.L. and Gilman, S.L. (1991) 'Appropriating the Idiom of Science', in D. LaCapra (ed.), *The Bounds of Race: Perspectives on Hegemony and Resistance*, Ithaca, NY and London: Cornell University Press, pp. 72–103.

Tabari, A. and Yahgeneh, N. (1983) *In the Shadow of Islam*, London: Zed Press.

Teltscher, K. (1995) *India Inscribed, European and British Writing on India 1600–1800*, New Delhi: Oxford University Press.

Terry, E. (1655) *A Voyage to East India*, London.

Tharu, S. (1996) 'A Critique of Hindutva-Brahminism', *Economic and Political Weekly*, 27 July: pp. 2019–2021.

Tharu, S. and Lalita, K. (eds) (1991) *Women Writing in India*, vol. 1, New Delhi: Oxford University Press.

Thiong'o, N. wa (1986) *Decolonising the Mind: The Politics of Language in African Literature*, London: James Currey.

Tiffin, C. and Lawson, A. (eds) (1994) *De-scribing Empire, Post-colonialism and Textuality*, London and New York: Routledge.

Vaughan, M. (1991) *Curing Their Ills: Colonial Power and African Illness*, Cambridge and Stanford, CA: Polity Press and Stanford University Press.

—— (1993) 'Madness and Colonialism, Colonialism as Madness', *Paideuma* 39: pp. 45–55.

—— (1994) 'Colonial Discourse Theory and African History, or has Postmodernism Passed us by?', *Social Dynamics* 20 (2): pp. 1–23.

Vecellio, C. (1598) *Habiti antichi et moderni di tutte il mondo*, Venice, 2nd edn.

Viswanathan, G. (1990) *Masks of Conquest: Literary Study and British Rule in India*, London: Faber and Faber.

Volosinov, V. (1973) *Marxism and the Philosophy of Language*, New York: Seminar Press.

Walkowitz, J. (1989) 'Patrolling the Borders, Feminist Historiography and the New Historicism' (Exchange and Seminar), *Radical History Review* 43:pp. 23–43.

Wallerstein, I. (1988) 'The Ideological Tensions of Capitalism: Universalism versus Racism and Sexism', in E. Balibar and I. Wallerstein, *Race, Nation, Class, Ambiguous Identities*, London and New York: Verso.

Warmistry, T. (1658) *The Baptized Turk, or a Narrative of the Happy Conversion of the Signior Rigep Dandulo*, London.

Warner, M. (1987) *Monuments and Maidens: The Allegory of the Female Form*, London: Picador.

Watson, J.F. and Kaye, J.W. (eds) (1868–1875) *The People of India: A Series of Photographic Illustrations, with Descriptive Letterpress, of the Races and Tribes of Hindustan*, 8 vols, London: India Museum.

White, H. (1987) *Tropics of Discourse: Essays in Cultural Criticism*, Baltimore, MD and London: Johns Hopkins University Press.

Williams, P. and Chrisman, L. (eds) (1994) *Colonial Discourse and Post-Colonial Theory: A Reader*, New York: Columbia University Press.

Williams, R. (1976) *Keywords, A Vocabulary of Culture and Society*, New York: Oxford University Press.

—— (1977) *Marxism and Literature*, Oxford: Oxford University Press.

Young, C. (1994) 'The Colonial Construction of African Nations', in J. Hutchinson and A.D. Smith (eds), *Nationalism*, Oxford: Oxford University Press.

Young, R. (1990) *White Mythologies: Writing History and the West*, London: Routledge.

—— (1995) *Colonial Desire: Hybridity in Theory, Culture and Race*, London: Routledge.

Yuval-Davis, N. and Anthias, F. (eds) (1989) *Woman–Nation–State*, London: Macmillan.

INDEX